Children and Childhoods 1

Children and Childhoods 1:
Perspectives, Places and Practices

Edited by

Peter Whiteman and Katey De Gioia

CAMBRIDGE
SCHOLARS
PUBLISHING

Children and Childhoods 1:
Perspectives, Places and Practices,
Edited by Peter Whiteman and Katey De Gioia

This book first published 2012

Cambridge Scholars Publishing

12 Back Chapman Street, Newcastle upon Tyne, NE6 2XX, UK

British Library Cataloguing in Publication Data
A catalogue record for this book is available from the British Library

ISBN (10): 1-4438-3456-4, ISBN (13): 978-1-4438-3456-8

TABLE OF CONTENTS

PREFACE

This volume is the first in the *Children and Childhoods* series. The series aims to report current research in early childhood and childhood education while challenging tradition and invoking debate about the nature of research in these and cognate fields. The complex, transdiciplinary nature of childhood is reflected in the transdisciplinary nature of the series. For example, children's voices will be heard alongside those of adults, practitioner-led action research may well sit beside experimental research, neo-liberal critique and cultural politics may join curriculum analysis.

Volume 1 draws on a range of papers presented at the innaugural *Children and Childhoods Symposium*, held at Macquarie University, Australia in 2010. The examination of how children and childhoods are seen (perspectives), where they are enacted (places) and how they are played out (practices) sets the scene for the series. Researchers, practitioners, policy-makers and others will find their interest piqued by the various paradigms represented as we hear about playgrounds, museums, hospitals, child care centres and other places in which children do childhood. I invite you to join me on an exciting journey of discovery as we are led through the detail of that complex construct we call childhood.

Peter Whiteman, Series Editor

CHAPTER ONE

PERSPECTIVES

PETER WHITEMAN, KATEY DE GIOIA
AND ZINNIA MEVAWALLA

Artists have painted it (e.g. *The Voyage of Life* by Thomas Cole), poets have written about it (e.g. *Michael* by William Wordsworth, *Songs of Innocence* by William Blake) and composers have imagined it in music (e.g. *Kinderszenen* by Robert Schumann). Childhood is omnipresent. It is a multifarious concept that is inextricably entwined with social, cultural and historical moments that influence and are influenced by a multitude of perspectives, places and practices. The manner in which these perspectives, places and practices are enacted by children, families and communities determines the nature of childhood experiences and defines the complex nature of childhood itself. This complex, contemporary notion is not without history. Generations of competing theoretical, philosophical, scientific and socio-historical ideologies have framed current constructions of childhood (Burman 1994; Cannella 2000). Notably, the majority of literature has been definitively Eurocentric. Childhood has often been conceptualised as a singular, universal phenomenon. In recognition of this, it is reiterated that a plethora of socio-culturally diverse histories (both written and unwritten) have influenced understandings of childhood. Nonetheless, surveying the theoretical and philosophical groundwork laid within Eurocentric traditions is pertinent to understanding some of the residual impacts of past eras upon current and future early childhood theory, research and practice (MacNaughton 2003; Woodrow 1999; Dahlberg, Moss, and Pence 1999; Wong 2007)

The Silent Child

The construction of the silent child is contextualised by a historical era in which children were seemingly invisible (Ariès 1962; Cannella and

Grieshaber 2001). Prior to the Age of Enlightenment, childhood was not seen as a distinctive phase of the lifespan in itself, but rather as the necessary precursor to adulthood. Children were therefore conceptualised by theorists such as Locke, as "blank slates" awaiting inscription from the experiences of life (MacNaughton 2003). In this sense, children were seen to start "life with and from nothing – as an empty vessel or *tabula rasa*" (Dahlberg, Moss, and Pence 1999, 44, original emphasis). Subsequently, Romantic-era philosophers such as Rousseau, Pestalozzi and Fröebel placed paramount importance on the role of education in enabling children to discover their inner nature (Dahlberg, Moss, and Pence 1999) in an environment that protects the innocence and naivety of childhood (MacNaughton 2003).

The silent child then, was one in constant need of protection and shaping – a child upon whom predetermined socially acceptable forms of knowledge, skills and attitudes were to be bestowed, in order for the child to function (conform) in accordance with the dominant socio-cultural norms and sanctions of the age (Dahlberg, Moss, and Pence 1999). This view has been exemplified by literature regarding the conditions of childhood experienced by children in the 18th and 19th centuries. For example, young children of means were sent to wet nurses for the first two-to-five years of their lives, while other children were placed into the workforce as apprentices and labourers (Turmel 2008).

Correspondingly, in educating the silent child, the role of practitioners was to protect and imbue children with the virtues that would enable them to contend with societal norms and practices (MacNaughton 2003). Woodrow (1999) has highlighted that the role of educators was to direct learning through the top-down imposition of power, by which means practitioners were to "confer rewards, sanction behaviour, and ensure conformity to the acceptable social order" (9). Similarly, Locke argued that the role of educators was to "dampen [children's] desires and their tendency to frivolity, so that reason can prevail" (as cited in MacNaughton 2003, 25). Conversely, Romantic philosophers such as Rousseau argued that educators were to play a facilitative role, letting nature take the primary lead in unfolding the child's journey to maturity (Rousseau [1762] 1968). This Romantic perception was the precursor to the development of views surrounding the individual child (MacNaughton 2003).

The Individual Child

Contextualised against the backdrop of the Post Industrial Revolution – the Period of Modernity, also known as the Scientific Period (19th, 20th and 21st centuries) brought with it a plethora of changes that have subsequently influenced meanings of childhood (Crain 1995; Turmel 2008). During the latter part of the 19th century, childhood was recognised as a separate period of the lifespan, leading to major reforms in legislation pertaining to child protection, education, and child labour (Turmel 2008). General progress in the 20th century was characterised by improvements in health, life expectancy and child mortality, therefore leading to further changes in the depiction of childhood.

In line with the philosophical beliefs of the era that focused on the discovery of knowledge through logic, reason and the scientific application of technology, notions of child development were particularly sharpened by scientific investigation during this period (Johnson, Christie, and Wardle 2005). Utilising scientific (positivist) methods and technologies for proving knowledge, investigations of children built upon Darwinian notions of humans having evolutionary predispositions toward maturation (Boardman, Smuts, and Hagen 1986). Twentieth century maturationists such as Hall, Gesell and Piaget studied children's development and defined universal categories for the ages and stages of children's normative development (MacNaughton 2003). This formed the basis of the individual child as one "who is a natural, rather than a social phenomenon, abstracted and decontextualised, essentialised and normalised, defined either through abstract notions of maturity…or through stages of development" (Dahlberg, Moss, and Pence 1999, 46).

The individual child then, was one that had been naturally endowed (genetically pre-programmed) with a set of "universal properties" (Dahlberg, Moss, and Pence 1999) that predetermined their progression into adulthood, regardless of the cultural context in which the child lived (Woodrow 1999). The linearity of the reductionist scientific thinking of the period compartmentalised the individual child into isolated developmental aspects (physical development, intellectual development, social development, and so on) that could be separately measured and ameliorated. The role of the individual child was to comply (without agency) with the linear progression into maturity by achieving a set of biologically defined milestones, passing through developmental stages at a particular time in life.

Accordingly, the role of the educator was to provide "Developmentally Appropriate Practice" (DAP), that is, practice that directed children to engage with age-and-stage appropriate content, materials and activities that had been engineered to address children's abilities to meet developmental norms (Bredekamp and Copple 1997). The "normalisation" of the individual child was furthered by behaviourist approaches to teaching children according to predetermined standards, measurement assessments and teaching practices that reinforced the existence of universal knowledge and truths. Correspondingly, behaviourists such as Pavlov, Watson and Skinner highlighted the importance of educators conditioning children (despite differences in situation or temper) to conform to the linearity of biological rules outside of the context of history or society (Cannella and Grieshaber 2001).

The end of modernism brought postmodern views to education during the 1980s and 1990s (Johnson, Christie, and Wardle 2005). Postmodernists questioned the existence of universal truths, postulating instead that truth is an interpretive and subjective phenomenon, therefore leading to the view that concepts such as childhood are socially constructed ideals (Wong 2007).

The Social Child

While Piaget (1962) maintained that children were thinking, investigating beings that actively engaged in the acquisition of skills, knowledge and understandings, Vygotsky (1978a) proposed that learning occurred in social contexts, and that there was a theoretical space – the "Zone of Proximal Development" – in which children can achieve greater understandings with the help of their peers, than that which they would have been able to accomplish singularly. Thus arose the social child, as one that was a co-constructor of knowledge, seeking, from infancy, to learn in the context of peer relationships (Curtis and Carter 2000; Hewett 2001; Millikan 2003). For social children, learning became a socially-located, collective action.

Contextualised against a "new sociology of childhood" (Prout 2011, 4), the emergence of the social child corresponded with the development of the *United Nations Conventions on the Rights of the Child* (United Nations 1989), which recognised children as active agents and citizens with a specific set of human rights. Following the lead of critical educators (such as Loris Malaguzzi from Reggio Emilia), contemporary understandings in early childhood subsequently sought to distance themselves from the memory of previously deficit views of children and childhood.

The social child, therefore, was framed as "beautiful, powerful, competent, creative, curious, and full of potential and ambitious desires" (Hewett 2001, 96). Pedagogical practices in turn became increasingly child-centred, child-focused and child-directed, where the role of the educator was to inspire discovery, investigation and capitalise on the teachable moment, procuring learning in the context of meaningful relationships by "truly listening" (Hewett 2001, 96). Reciprocity of learning was a particularly pertinent point, where to learn was "not to pass information along or replicate thinking, but to advance thinking" (Hewett 2001, 98). The social child was therefore educated in the context of relationships, as relationships create conflict which creates cognitive disequilibrium and an opportunity to question one's assumptions and ideas.

Illustrations of the social child abound in what could be construed as seemingly inconsequential, common events. For example: the act of obtaining a new bookcase for the family room. After coming to agreement on the style, family members purchase their new furniture, only to realise as it is brought from the warehouse area that the real adventure is about to begin as it becomes clear that the assortment of flat, slim boxes means that this bookcase requires assembly. Once home, the children help unpack the boxes then stand back and observe as their parents begin the process of assembling the new acquisition. Instructions are read, tools, screws and other small accessories are sorted and the item begins to take shape. At times, someone will read from the instructions. At other times, one parent will demonstrate to the other how they believe the components should be fitted together. Other interactions will take the form of a parent speaking quietly to himself or herself as they talk their way through a particularly intricate procedure. At other times, one parent might explain something to the other, while extracting only two types of screws from the large variety in the pack to illustrate their point. Eventually, a new bookcase stands in the corner of the room. To the untrained eye, this appears to be quite ordinary. To an observer versed in learning as socially located, collective action, this could be quite an extraordinary event.

An important concept linked with the social child is that of scaffolding. A new building is often surrounded by scaffolding, a temporary structure that remains in place until the building itself is complete. The social child was often similarly surrounded. Scaffolding in childhood can be thought of as support strategies employed by experts (the more knowledgeable) as they support novices (the learners) in their quest to become experts. For the social child, scaffolding was good pedagogy.

Wood, Bruner and Ross (1976) named five strategies that experts utilise in their support of novices:

- Recruitment – engaging the novice
- Reduction of degrees of freedom – simplifying the elements of the task at hand in order that the novice can recognise the requirements
- Marking of critical features – pointing out relevant responses and their components
- Maintenance of direction – ensuring that the novice's interest in the task remains
- Demonstration – modeling solutions.

Returning to the new bookcase, aspects of this framework can be clearly seen:

- Recruitment – the whole family is excited by the new furniture and keen to place it in the family room
- Reduction in degrees of freedom – only two types of screws were removed from the large collection while one parent explained something to the other
- Marking of critical features – as the bookcase took shape, one parent's achievements were applauded by the other with accompanying explanations for the success
- Maintenance of direction – everyone voiced their delight as the project moved towards completion
- Demonstration – as small hurdles were met along the way, one parent offered advice to the other by showing how they thought particular components should be assembled.

Scaffolding was evident in more formal learning environments as well. Teachers were experts and children were novices. Content gave way to process and scaffolding became commonplace. Interestingly, the notion of "expert" was widened, as the social child was acknowledged as an expert in his or her own right. For example, it is plausible that one of the children returned to kindergarten a few days after the bookcase experience, and was completing a large wooden jigsaw puzzle with another child. Explanations of which piece went where were punctuated with demonstrations of how a piece could be rotated to fit, success was applauded and one child removed a few pieces at a time from the large array that eventually needed to be placed. There were no printed instructions as there were for the bookcase, but aspects of scaffolding were clearly evident.

Children can understand aspects of scaffolding. The following interview is an extract from a larger discussion that took place between a researcher and Aaron, a preschool aged child. They were watching some short video clips that Aaron had recorded of music making in his home, and Aaron was sharing his thoughts on what was happening with his brother, Ethan, and his mother.

Aaron:	Oh yeah, that's my brother playing the violin. Daniel's crying. He's playing I wish you a merry Christmas.
Researcher:	He is. What's he playing?
Aaron:	His violin.
Researcher:	And is there other music happening there as well?
Aaron:	No.
Researcher:	Just your brother? I wonder what your mum's doing.
Aaron:	She's playing the piano, playing the songs that Ethan should play.
Researcher:	Why is she playing the sounds that Ethan should play?
Aaron:	So he knows the sound that he should play.
Researcher:	That's pretty clever isn't it? How does mum know what to play?
Aaron:	Because she looks at the book.
Researcher:	Really?
Aaron:	And then my brother learns how to play.
Researcher:	So, is the book really important when you play music?
Aaron:	Yes.
Researcher:	Yeah? What's in the book?
Aaron:	But when you've fully learnt and you're actually a really good musician you don't need the book any more.
Researcher:	Ooh, is your mum really good and doesn't need the book?
Aaron:	No. She still needs her book.

Aaron is a social child. He seems to have an understanding of various ways in which Ethan is scaffolded, and in turn, his mother. In this case, Ethan is scaffolded by his mother, who is in turn, scaffolded by the printed music. Aaron understands this because as part of his early learning experiences he has regularly been both scaffolder and scaffolded.

The Cultural Child

The historical establishments of theorists such as Vygotsky, Bronfenbrenner and Malaguzzi have all led towards the eminence of socio-cultural theories, which explore the importance of communities, families and the role of the context upon the individual (Vygotsky 1978b; Rogoff 2003; Bronfenbrenner 1986). Contemporary early childhood practices have adhered to the recognition of the importance of relationships, critical reflection and the authenticity of programming and planning in early settings (O'Connor and Diggins 2007; Fleer et al. 2006; Hujala et al. 2009; Nimmo 2002).

Following on from the development of the *United Nations Convention on the Rights of the Child (1989)* and the principles underlying education in Reggio Emilia, recent understandings of childhood have framed children as citizens that actively engage with the world (Millei and Imre 2009). The cultural child, therefore, is seen as one imbued with critical tools, able to critically question and engage with the power structures in society. This view of childhood has surfaced from increased awareness of equity and social justice issues surrounding diversity and inclusive education (Diaz Soto and Blue Swadener 2002; Hawkins 2009; Keesing-Styles and Sumsion 2007; Pelo 2006). The role of the educator is to engage in collaborative partnerships with families and communities in order to better understand children's critical knowledge, interests and current understandings (Hewett 2001; Hughes and MacNaughton 2002; Swick 2003) and further provide children with the tools to critically question the power structures in an attempt to transform society.

The recent focus on child-centred sociocultural models, has forced educators to take a closer look at recognising the increasing importance of collaborative partnerships with families and members of the local and wider community. Bronfenbrenner's theory (1979), which proposes the multitude of layers impacting on children both directly and indirectly, emphasises the importance of relationships between children, adults, families and the community.

The notion of partnerships with families in early childhood setting continues to be subject to discussion and debate (Brown et al. 2002; Hughes and MacNaughton 2002; Lubeck and deVries 2000). While Westernised literature supports this concept, careful conversations pertaining to deconstructing the notion of "partnerships" should be contextualised within individual settings. A study conducted by De Gioia (2003) explored continuity of care-giving practices for very young children between home and early childhood setting. One of the overarching findings identified effective partnerships as key. Discontinuity was an issue when partnerships were not established and maintained, and covert practices in the early childhood settings resulted.

The importance of successful communication for continuity between home and setting was acknowledged by a parent in the following manner:

> What I wanted them to do was to come and speak to me so that we could talk about it together and then decide what was best for Olivia so that I could follow through with it at home as well (Hetti, Mother, second generation Australian).

A further two parents also acknowledged the significance of developing trust relationships which incorporated the exchange of valuable information about home practices and centre processes.

> Letting them "in" on the family - getting them to know us (Mei, Mother).

> This [communication] also helps child to adjust easier because [there] is [a] good relationship between carers and parents (Olin, Mother).

This was also reinforced by educators. For instance:

> [We need to] build up friend [ships/] relationship with parents so it's made relaxed and ease into exchange information between us (Xanthe, Educator, Long Day Care Centre).

However, there were family members who had chosen not to share information about home practices with educators. In one centre, interviews were conducted with family members who had all recently arrived in Australia as migrants (n=8 parents). While these family members were able to articulate their reasons for choosing the centre in their interviews; *it represented Australia; they could learn English*, the educators were unaware of this and believed that family members were working counter to their philosophy by not sharing practices. Family members were open in their conversations with the researcher but the questions did explicitly centre around practices and reasons. While studies have supported this finding (see, for example, Wise 2002; Ebbeck and Glover 2000), it highlights the necessity for educators to deconstruct the notion of partnership, ensuring that families have an understanding of the terminology in the context of that particular early childhood setting. Further, the discussion of practices enables families and educators to come to shared understandings and determine opportunities for negotiating differences where needed. Bess explained:

> … we do quite a bit of what the parents ask, but what we'll do is we try and reach a solution that we're both happy with. Sometimes we need some negotiation, [for example] "I understand this is what you want, this is what we can do, do you think that you'd be happy with that?" A lot of families are… (Director, Long Day Care Centre).

When conversations occur and negotiation is the result of discontinuity, partnerships flourish. Meaning is shared, understanding strengthened and both parties feel empowered.

The cultural child is framed in the understanding that early childhood settings are inextricably linked to the community in which they are situated; they are hubs for connections, advocacy and possibilities. Opportunities begin with the mindset of educators who define community as extending beyond the gates of the setting and not confined to the community within. This enables educators to consider broader and more relevant approaches to working with the community. Influences in framing the cultural child acknowledge the relevance of context and authenticity in these connections, determining that a "one size fits all" approach is unrealistic and incongruous. For instance, a small rural suburb on the outskirts of metropolitan Sydney has developed an approach to transition to school which has taken into account *their* community needs which they have reflected on and adapted over the past years. This has brought together a community in assisting children in the transition to school.

A community organisation supported through State Government funding identified a need for young mums to connect to each other and services to support them in the parenting role. Slowly, slowly, through building partnerships with these families, the numbers increased and two playgroups were in operation over the week, in a small demountable classroom at the back of a local school. Playgroups consisted of time for children to come together to play and information sessions for family members or caregivers. The Coordinator believed that the families would benefit from an early childhood teacher at the playgroups to guide pedagogy, curriculum and in discussions of transition to school. Some family members had privately expressed their fear of their children starting school based on their own negative experiences. The local child care centre was approached and discussions commenced between the Director and Playgroup Coordinator. Outcomes included looking for ways to incorporate community into the transition to school and the teacher from the child care centre being released to spend 2 hours, once a week at the playgroup; particularly to support children and families transitioning into school.

Community meetings were arranged. Being such a small suburb, residents knew each other and were always willing to support local projects. The main street held the majority of businesses down both sides; newsagency, café, mini market, butcher and clothing store. There were two schools, one public school and a Catholic school situated in this community. Both sent representatives to the meeting and later became part of the project team. The Director and Playgroup Coordinator presented information about transition and benefits for children, families, early childhood settings, schools and communities. A small start to this project has had significant outcomes, which have built slowly from reflection, determination and realisation of the importance of community working together. Approximately halfway through the year all children starting school in the following year receive a tee-shirt which acknowledges this Playgroup milestone. They wear it to the local shops, which prompts the business community to acknowledge this significant event (usually with a token gift such as; free milkshake, drink bottle, frankfurt and cap) through conversation prompted from information sheets developed by the project team. Visits to schools also became part of the day for playgroup members accompanied by their child care centre friends who were also starting school the following year. These visits were across schools where the conversation was about what happened at schools and environmental aspects, not about one sector in competition with the other. Kindergarten teachers anecdotally report changes in children's confidence when starting school and the ease with which they settled in.

This project worked for *this* community; however, it may not work in larger suburban parts of Sydney. The consideration here is to determine the needs in the community and advocate for experiences to meet the needs which are realistic to the community. Connections grow communities and understanding, giving children a presence and visibility which acknowledges the valid contributions they have. .

Reframing children over the years has led us to a space where collaborations and partnerships are critical. They define our pedagogy and force us to rethink children and families both within and beyond the early childhood setting. The location or *walls* which have held learning now extend to possibilities and places which allows children to construct knowledge as they co-construct culture. The imperative now is to ensure that early childhood does not become stagnant within this frame but rather, with reflection and ongoing critical dialogue, extends to places, perspectives and practices beyond current possibilities.

References

Ariès, Phillipe. 1962. *Centuries of childhood*. London: Cape.

Boardman Smuts, Alice, and John W Hagen. 1986. *History and research in child development*. Chicago: Society for Research in Child Development.

Bredekamp, Sue, and Carol Copple. 1997. *Developmentally appropriate practice in early childhood programs*. Washington, DC: National Association for the Education of Young Children.

Bronfenbrenner, Urie. 1979. *The ecology of human development. Experiments by nature and design*. Cambridge, MA: Harvard University Press.

—. 1986. "Ecology of the family as a context for human development research perspectives." *Developmental Psychology* no. 22:723-742.

Brown, Elizabeth Glyn, Carolynn Amwake, Tim Speth, and Catherine Scott-Little. 2002. "The Continuity Framework: A tool for building home, school and community partnerships." *Early Childhood Research and Practice* no. 4 (2).

Cannella, Gaile S., and Susan J. Grieshaber. 2001. "Identities and possibilities." In *Embracing identities in early childhood education: 'Diversity and possibilities'*, edited by Gaile S. Cannella and Susan J. Grieshaber. New York: Teachers College Press.

Crain, William C. 1995. *Theories of development: Concepts and applications*. 3rd ed. Englewood Cliffs, NJ: Prentice Hall.

Curtis, Deb, and Margie Carter. 2000. *The art of awareness: How observation can transform your teaching*. St Paul MN: Redleaf Press.

Dahlberg, Gunilla, Peter Moss, and Alan Pence. 1999. "Constructing early childhood: What do we think it is?" In *Beyond quality in early childhood education and care: Postmodern perspectives*, edited by Gunilla Dahlberg, Peter Moss and Alan Pence. London: Falmer Press.

De Gioia, Katey. 2003. *Beyond cultural diversity. Exploring micro and macro culture in the early childhood setting*. PhD thesis, School of Applied Social and Human Sciences, University of Western Sydney, New South Wales, Australia.

Diaz Soto, Lourdes., and Beth Blue Swadener. 2002. "Toward liberatory early childhood theory, research and praxis: Decolonizing a field." *Contemporary Issues in Early Childhood* no. 3 (1):38-66.

Ebbeck, Marjory, and Ann Glover. 2000. "Immigrant families in early childhood centers: diverse expectations." In *Landscapes in early childhood education. Cross-national perspectives on empowerment - a guide for the new millenium.*, edited by Jacqueline Hayden, 239-249. New York: Peter Lang Publishing.

Fleer, Marilyn, Suzy Edwards, Marie Hammer, Anne Kennedy, Avis Ridgway, Jill Robbins, and Lynne Surman. 2006. *Early childhood learning communities: Sociocultural research in practice.* Frenchs Forest: Pearson Education Australia.

Hawkins, Karen. 2009. Teaching for social justice: A pedagogy for twenty-first century early childhood education. In *AARE 2009 International education research conference*, edited by Australian Association for Research in Education Conference. Canberra.

Hewett, Valerie Mercilliott. 2001. "Examing the Reggio Emilia approach to early childhood education." *Early Childhood Education Journal* no. 29 (2):95-100.

Hughes, Patrick, and Glenda MacNaughton. 2002. "Preparing early childhood professionals to work with parents : the challenges and diversity and dissensus." *Australian Journal of Early Childhood* no. 27 (2):14-20.

Hujala, Eeva, Leena Turja, Maria Filomena Gaspar, Marika Veisson, and Manjula Waniganayake. 2009. "Perspectives of early childhood teachers on parent-teacher partnerships in five European countries." *European Early Childhood Education Research Journal* no. 17 (1):57 - 76.

Johnson, James E, James F Christie, and Francis Wardle. 2005. *Play, development, and early education.* New York: Pearson Education.

Keesing-Styles, Linda, and Jennifer Sumsion. 2007. "Connections, dissension and dialogue: The role of teacher education in promoting social justice." In *Theorising early childhood practice: Emerging dialogues*, edited by Linda Keesing-Styles and Helen Hedges, 211-230. Castle Hill: Pademelon Press.

Lubeck, Sally, and Mary deVries. 2000. "The social construction of parent involvement in Head Start." *Early Education and Development* no. 11 (5):633-658.

MacNaughton, Glenda. 2003. *Shaping early childhood: Learners, curriculum and contexts.* Berkshire, United Kingdom: Open University Press.

Millei, Zsuzsa., and Robert. Imre. 2009. "The problems with using the concept of 'citizenship' in early years policy." *Contemporary Issues in Early Childhood* no. 10 (3):280-290. doi: http://dx.doi.org/10.2304/ciec.2009.10.3.280.

Millikan, Jan. 2003. *Reflections: Reggio Emilia principles within Australian contexts.* Castle Hill, NSW: Pademelon Press.

Nimmo, John. 2002. "Nurturing the spirit to teach : commitment, community and emergent curriculum." *Australian Journal of Early Childhood* no. 27 (2):8-12.

O'Connor, Angela., and Cathy Diggins. 2007. *On reflection: Reflective practice for early childhood educators.* Lower Hunt, NZ: Open Mind Publishing.

Pelo, Ann. 2006. "At the crossroads: Pedagogical documentation and social justice." In *Insights : behind early childhood pedagogical documentation.*

Piaget, Jean. 1962. *Play, dreams and imitation in childhood.* Translated by C. Gattegno and F.M.Hodgson. London: Routledge and Keegan Paul.

Prout, Alan. 2011. "Taking a step away from Modernity: reconsidering the new sociology of childhood." *Global Studies of Childhood* no. 1 (1):4-14. doi: http://dx.doi.org/10.2304/gsch.2011.1.1.4

Rogoff, Barbara. 2003. *The cultural nature of human development.* New York: Oxford University Press.

Rousseau, Jean-Jacques. [1762] 1968. *The social contract.* London: Penguin Books.

Swick, Kevin J. 2003. "Communication concepts for strengthening family-school-community partnerships." *Early Childhood Education Journal* no. 30 (4):275-280.

Turmel, Andre. 2008. *A historical sociology of childhood: Developmental thinking, categorization, and graphic visualization.* Cambridge: Cambridge University Press.

United Nations. *Convention on the rights of the child*, August 15, 2009 1989. Available from http://www2.ohchr.org/english/law/crc.htm

Vygotsky, Lev S. 1978a. *Mind in society: The development of higher mental processes.* Cambridge, MA: Harvard University Press.

—. 1978b. *Mind in society: The development of higher psychological processes.* Cambridge MA: Harvard University Press.

Wise, Sarah. 2002. "Parents' expectations, values and choice of child care. Connections to culture." *Family Matters* (61):48-55.

Wong, Sandie. 2007. "Looking back and moving forward: Historicising the social construction of early childhood education and care as national work." *Contemporary Issues in Early Childhood* no. 8 (2):144-156. doi: 10.2304/ciec.2007.8.2.144.

Wood, David, Jerome E. Bruner, and Gail Ross. 1976. "The role of tutoring in problem solving." *Journal of Child Psychology and Psychiatry* no. 17:89-100.

Woodrow, Christine. 1999. "Revisiting images of the child in early childhood education: Reflections and considerations." *Australian Journal of Early Childhood* no. 24 (4):7-12.

CHAPTER TWO

RETHINKING PEDAGOGICAL PRACTICES: HOW CAN TEACHERS IN EARLY CHILDHOOD SETTINGS BE SUPPORTED PROFESSIONALLY TO EXAMINE THEIR PRACTICES?

FAY HADLEY

This chapter reports on a one-year project that was implemented with a community based child care organisation that operates three child care centres[1] in Sydney, Australia. The organisation employed an academic consultant to work with the qualified staff and Directors in regard to planning, programming and pedagogical documentation. The project was situated within a change management theoretical framework. Change management requires the leadership to create a space and vision for examining and reframing practices. For this project, this enabled the organisation to transform their pedagogical practices. This project involved several stages to implement the change over a period of a year. At the completion of the project the role of the consultant was evaluated. This chapter will explore the effectiveness of the consultant in terms of managing the changes to planning and programming processes. Conclusions will be drawn as to the support qualified staff require to transform their pedagogical practices and how a change management approach can support professional learning.

[1] Centres in this article are places for children 0-5. There is at least one university-qualified teacher (three-four year trained) and/or Diploma staff (2 year trained) in long day care centres in Australia.

Supporting the professional learning of qualified staff

The Organisation for Economic Cooperation and Development (2006) *Starting Strong II* review identified that early childhood professionals need quality, participatory approaches to training to ensure that they "take responsibility for the pedagogical choices that appropriately serve the children in their care" (p. 18). This project was significant given the introduction of National Early Years Learning Framework (EYLF) (Department of Education Employment and Workplace Relations 2009)[2]. The EYLF advances core principles and practices that early childhood staff can apply when developing a contemporary early childhood curriculum. Qualified staff, therefore, need to be confident in their ability to use this document and to make evidence-based and theoretically sound pedagogical decisions. As Hahs-Vaughn & Yanowitz state:

> Today's teachers are expected to be more than just providers of information. To effectively guide their students, teachers need to be reflective practitioners, using research-based pedagogy in and adapting it to their own particular classroom (2009, 422).

Jaruszewicz & White (2009) argue that to create a space for professional learning and change, leaders of the program need to undertake intentional actions to develop a culture that challenges professional growth. Previous research has found that models of professional learning that include academics or expert external consultants have had positive effects on teachers' practices (Evans, Lomax, and Morgan 2000; Hahs-Vaughn and Yanowitz 2009). Other research has found that when professional learning is undertaken outside of the workplace, it is more difficult for the participants to implement changes in their workplaces (Morgan 2003). Research has shown that professional learning is more successful when the training is implemented in the workplace, provides both off site and on site support and is aligned with outcomes and expectations (Morgan 2003; Fiene 2002; Campbell and Milbourne 2005). Much of this research has focused on the school sector. As there have been limited studies that have examined educational change in the early childhood sector (see Kilgallon, Maloney, and Lock 2008) this study aimed to investigate the teachers' perceptions of the value of the external consultant in supporting them in implementing pedagogical changes.

---

[2] The Early Years Learning Framework is mandatory from 2012 and had been sent to all Australian prior-to-school settings in July 2009.

Change management framework

The management literature (both in the business and education fields) addresses processes and steps that are needed to undertake change within an organisation (Dubrin, Dalglish, and Miller 2006; Duigan 2006; Hiatt and Creasey 2003). It is crucial within this change management framework for leaders of the organisation to create a space and vision for examining and reframing practices (Kotter 1990). Kotter (2007) argues that leadership plays a critical role in the beginning of the change management process to ensure effective change is enacted. He argues that the leader creates a sense of urgency within the staff, assembles a group who believe in the change and creates the vision for the change. Changing the culture of an organisation only occurs at the end of the implementation stage, once (or if) the staff believe that the changes were effective. Therefore, for change to be imbedded within the organisation, staff beliefs and attitudes need to be transformed (Kotter and Schlesinger 2008; Kotter 1990).

The *Appreciative Inquiry Model* was developed in the mid 1980s by David Cooperrider and associates. This model was developed from research undertaken by Cooperrider (2001) that focused on how an organisation developed, evolved and managed change. Cooperrider and Suresh (1987) argued that for organisations to be transformational in their change they needed to move beyond conventional action research.

The appreciative inquiry approach is based on the premise that organisations change in the direction in which they inquire. This means not only focusing on the problems, but also recognising the strengths and how the organisation can move forward. The *Appreciative Inquiry Model* is an effective approach to changing organisational culture and offers an exciting way to re-think the way organisations operate. This model includes 4 stages. These are:

1. Discover – the organisation identifies both their strengths and weaknesses;
2. Dream – the future vision and direction the organisation wants to implement;
3. Design – develop strategies and changes that will move the organisation towards the vision; and
4. Destiny – implement and evaluate the changes (adapted from Srivastva and Cooperrider 1990).

This model was implemented for this 12-month change management project and is discussed below to provide contextual background to the research study on the evaluation of the consultant's role. This chapter reports the findings collected from interviews conducted with the teachers after the 12-month project. The main aim of this project was to identify the needs and resources required by the qualified staff[3] to implement documentation that met both the state and federal government accountability requirements, as well as contemporary approaches to planning. The consultant aimed to discover:

- What were the current strengths of approaches to documentation in the three centres?
- How did the current documentation processes meet accountability requirements and contemporary approaches to planning?
- What supports and resources did the qualified staff need to ensure their program and documentation meets accountability requirements and contemporary approaches to planning?

Utilising the appreciative inquiry model in data analysis requires the ideas, themes and views to be commonly agreed upon. This means that although the data are collated, they are not deemed quantifiable or sorted into themes like other approaches to data analysis (Bushe 1995). Once the data have been generated and organised, this is reported to the group so they decide collectively on the direction to be taken. This approach to the data provides an opportunity "to generate new theory that will have high face value to members of the organization" (Bushe 1995, 15).

1st stage: Discover and management rethinking

The first stage involved the management team rethinking what forms of professional learning should occur and whether the resources were being effectively utilised. This research project was commissioned by the organisation's board with the aim to improve the capacity of qualified staff in the three centres to document children's learning to meet the Quality Improvement Accreditation System requirements[4], Early Years Learning

[3] Diploma (two-year TAFE qualification) and degree trained (three or four-year university degree) staff.

[4] The Quality Improvement Accreditation System has since been revised as a part of the National Quality Reform Agenda, but at the time of the project it required developmental milestones being met as well as an emphasis on family participation.

Framework (DEEWR 2009) and contemporary approaches to pedagogical documentation. The whole-of-organisation strategy provided the opportunity to develop a culture that supported pedagogical change.

The Council of Australian Government's reform agenda provided impetus for implementing the changes due to the new national accountability requirements. This external accountability required staff to implement changes. In terms of enacting this change management process and building this culture, the organisation recognised that this required:

- a sustained period of time;
- a whole-of-organisation support;
- a critical mass where all of the qualified staff needed to be involved in the training; and
- reviewing current practices in relation to documentation.

The commitment of the organisation to include budgetary funds and the engagement of senior management and centre Directors provided an opportunity for staff to implement the pedagogical changes to programming and planning.

2nd stage: Dream and needs analysis

The second stage involved engaging an academic consultant to understand current practices in the three centres, including identifying needs and resources required by the qualified staff. The role of the external consultant in this project needed to balance contemporary knowledge and approaches with what could be implemented at a practical level in busy long day care settings. This also required an organisational "fit" between the external consultant and the senior management's expectations of programming and planning.

In this stage a needs analysis was undertaken to inform future directions in terms of pedagogical practices and documentation. This stage included questionnaires, observations and semi-structured interviews to elicit knowledge about the strengths, current practices and the challenges the qualified were facing in terms of programming and documentation. Documentation examples were also collected at this stage. This dream and needs analysis stage created a space to begin to develop organisational goals as well as individual action plans for each centre.

The results for the organisation as a whole (strengths and issues for further discussion) were presented at a staff training day in April 2009. The strengths included working well as a team, children were provided with choices, children's interests were incorporated into the program and children and staff had developed close relationships. In terms of the organisational goals it was evident that staff recognised issues of documentation and use of appropriate formats within a contemporary framework. The aspects that staff felt needed attention included documenting children's choices and interests in planning and programming, indoors, outdoors and group times, documenting links clearly, and strengthening pedagogical documentation.

3rd stage: Design and working party

Action research involves collaboration between participants to provide a depth of analysis as well as opportunities to share findings in the hope that changes can be developed and implemented to improve the practices (Cohen and Manion 1986). The cycle, referred to by Kemmis and Wilkinson (1998), of plan, act, observe and reflect is not so clear-cut - it is a spiral that the researcher has little control over. The important issue of action research is being self-critical. The third stage involved negotiating action plans which were cognisant of management expectations and underpinned by contemporary early childhood practices. This stage also required the plans of actions to be compatible with the professional and industrial landscape. The organisational goals were developed in consultation with the CEO and three Directors. The individual action plan for each centre was developed in consultation with each staff team.

The outcome of this initial data analysis at the organisational level was the formation of a small working party to review documentation, processes, formats, expectations and requirements. The members of this group were handpicked and included the three Directors, one qualified staff member from each centre and the academic consultant (N=7). This small working party met fortnightly for a period of three months to reconceptualise the systems and templates used for programming and planning across the three centres. Systems and templates, alongside a detailed policy, were developed for the daily diary, the programming plan (indoor and outdoor classroom and group times), portfolios, projects and displays. The external consultant worked closely with the qualified staff and Directors throughout the process.

4th stage: Destiny – Implementation and evaluation

The fourth stage involved implementing the pedagogical changes and evaluating these changes. The goals and action plans developed in the small working party and with the individual centres were implemented with the support of the academic consultant throughout the 2009 year. During this stage of the project the academic consultant spent significant time in each centre with the qualified staff explaining the systems, templates and addressing any questions or issues as they arose. These systems and templates were implemented gradually, explained to the qualified staff and supported individually as needed. Family memos were also distributed as each system and template was introduced, to ensure families were aware and informed of the changes being introduced.

In terms of each centre the "pre" questionnaire was analysed, and results presented to each centre at a staff meeting. From this dissemination an individual plan of action was developed for each centre. This individual plan of action was implemented in each centre where the academic consultant provided support, mentoring and resources as necessary. The academic consultant worked closely with the Director of the centre in terms of implementing the required changes. Each centre focused on changes that reflected their results. For example, two of the centres focused on improving the outdoor program, and the other centre focused on ensuring the documentation and links to planning were evident in their day-to-day practices. At the completion of the 12 months, a "post" questionnaire was completed by the staff, samples of documentation were collected and a questionnaire was completed by the families. A final report was presented to the organisation's board, the CEO and each centre. A summary of the project was presented to each centre at an end-of-year staff meeting.

Methodology and research design

Using a phenomenological approach, the research investigated early childhood teachers' and directors' perceptions of the effectiveness of the external consultant. Phenomenology identifies "phenomena" through the eyes of the participants and is a reflection and interpretation of these experiences (phenomena) from the participants' perspectives. This approach is a "way of seeing" and helps create opportunities for new understandings (Husserl 1965; Lester 2001; Lyotard 1991; Schutz 1972; Stamage and Kreiger 1987; van Manen 1990; Heidegger 1962).

As the study was investigating the effectiveness of the external consultant's role (the researcher) within the organisation it was recognised that some participants may not have felt comfortable being interviewed. Three aspects were included to help alleviate this issue. Firstly, there was no obligation for participants to be involved in the study. Secondly, a research assistant (with no association with the organisation) conducted the interviews to maintain impartiality and credibility of the data collected. Finally, the data were not collected until the consultant's contractual arrangements with the organisation had expired.

After receiving Human Research Ethics approval, the invitation for the qualified staff (N=16) to participate in the research was delivered by the research assistant, via the Director in each centre. The information letter disclosed that an aim of the research was to evaluate the researcher's role as an external consultant to the organisation. Participants who chose to be involved then posted the consent form to the research assistant who then organised a time and place for the interview to be conducted. The interview included the following questions:

1. Have you benefited from the external consultant working with you and the setting? Why or why not?
2. Do you see any benefits for the families and children since you have been working with the external consultant? Why or why not?
3. Have you seen changes in the setting since you have been working with the external consultant? Please explain.
4. What else would you like to have had happen, or done differently? Why?

Nine participants[5] across the three centres chose to participate in the research study. This comprised of Centre 1 = 4 (including the Director); Centre 2 = 4 (including the Director) and Centre 3 = 1. This represented 56% of the qualified staff in the three centres. Interviews were conducted at the beginning of the year, and this may have impacted on how many qualified staff chose to participate in the research as this is a busy time in long day care centres in terms of settling new children and families.

---

[5] For this chapter staff are not identified by position (for example director, teacher of 3-5 room) to ensure anonymity of participants who were involved in this research.

Data from the interviews were transcribed, sorted and analysed with the use of QSR NVivo 8 (QSR International, 2009). NVivo is a qualitative software program that allows for the data to be compared and analysed across attributes (Bazeley 2007; Richards and Richards 1992; Murphy 2000; Welsh 2002; Dey 1993; Morse and Richards 2002). The data were firstly coded in relation to the interview questions and then analysed to determine findings that were representative across all three centres.

Findings

Benefits of the external consultant

Across the three centres the staff highlighted several aspects of the external consultant that supported them in examining their practices. Firstly, staff noted that a high level of enthusiasm, approachability and having an ability to generate respect were important attributes of the consultant in galvanising support in the centres. The benefit of a sustained period of time that the consultant was involved with the organisation was perceived as imperative to staff developing a relationship and rapport with the consultant. The sustained period was also seen as a way of supporting staff in implementing change. For instance, staff noted:

> For deeper thinking…when they really do have to reflect on their thinking, it needs to be more sustained. (staff 1, centre 3).

> I think we have benefited, in that we haven't just gone to one day training or one evening of training and then have to come back and grapple with it. Any questions we have about it we've been able to ask [consultant] and to refer things to her and to ask her; to take observations to her and say "what do you think" (staff 1, centre 2).

The staff also discussed the importance of the consultant providing technical support and expertise, to both reaffirm their beliefs as well as challenge them. For example:

> Walking through with her, it was just like she got it. She got what I was thinking and it was just nice to have someone…she was kind of backing me up on a few things that we were talking about, and stuff. I found that really quite helpful (staff 1, centre 1).

> Actually being able to work with an academic. Having [consultant's] insight into how things can be and how you can do things to make them run better and smoothly…before you get stuck in a rut (staff 2, centre 2).

> Obviously our points of view were not always the same, so just to have a different opinion and to push me (staff 1, centre 3).

> Sometimes she could give guidance that I couldn't, and they took that on board (staff 2, centre 1).

The staff also noted that the changes being implemented were achievable as they were broken down into smaller tasks. By not focusing on the whole change, but working on parts and developing mastery the staff felt this made it an easier transition.

> Yeah. Breaking it down – like, say, if they're looking at the programming and breaking that down into parts. So it's not go and read this and come back with some thoughts. It's about breaking that down into parts and really concentrating on parts of it; giving them something to do (staff 1, centre 3).

> So I think this helps us recognise ours own value. You know what you can do. We thought we couldn't do (programming) like this. We just said, "that's so hard". At the beginning it's so hard. But now, everyone is used to daily diary, report, portfolio and program (staff 3, centre 2).

Staff also commented on the consistency of information being given across the three centres. This collective information ensured that everyone was clear about the content, expectations and process in relation to programming, which is very different to when one or two individuals go to a course and bring that information back to the centre. This collective approach also helped consolidate the teams in the centre, in terms of working well together and collectively understanding what needed to occur. Staff noted:

> There's much more focus again for the teams to work together, to evaluate, to look at what they're next moving towards which has come out of the programming and planning project. I think that there's more of a team understanding now (staff 2, centre 1).

> I think this year will be a really good year for them to consolidate and to really start moving ahead (staff 1, centre 3).

Finally, staff discussed the high level of motivation and confidence that is now exhibited about planning and programming.

> I think that's from [consultant] and everyone taking responsibility, and everyone should think, "I'm a master in this room you're not only a worker...you should take responsibility" (staff 3, centre 2).

> So you can see the changes in staff attitudes and what they think, because they can teach children that this is what you want and this is what you don't want and that comes back to that intentional teaching. Somehow, I don't know how that got lost, but it did get lost for a few years (staff 1, centre 3).

Benefits for children

The staff in all three centres noted that the changes to programming and planning had benefited the children. In particular, the staff discussed the program and planning had become more intentional and focused on what they wanted to not only teach the children, but also what the children wanted to learn. This had occurred through the processes that had been established in terms of planning, programming and documenting, and how this had ensured the staff listened to and adapted the program to meet the needs and interests of the children. For instance, staff stated:

> I think they (children) are seeing themselves reflected a bit more than they used to in terms of the displays...I think the quality of the program that the children receive is better than it was as well because the staff have to have objectives in mind. What are the children going to learn in a group in the room, and each individual child? I think that's focused the staff to be more intentional (staff 2, centre 1).

> Families comment on the changes to the program and how they see that has benefited their child – through their involvement, engagement and keenness to come to the centre…the children have benefited a lot through this. They're actually being more challenged than they were (staff 4, centre 3).

Benefits for families

The staff felt the families also benefited from the changes to the planning, programming and documentation. Staff discussed how more informed families were about the learning occurring in the centre for both their individual child as well as for the group their child was in:

> I think in terms of the programming and planning project they're getting a lot more information about how their children are learning, what they're learning, and what their children do here every day. So through the daily diaries they have a much better grasp of what actually happens in a day and that, yes, there is teaching and learning happening in the centre. The biggest response we've had has been to the environments, the changing

> environments and the reports that we've been handing out (staff 2, centre 1).

> The parents certainly notice the difference. Some of the feedback we got was around "it seems the staff really know my child now". Parents are seeing the link between "oh yes, they really do have that interest at home", or "do you know what, this is a totally new interest. I didn't know they were as interested in this as what you're telling me they are" (staff 1, centre 2).

Staff discussed how relationships with the families had evolved and developed over the time the project was conducted. This relationship also impacted on how families felt connected to the centre, and comfortable about leaving their child each day. For example, the staff stated:

> I think they feel more relaxed and in this last couple of years they've just sort of rushed in and rushed out. But this year they seem more relaxed and they sit on the lounge where I've got my daily diary and have a read with their children and they sort of spend a little bit more time before they're running off to work or university or wherever (staff 2, centre 2).

> Parents do come and enjoy the room. Parents do come and say, "look at the beautiful lights and look at the curtains". They do come and they say, "okay, mummy is going to work. When you want mummy I am here on the photo frame" and they show their photo. So you feel that, okay, they are happy (staff 3, centre 1).

Staff noted that even though families were not involved in the changes made to the programming and planning this did not create negative comments. All families were kept informed about the project through regular memos and each change was explained both in memos and through conversations with families.

Things to improve

The staff in all three centres noted that they wanted to have more time to work with the consultant and discuss changes being implemented.

> It wasn't enough actually, because finally we have to wind up in that two hours. Then I guess it's also that not everyone can take that time out and come and sit down. I myself can't do it too, because I have young one now. I haven't got anyone to look after her, so it's a bit hard to organise that sort of meeting where five people, six people sit down together and do things (staff 3, centre 1).

> So I think in terms of what support the staff need, I think it is just more time getting to implement it, more time helping to really unpack it and to look at each outcome and what we are already doing, and what ways we could challenge the children further on particular outcomes; because I think it is a pedagogical approach as well (staff 1, centre 2).

They felt that the meetings with the whole team could have been more collaborative and informal where staff could provide their ideas to share. This would have helped all staff to feel included in the changes and decisions being made. These meetings tended to be more about information giving, as the negotiation about the processes and changes happened in the small working party with the qualified staff. For example, they noted:

> I think maybe giving the staff time to share their ideas with her as well. A lot of the meetings that we had were Directors and [consultant], and then the Directors took it back to the staff, which I think was necessary for a lot of the things but in terms of - and I guess we needed to then coach and train the staff, but I think some of the best things that came out were when the staff just had informal discussions with [consultant] when she came in (staff 2, centre 1).

> For a while there was an issue with the child care workers feeling they were left behind and missing out. Then we were bringing them into the whole group discussions of unpacking the outcomes (staff1, centre 2).

Interestingly, staff discussed the dilemma of implementing changes too quickly as opposed to a slower pace until all have achieved mastery or felt comfortable with the change. One staff member discussed this dilemma in pondering whether the changes that occurred would have happened if the project had been implemented more slowly over a longer period of time. She stated:

> Sometimes I felt like it moved a little bit too fast, but in hindsight perhaps it moved at the right speed that it just kept going. Sometimes I felt like we needed a breather, but you know, I think that what happens is sometimes it takes years to implement something, because we back off it a bit, a lot. We just go, "oh this is too hard" (staff 1, centre 3).

Discussion

The findings of this study support current research literature on the importance of qualified staff being provided opportunities for professional learning to engage with educational change (Jaruszewicz and White 2009). The participants in this current study noted that the external consultant was a support to enabling change and challenging staff's approaches to programming and planning. In this study, staff recognised the importance of the consultant not only affirming them but also challenging them by providing constructive feedback over a sustained period of time. For instance, one staff member noted: *I like input from external people...it takes time to understand and to develop more (staff 1, centre 3).* The role of an external consultant and prolonged engagement with professional learning is supported by previous research that has been conducted in early childhood settings in the United States of America (see Fiene 2002; Campbell and Milbourne 2005).

The staff in this study also discussed the importance of establishing an organisational culture that embraced change. The staff perceived that this positive attitude ensured engagement with the changes to planning and programming. This pedagogical shift in the way the staff planned their curriculum was supported by the change management approach implemented by the organisation. Killgallon et al. (2008) also found that teachers noted that when there was a positive attitude or approach to the educational change this contributed to their coping skills. This research noted that:

> Knowing the change "wouldn't go away" resulted in participants ... adopting a proactive stance, and contributed to their willingness to be informed and actively engaged in the change process (Kilgallon, Maloney, and Lock 2008).

The issue of who decided on the changes and how they were implemented was contentious. Implementing the Appreciative Inquiry Model did require balancing the expectations of management with the needs of the qualified staff. For this study, the small working party was deemed to be the most effective way of developing a systems approach across the three centres, and the decision was made that the qualified staff would lead this working party. Historically in Australia, long day care centres have enjoyed flat management structures whereby all staff (qualified and experienced) contribute to and document children's learning. This can include writing daily diary entries, writing observations for individual children's portfolios and planning experiences in the program. This study's findings indicated that a shift in pedagogical responsibility was, at the beginning, challenging for some of the staff. The staff (on reflection) saw the benefits of this approach as their confidence levels in meeting expectations increased, although they also recognised it increased their responsibility for leading the program.

Another area that created philosophical discussion related to the involvement of families in the centres' programming and planning. Historically, and prevalent in the early childhood literature, is the concept that as families are the "child's first teacher" (Department of Employment Education and Workplace Relations (DEEWR) 2009) they must be involved in the programming and planning for their children in the early childhood setting. Again, early in the project a decision was made (by both the management and the working party) that families would be informed of the changes but that they would not be asked to contribute to the changes being discussed and implemented. The rationale for this was that the changes being discussed related to pedagogical decisions about what was appropriate programming systems that also met the external accountability systems and the qualified staff should take the leadership role in terms of pedagogy and curriculum decisions in the program. This decision recognised that families are (and should be) involved in the centres, but that the broader curriculum decisions and directions being undertaken required engagement of the qualified staff.

Limitations

As this study was undertaken in one early childhood organisation in Sydney, Australia, there are some limitations to the findings that need to be considered. First, the measurement of the success of the changes being implemented was based on the staff's perceptions. To strengthen the findings other tools that measure pedagogical documentation and quality environments and standards could be used. For example the Quality Improvement Accreditation System scale (National Childcare Accreditation Council 2002) or *The Early Childhood Environment Childhood Rating Scale revised edition (ECERS-R)* (Harms, Cryer, and Clifford 1990).

Second, due to the small sample of participants the findings may reflect a bias for the consultant's role in the change management process. Qualified staff who did not value the role may have chosen to opt out of the research. It should be noted that one of the centres only had one staff member's perspective. This centre did find the change management process difficult at times, and their perspectives may not mirror that of the other participants.

This project was based on one organisation and its approach to utilising a change management framework to rethink its pedagogical practices and documentation systems. Therefore, this change management process would need to be replicated across several organisations, utilising an external consultant to evaluate if the processes and strategies utilised are transferable to other early childhood settings.

Significance

Given the increased focus on the early years (Shonkoff and Phillips 2000; Department of Education 2001), educational outcomes and what is argued to be appropriate to teach young children, a process to support qualified staff in examining their pedagogical practices is pertinent. Providing a culture of examining practices allows for qualified staff to critically reflect and examine teaching practices (Fiene 2002; Riley and Roach 2006). The appreciative inquiry approach provides a process for organisations to move beyond focusing on solving problems to dreaming and inquiring on what could be. As the field of education around the world is becoming more focused on external accountabilities and outcomes, this approach provides educational organisations an avenue for enacting change differently.

The role of the external consultant is an important contributor to professional learning. This outsider can be an impetus for change, allowing the staff to examine other ways of practicing their teaching and leading to a critical inquiry of what they do and why. Webster-Wright (2009) argues that reframing professional learning to include a critical inquiry process with academia and community can result in transformative practices. In this study, the staff noted the importance of being supported and challenged by the consultant. For instance, one staff member staff stated:

> Challenge is a good thing. If you're [not] challenged you just feel everyday is the same…if you get used to no challenge you lose yourself (staff 3, centre 2).

Staff did note that they wanted more time with the consultant to ponder planning and programming. Further research would be valuable to investigate how the external consultant's role supports educational change, and what length of involvement is needed for this change to be sustained.

Conclusion

This project enacted a change management framework to rethink and reframe pedagogical practices. For this organisation, investing in a whole-of-organisation approach to professional learning created a space for contemporary approaches to programming and planning to be examined, and changes to be implemented successfully across the organisation. Having an external consultant act as a critical friend, utilising an appreciative inquiry model over a sustained period of time, created a space for change to emerge. The commitment from leadership and the staff seeing the changes were needed have been highlighted in other appreciative inquiry studies (see Bushe 2010). While this chapter reports on one small project, there is potential for this model to be implemented with other early childhood centres to ensure engagement with contemporary practices and pedagogies.

References

Bazeley, P. 2007. *Qualitative data analysis with NVivo*. London Sage Publications.

Bushe, G.R. 1995. Advances in appreciative inquiry as an organization development intervention. *Organization Development Journal* 13 (3):14-22.

—. 2010. A comparative case study of appreciative inquiries in one organization: Implications for practice. *Review of Research and Social INtervention* 29:7-24.

Campbell, P. H, and S. A Milbourne. 2005. Improving the quality of infant-toddler care through professional development. *Topics in Early Childhood Special Education* 25 (1):3-14.

Cohen, L., and L. Manion. 1986. *Research methods in education*. 2nd ed. Australia: Croom Helm Ltd.

Cooperrider, D.L. 2001. Positive image, positive action: The affirmative basis of organizing. In *Appreciative Inquiry: An Emerging Direction for Organization Development*, edited by D. L. Cooperrider, J. Peter F. Sorensen, T. F. Yaeger and D. Whitney. Champaign IL: Stipes Publishing L.L.C.

Cooperrider, David L., and Srivastva. Suresh. 1987. Appreciative inquiry in organizational life. *Research in Organizational Change and Development* 1:129-169.

Department of Education, Employment and Workplace Relations (DEEWR). 2011. Policy agenda.

—. 2009. *Regulation impact statement for early childhood education and care quality reforms.* 2009 [cited August 18 2009]. Available from http://www.coag.gov.au/coag_meeting_outcomes/2009-07-02/docs/RIS_for_early_childhood_development.pdf

—. 2009. *Belonging, being and becoming. The early years learning framework*. ACT: Commonwealth Government.

Dey, I. 1993. *Qualitative data analysis: A user friendly guide for social scientists*. New York: Routledge.

Dubrin, A, C Dalglish, and P Miller. 2006. *Leadership*. 2nd ed. QLD: John Wiley and Sons Australia, Ltd.

Duigan, P. 2006. *Educational leadership. Key challenges and ethical tensions*. Melbourne, Victoria: Cambridge University Press.

Evans, M, P Lomax, and H Morgan. 2000. Closing the circle: Action research partnerships towards better learning and teaching in schools. *Cambridge Journal of Teacher Education* 30:405-419.

Fiene, R. 2002. Improving child care quality through an infant mentoring project. *Child and Youth Care Forum* 3 (2):75-83.

—. 2002. Improving child care quality through an infant mentoring project. *Child and Youth Care Forum* 3 (2):75-83.

Hahs-Vaughn, D, and K Yanowitz. 2009. Who is conducting teacher research? *Journal of Educational Research* 102 (6):415-424.

Harms, T, D. Cryer, and R.M. Clifford. 1990. *Infant/toddler environment rating scale*. New York: Teachers College Press.

Heidegger, M. 1962. *Being and time*. Translated by J. Macquarrie and E. Robinson. Oxford and New York: Blackwell/Harper and Row.

Hiatt, J, and T Creasey. 2003. *Change management: The people side of change*. Colorado, USA: Prosci Learning Center Publications.

Husserl, E. 1965. *Phenomenology and the crisis of philosophy. Philosophy as rigorous science and the crisis of the European man*. United States: Harper and Row.

Jaruszewicz, Candace, and Mary White. 2009. The Teachergarten: Creating an Environment Conducive to Meaningful Teacher Growth. *Early Childhood Education Journal*, 171-174.

Kemmis, S., and M. Wilkinson. 1998. Participatory action research and the study of practice. In *Action research in practice: Partnerships for social justice in education*, edited by B. Atweh, S. Kemmis and P. Weeks. London Routledge.

Kilgallon, Pam, Carmel Maloney, and Graeme Lock. 2008. Early childhood teachers coping with educational change. *Australian Journal of Early Childhood* 33 (1):23(7).

Kotter, J. 1990. *A Force for change : how leadership differs from management*. New York: Free Press.

—. 2007. Leading change. Why transformation efforts fail. *Harvard Business Review* January:96-103.

Kotter, J., and L. Schlesinger. 2008. Choosing strategies for change. *Harvard Business Review* July-August:130-139.

Lester, S. 2001. *An introduction to phenomenological research* 2001 [cited 19/11/2001 2001]. Available from www.devmts.demon.co.uk/resmethy.htm

Lyotard, J.F. 1991. *Phenomenology*. USA: State University of New York.

Morgan, G. 2003. Staff roles, education and compensation. In *Early childhood education and care in the USA* edited by D. Cryer and R. Clifford. Baltimore: Brookes.

Morse, J. M., and L. Richards. 2002. *Readme first for a users guide to qualitative methods*. Thousand Oaks, California: Sage Publications Inc.

Murphy, John. 2001. *Empowering grass-roots groups to strengthen communities*. 2000 [cited 23/01/01 2001]. Available from www.communitybuilders.nsw.gov.au

National Childcare Accreditation Council. 2004. *About quality improvement and assurance*. National Childcare Accreditation Council. 2002 [cited 16th April 2004]. Available from http://www.ncac.gov.au/quality_systems/quality_systems_index.html

QSR International. 2009. *NVivo 8* Computer Software. Doncaster, Vic: QSR International.

Richards, Lyn, and Tom Richards. 1992. Hard results from soft data. Issues in qualitative computing. Paper read at British Sociological Association Annual Conference, at Manchester.

Riley, David, and Mary Roach. 2006. Helping Teachers Grow: Toward Theory and Practice of an "Emergent Curriculum" Model of Staff Development. *Early Childhood Education Journal* 33 (5):363-370.

Schutz, A. 1972. *On phenomenology and social relations; selected writings*. Chicago: University of Chicago Press.

Shonkoff, J. P, and D. A Phillips, eds. 2000. *From neurons to neighbourhoods: The science of early childhood development. Committee on integrating the science of early childhood development*. Washington, DC: National Academy Press.

Srivastva, S, and D Cooperrider. 1990. *Appreciative management and leadership: the power of positive thought and action in organizations.* . San Francisco, USA: Jossey-Bass.

Stamage, S.M., and R.E. Kreiger. 1987. *Adult education and phenomenological research: New directions for theory, practice and research*. Florida: Publishing Company.

van Manen, M. 1990. *Researching lived experience: Human sciences for an action sensitive pedagogy*. London: Althouse.

Webster-Wright, Ann. 2009. Reframing Professional Development Through Understanding Authentic Professional Learning. *Review of Educational Research* 79 (2):702-739.

Welsh, E. 2002. Dealing with data: Using NVIVO in the qualitative data analysis process. *Qualitative Social Research* 3 (2).

CHAPTER THREE

USING PRACTITIONER INQUIRY TO PROMOTE REFLEXIVITY AND CHANGE IN INFANT-TODDLER EARLY CHILDHOOD PROGRAMS

SHEILA DEGOTARDI, ANTHONY SEMANN AND WENDY SHEPHERD

Introduction

Like many other countries, Australia is experiencing a rapid growth in the number of children enrolled in formal early childhood programs (United Nations Children's Fund 2008; Office of Early Childhood, Education and Child Care 2008). With the care of infants and toddlers increasingly shared between home and early childhood centres, attention is drawn to the quality of infant-toddler early childhood programs (Warrilow et al. 2002; Phillips and Adams 2001). The widely accepted view that the quality of early experiences significantly impacts on children's development and wellbeing is supported by robust and enduring evidence that children in high-quality infant-toddler settings fare better developmentally, than those in poor quality settings (e.g. Deynoot-Schaub and Risken-Walraven 2006; NICHD Early Child Care Research Network 2001, 1998, 2000; Burchinal et al. 2000; de Schipper et al. 2008; Fein 1995; Howes, Hamilton, and Matheson 1994). It is of concern therefore, that research suggests that the quality of these infant-toddler programs is often lower than that of programs for preschool-aged children (Howes, Phillips, and Whitebook 1992; Goelman et al. 2006; Phillipsen et al. 1997). For this reason, researchers are turning their attention to investigating factors that support the provision of quality programs within these programs.

The level of quality in early childhood centres is closely aligned with structural elements such as staff qualifications, salaries, adult-child ratios and managerial support (NICHD Early Child Care Research Network 2002; Sumsion 2005; Semann and Sims 2010). In infant-toddler programs, observations that staff tend to be less qualified and have less experience than staff employed with preschool-aged children are concerning (Phillipsen et al. 1997; Ireland 2007), as structural factors not only contribute significantly to program quality, but are also major sources of staff status, morale and retention (Sumsion 2005; Warrilow et al. 2002). In the context of a shortage and high turnover of early childhood staff (Community Services Ministers' Advisory Council 2006), there is an impetus to develop models that support the ongoing professional learning and status of infant-toddler staff.

The Potential of Professional Learning

Professional learning programs have long been considered a means of supporting the direct, day-to-day contributions of practitioners and, as a consequence, have the potential to address concerns about quality and staff status (Warrilow et al. 2002). The deliberate act of seeking further knowledge prompts practitioners to seek new ways of engaging with both theory and practice in their professional context (Semann et al. 2009). By validating and extending sound, effective practice, professional learning programs also contribute towards feelings of self-competency and professional agency, and thus raise the status of early childhood professionals (Waniganayake et al. 2008).

Traditional professional learning approaches have tended to comprise the delivery of one-off presentations or workshops, yet recent research indicates that conceptual knowledge and operational skills can be more effectively enhanced though practitioners' engagement in more longer-term professional learning program such as practitioner inquiry or action learning projects. Waniganayake et al. (2008), for example, argue that there is a greater possibility of change and quality enhancement when practitioners receive ongoing support over time, are actively involved in the learning process, have opportunities to apply new knowledge in their workplace and to discuss their developing practice with 'trusted' others (see also Warrilow et al. 2002; Kilgallon, Maloney, and Lock 2008). Practitioner inquiry is one long-term professional learning approach that can satisfy these conditions.

Practitioner Inquiry as a Paradigm for Change

Practitioner inquiry is an approach to professional learning whereby practitioners deeply explore their own practice (Goodfellow and Hedges 2007). It affords opportunities to develop and test new ideas, respond to real-world challenges and engage reflectively with theories and research. In this way, practitioner inquiry projects seek to promote an increased awareness of the basis of professional decision-making and judgments by encouraging practitioners to "recognise and articulate the complexities of their work and the values that lie at the heart of professional practice" (Goodfellow 2005, p.48).

Such programs have the potential to promote reflexive engagement, in which practitioners think deeply about the ways in which their beliefs, experiences and reactions to new ideas contribute towards their evolving practice, shape their understanding of their own role, and impact on how they conceptualise the experiences of the children with whom they work. Reflexivity is an intentional, emotional and cognitive process that requires practitioners to tune in to and critically reflect on often-taken-for-granted values and beliefs. This enhanced self-knowledge becomes a catalyst for examining the basis of the way in which individuals perceive and act in the real world and thus enables practitioners to develop a richer understanding of their own practice (Maton 2003; Sumsion 2005). As Sumsion writes, reflexivity involves

> challenging our own assumptions and engaging in ongoing internal dialogue and conversations with others about how to respond imaginatively, courageously, and with integrity to the troubling questions that arise when we unsettle the status quo. In requiring a continual rereading and rewriting of our-selves and our practice, reflexivity keeps alive the possibility of seeing and acting differently (pp. 197-198).

In this way, practitioner inquiry constitutes a "paradigm for change" (Orland-Barak 2009) that allows practitioners to build both evidence-based practice and practice-based evidence that directly contributes towards enhancing the quality of their own teaching and programs.

The Present Study

This chapter describes the pedagogical attitudes and outcomes expressed by infant-toddler practitioners who participated in a 6-month practitioner inquiry professional learning program in Canberra, Australian Capital

Territory. By joining the program, participants committed to the attendance of five 3-hour sessions in which they would engage with and discuss a range of theoretical ideas related to infant-toddler curriculum and pedagogy. Practitioners were asked to commit to a level of critical reflexivity about their reactions to the session content, and how it could relate to and be applied in their own context. This reflexive component required participants to use reflective diaries to respond to provocation questions and practical exercises that were provided by the professional learning facilitators at the conclusion of each session. These diary entries then became the topic of discussion and debate at the beginning of the subsequent session.

Five content areas were addressed by the professional learning sessions:

Historical and contemporary beliefs and images of infants and toddlers prompted participants to explore and debate how infant-toddler experiences, learning and care are conceptualised and theorised about in each of the general, academic and professional communities.

Characteristics of infant-toddler curriculum deconstructed the elements and attitudes that can underpin infant-toddler curriculum, including the provision of authentic learning experiences, notions of respect and relationships, ideas about infant agency and problem-solving capabilities, and the importance of a calm learning environment.

Relationships and interactions promoted the importance of sensitive, responsive and authentic communication, as well as factors that can promote adult-child and peer relationships in infant-toddler programs

Environments and materials challenged participants to consider the diverse ways in which environments for infants and toddlers could be provisioned, and the impact those environments and materials have on pedagogy and relationships.

Planning for and documenting experiences and learning encouraged participants to explore the unique ways in which they can document the learning, teaching and relationships that take place within an infant-toddler program.

In this chapter we present and discuss the perspectives of the participants, focusing on the ways in which their ideas about their work, their infant-toddler curriculum and their pedagogy changed as they progressed through the practitioner inquiry project. We draw on written and verbal reflections collected during the course of the program to illustrate practitioners' increasing levels of critical self-awareness of their own practices and resulting reported changes in their programs.

Method

Participants

Participants were twenty early childhood practitioners working directly, or in a supervisory role of those working directly, with infants or toddlers in an early childhood centre. Of the twenty participants, eighteen worked in community-based not-for-profit childcare programs, one in an employer-sponsored program, and one a privately-owned centre. Two participants were centre directors, while the others identified themselves as room leaders (n=17) or "educator" (n=1), and had a wide range of experience: less than 1 year (n=1); 1-3 years (n=3); 3-6 years (n=4); 6-10 years (n=6); more than 10 years (n=6). Most worked with the birth - 2 year age group (n=15) with the remaining working with 2-3 year-old children.

Data Generation

Survey data. Two electronic surveys generated data about participant perspectives and attitudes towards their work and infant-toddler pedagogy. The entrance survey was delivered prior to the commencement of the program, and included demographic questions and a series of open-ended questions. The exit survey was delivered after the final session, and asked participants to reflect on any changes in thinking or practice over the course of the program (See Table 1).

Table 1: Entrance and Exit Survey Open-ended Questions

Entrance Survey
What do you think are the three or four most important characteristics of a high-quality infant-toddler program?
What or who would you say supports you the most in your work?
What or who would you say constrains what you can do or achieve?
Please list the most important three or four things that you hope to gain from participating in this action-research project.
Exit Survey
What (if anything) would you say has been the greatest change in your views about your work over the past 5 months?
What (if anything) would you say has been the greatest change related to your thinking about, or delivery of your curriculum for, infants and toddlers in your room/centre over the past 5 months?
What (if anything) would you say has been the greatest change in the feelings and/or experiences of infants and toddlers in your program over the last 5 months?
What were the most significant features of the program for your own thinking and practice?

Interview data. A sub-set of participants volunteered to be interviewed over the course of the project: even participants for a mid-way interview after the third professional learning session, and five for a final interview after the conclusion of the program. The aim of these interviews was to provide interested participants with an opportunity to share information about their direct experiences and thoughts in a more detailed manner than that permitted by the online survey. Examples of the open-ended interview questions are provided in Table 2.

Table 2: Examples of mid-way and final interview questions

Mid-way Interview

What were your most pressing concerns about your work or your program before you started?

Have any of these concerns changed in any way since you started this program? If so, can you tell me how and why you think they have changed.

What (if any) workshop ideas have had the most impact on you so far?

Have there been any ideas that i) have made you uncomfortable/uneasy; ii) that you found unrealistic or impractical?

Final Interview

Has any of the information presented or discussed during the workshops impacted on you in terms of your thinking or your practice?

Are there any ideas or information that you found confronting or challenging or difficult in any way?

Has anything changed in the way in which you feel about your work since you started the project?

Data Analysis. The transcribed survey and interview responses were analysed using an interpretive, thematic analysis approach (Maykut and Morehouse 1994; Braun and Clark 2006). The data were read and margin notes were made to identify key points related to participants' perspectives about their work, curriculum and pedagogy. In keeping with the present focus, particular attention was paid to evidence of change and indicators of reflexive awareness related to challenges and changes. Once margin notes were complete, these notes were compared and contrasted with each other in order to develop and then articulate key themes that emerged from the data (Strauss and Corbin 1998).

Results and Discussion

Two main themes emerged from the survey and interview data. The first related to curriculum challenges and changes that were experienced by the practitioners as they entered, progressed through and completed the project. The second theme related to views about their professional status and development. In the following section, these themes and related sub-themes are discussed. Extracts from the data are used to exemplify the responses in each theme, and the source of each extract is identified as follows: (EntS) = Entrance survey; (ExS) = Exit Survey; (MW#) = Midway interview identified by number; (F#) = Final interview identified by number.

Understanding of Curriculum: Changes and Challenges

The entry survey responses suggested that participants attributed the notion of high quality infant-toddler programs to four broad pedagogical and structural elements. As Table 3 illustrates, the notion of responsiveness and a positive emotional climate featured in most participants' responses. While the notions of responsiveness and emotional wellbeing are consistent with attachment-based pedagogical approaches (e.g. Harrison 2003; Honig 2002; Raikes 1996), it has been argued that concentration on such characteristics can downplay professional status of early childhood practitioners through the emphasis of the "motherhood" role (Ailwood 2008). Practitioners also expressed the importance of a stimulating curriculum, but responses were generally restricted to notions of physical, sensory and exploratory play. While the importance of physical and explorational play reflects infants' sensorimotor approach to learning and developing, some have argued that a strong focus on these aspects can cause practitioners to overlook social and communicative qualities of infant play (Degotardi and Pearson 2010), as well as the learning opportunities found in other experiences that make up the infants' day (Gonzalez-Mena and Widmeyer Eyer 2007).

The interview and the exit survey responses suggested that practitioners had added depth to their initial understanding of curriculum by considering how some of the principles that were promoted during the workshops may enrich the curriculum in their rooms. Four main principles featured strongly in these responses.

The notion of respect. Early workshops challenged participants to explore the concept of respect for infants and toddlers and how this can be made evident in their work. Participants appeared to have cast a critical eye over their own and team-members' practices to reconsider "The way we treated and respected the children (MW2)." Some looked closely at how they interacted with the children, giving stronger consideration to allowing children time to respond and listening closely to children's perspectives and needs:

> It's a challenge that you really need to listen more than you do, and asking children questions before we do things (F1)

> Over the past 5 months the staff have had a look at their own practices in regards to respect for children by always ensuring that they inform the children of what is going to happen next. (ExS)

Table 3: Practitioner-identified characteristics of high-quality infant-toddler programs.

Characteristic	Examples from Survey
Responsiveness	"High responsiveness to individual needs"; "catering to their interests and developmental needs"; "respect and listen to infants' and toddlers' words"; "intuitive carers"
Emotional climate	"Laughter"; "feel safe"; "loving"; "feeling good about themselves"; staff who take time to bond with children and families'; "relaxed; "lots of support and cuddles:; "positive interactions".
Stimulating curriculum	"being active"; "sensory exploration"; "physical development"; "variety of activities"; "knowing all children…learn differently through play", "having a wide range of resources on offer".
Centre supports	"Having a team that supports parents, children and each other"; "having adequate programming and planning time"; "lower ratios".

Others commented about how they felt that this shift in thinking and practice appeared to have impacted on children's response to them:

> The fact we are more respectful – listening to children and to their lives. They respond to staff more (F5)

> We have found that children will come when asked. We tell the children what we are going to do and they seem to appreciate that. (MW7)

Considering children's perspectives. Related to the notion of respect, practitioners were challenged to deepen their appreciation of children's perspectives. One workshop reflective exercise seemed particularly useful in prompting this change:

> I also found it challenging when we had to take the children's point of view – sitting on the ground and listening. It was interesting to do this and it gave me a different point of view…you notice things when you do this and the children notice that you are sitting and stopping to listen to them. After doing this I can see more things, tuning my ears to their talk, I am there for them. I feel delighted when I understand them better. (F3)

Overall, practitioners reported an increased awareness of and respect for children's agency, both in terms of their intentions and their ability to be active in their own learning:

> I have been thinking more about "how do I give them more say in what happens in their day?…giving them more choices." If they do not want to do something, asking ourselves "does it have to be done now?" (F4)

> [We are] offering more of a challenge. Not helping them, but letting them work some things out for themselves. (F2)

A sense of calm. Some participants credited the level of respectful responsiveness described above to a developing sense of calm in their room:

> We have been able to keep the environment calm which I think is because of the way we are communicating with the children. (F5)

Moreover, instead of rushing to "do what 'has' to be done" (EntS), practitioners appeared to respond to the call from workshop presenters to make a conscious effort to slow down and take their time to be with the children. The most significant change reported by one participant was:

> Slowing down: putting other things on hold to actually spend time with the children to just be there to support their play and be involved in helping stimulate their experiences. (ExS)

Another stated that:

> I believe that I have softened a little and am more focused on what works for the child rather than what I need to do. (ExS)

These changes were summed up by one participant who described her room as:

> Very calm, very happy, very settled…children not having tantrums. People walk in to the room and say "Wow! It is so calm. Is it always like this?" (F3)

Enhanced understanding of curriculum and the learning environment. Many participants reported that they participated in the practitioner inquiry project to find out "more about curriculum for infants and toddlers" (MW4) and noted pressure from other practitioners and families to adhere to a particular view of "curriculum":

> I wanted to let my parents know that we were doing as much as the older rooms but in different ways. (MW2)

Their responses suggested that an engagement in this project extended their ideas about curriculum content beyond those reflected in traditional play-based programs. Participants now referred to child-led investigations, interactions and routines, thus reflecting a deeper awareness of the learning potential of a wide range of experiences that have been argued to comprise a rich and holistic curriculum for this age group (Gonzalez-Mena and Widmeyer Eyer 2007; Greenman, Stonehouse, and Schweikert 2008).

> The curriculum in the nursery has changed so that it is more child oriented and focuses on more time for exploration and experimentation through play and interaction. (ExS)

> It's really reminded me to show respect to each child with some of the simple things which might get overlooked, such as hand washing, face washing. (ExS)

There was also a deeper appreciation of the need to engage with contemporary ideas about materials and learning environments:

> I am conscious of providing a natural environment for the children and am striving to provide authenticity in environment and experiences. (ExS)

Statements such as, "The curriculum now belongs to the children and the staff" (ExS) and "I am more flexible to the interests of the children which then take us on a journey" not only suggest that practitioners were including children in the decision-making process, but also increased confidence in their own ability to make informed choices:

> The experiences I provide are more thought out from use of my own imagination, having to really think about what can we do to stimulate the children which we have to create instead of going to a cupboard and pulling out a store-bought toy or plastic toy to provide that stimulation. (ExS)

Some listed implementing such changes as a major challenge throughout the project: "It is one of the challenges of child care to do it differently" (F3). However, most reported a level of critical engagement with ideas about curriculum:

> I am still in the process of getting my head around this...we will be going over the program and thinking about the way observations are done, into routines as well as play-based experiences. (F5)

> Little by little I am making changes, trying things out. (ExS)

Professional Growth and Development

The second main theme to emerge from the data related to practitioners' professional growth, status and development. Consistent with the goals of professional learning programs (Waniganayake et al. 2008; Warrilow et al. 2002), participants stated that they were motivated to enrol in the program by a desire to learn about new ways of approaching infant-toddler pedagogy: "to get a new view of working with infants and toddlers" (MW1), "to get new ideas" (MW6) and "looking for different ways to plan and program" (MW2). In the entry survey, however, participants identified a range of factors that currently constrained their practice. The first constraint reflected concerns raised in the literature about the structural elements of quality in early childhood programs (Goelman et al. 2006; Phillips et al. 2001), with the participants identifying limitations related to "budget, committee, paperwork", "money, staff ratios" and "resources and time" and "lack of support staff". Communication and partnership constraints were also identified, including "communication with management and staff", "ensuring all staff work as a team" and "parents". Finally, many of the practitioners expressed doubts about their professional competence, in particular "myself, as I have a lack of self-confidence" and a need to "learn if what I am doing is right". These personal acknowledgments, when taken together with the other reported constraints seem to echo concerns that have been raised about the perceived low professional status of infant-toddler practitioners (Sumsion 2005; Warrilow et al. 2002).

During the course of the project, the practitioners' responses suggested that some of them were finding new ways to address some of these constraints. Four sub-themes were reflected in the data.

Motivation to learn with and from others. While the majority of participants responded to the entry survey question about current support by nominating team members and their directors as prominent support resources, the interviews uncovered a strong desire to network with practitioners from other centres. One participant stated “Working in the nursery you might feel isolated within the centre” (MW5), while another, who had enrolled with other team members, said “We thought we should see and talk to others about what they are doing” (MW7).

As the program progressed, the participants’ appreciation of learning with and from others was reinforced, with some seeing it as a distinguishing feature of this program:

> It is very different from others I have seen and been to…I liked how it was not just talking, it was sharing ideas. (MW3)

> Part of it was being in the room with colleagues. Coming together and getting to know other people, sharing ideas and seeing that other people had the same problems was helpful. (MW5)

Ongoing contact. The progressive nature of the program was also viewed favourably, as the regular professional learning sessions seemed to promote feelings of collegiality and trust that underpin effective professional learning programs (Waniganayake et al. 2008; Semann et al. 2009). The ongoing contact also seemed to provide opportunities to explore the program content material in a greater depth than would have been afforded by one-off professional learning models. Participants claimed “For me it is better than reading 5 books. It was better to attend 5 sessions.” (F3) and “Coming monthly has reinforced those messages.” (F2). The benefits of the long-term nature of the project for the reflexive enhancement of knowledge and practice was summed up thus:

> the continual nature of the program allowed the information to sink in further, try new things and really reinforce what and why I’m doing something, coming back over a long time periods was very worthwhile (ExS)

Improved morale, status and empowerment. Participants’ responses suggested that the program had boosted their self-confidence and esteem. Some stated that they were feeling “a lot more positive” (F5), that they were “enjoying them (the toddlers) more now” (F1) and that the program was “motivating and confirming that I am doing a good job” (MW2). Others found that the program reinforced the importance of their role.

When asked about the most significant change in her own thinking as a result of the program, one participant responded:

> Probably that I do have a big influence on their lives…remembering that I am in an important role/profession and that is why I get paid for what I do. What we do affects lives. (F2)

The enhanced view of the practitioner's role seems to have given rise to a sense of empowerment among some practitioners regarding their ability to raise expectations of themselves, their team and the wider community:

> I have started thinking about having the professional conversations that you don't have everyday – having a vision is very important to empower staff for their ownership over what is happening and the changes we are making. (MW5)

> It made me realise how important it was to be an advocate for the children and these ideas. The workers need to band together to get that. (MW2)

Ongoing challenges. Finally, it is important to acknowledge that practitioners experienced a range of challenges throughout the program. Some struggled with ways to implement the ideas shared throughout the program, stating, for example:

> A lot of the things sound really good when we talk about them at the course, then when you come back it doesn't work. It makes me feel bad (MW3).

Others acknowledged the difficulty of being the only member of the team attending the professional learning program, with comments like "There is still the problem that everyone is not on the same page" (MW2) and "I need to make time to take my team on this journey with me" (ExS) demonstrating the struggle that they experienced when trying to share their new ideas and thinking with other practitioners in the centre. Consistent with practitioner inquiry challenges reported by Goodnow (2005), some participants also experienced difficulty working within management constraints, as the following response illustrates:

> How am I going to make it work for me in my setting? How to be an advocate for babies and then management saying "this is not going to happen…we can't get more staff...it is not viable to" so we know it is important, but what do we do when management says "no"?. (MW2)

Conclusions

This chapter has described the responses of infant-toddler practitioners to a 6-month practitioner inquiry program that aimed to support their professional learning and practice. While this project and its findings are exploratory, the perspectives presented have relevant implications for those who seek to use professional learning programs to enhance the quality of infant-toddler programs.

The findings emphasise the important role played by professional learning programs in enhancing practitioners' understandings of very young children. Not only did the program appear to bring about a broader understanding of the nature of infant-toddler curriculum, but by enabling practitioners to explore and critique their current understandings and images of infants and toddlers, the program appeared to promote a deeper consideration of the perspectives and experiences of these children. The focus on being perceptive of infants' and toddlers' thoughts and intentions, as well as their physical and emotional needs, challenged practitioners to explore notions of respect, communication and agency, which they then translated into their program. Simple modifications such as making the children's belongings more accessible to them, asking for permission or notifying infants before moving them, and allowing infants and toddlers time and space to explore and solve problems reflected a contemporary image of these very young children as agents in their own experiences, learning and development (Sorin 2005; Degotardi and Davis 2008). The observation by some that these small modifications gave rise to a new level of cooperation between themselves and the children not only suggests that staff-child relationships were being supported, but also that infants and toddlers were being encouraged to be active, contributing citizens to their educational program (Australian Government Department of Education, Employment and Workplace Relations 2009; Dahlberg and Moss 2005).

Responses from the participants support the benefits of particular aspects of professional learning programs. The findings highlight the importance of developing collegial support networks that extend beyond the centre walls (Warrilow et al. 2002). The sustained nature of the program was seen as a particular strength, with participants reporting that the opportunity to put theory into practice and then discuss these experiences supported them as they made changes to their practice and programs. Participants valued the opportunity to discuss and learn from each other's experiences, both positive and negative, and engage critically with the program content presented to them (Kilgallon, Maloney, and Lock 2008). The reflexive component of the program was affirming for some, as they gained confidence to express their views and opinions in a supportive group context. For some though, this aspect brought discomfort, as new ideas were presented that challenged their previously-accepted practices. This unease is an acknowledged aspect of reflexive practice, as it is the conflict between existing beliefs or values and new information or evidence that brings about the process of change (O'Connor and Diggins 2001). Moreover, while the content of the program resonated with particular practitioners' own beliefs about infant-toddler pedagogy, they expressed frustration at trying to bring about change within the constraints of their own programs and managerial structures. Ebbeck and Waniganayake (2003,) cite Dunphy's (1986) descriptions of individuals within an organisation to propose that early childhood practitioners' reactions to change can fall along a continuum from that of a "learning" stance, whereby individuals embrace change as an opportunity for growth, to the possession of a "self-defeating" stance, whereby individuals see change as unachievable and a threat to self-esteem. As Kilgallon et al. (2008) argue, however, by linking theory to practice, reflexive engagement prompts practitioners to develop a deeper recognition of the limitations of their own educational contexts and, by doing so, supports them in their quest to address these challenges. The reflexive discussions that took place during the professional learning sessions highlighted to both the researchers and program participants that change presents significant challenges as participants seek to reconcile new individual ways of thinking and acting with the collective pedagogical beliefs, practices and provisions at an organisational level.

Given the constraints that were identified by participants at the commencement of the project, it was encouraging to note the number of the practitioners who reported a positive change in their attitudes towards their work at its conclusion. Their responses suggest an increase in teaching confidence. Some participants also reported a sense of professional empowerment and agency that they had already taken to their workplace and hoped to take into the future. By embracing a leadership and advocacy role, the findings suggest that participation in the project instilled an enhanced sense of professional self-worth. Not only does an increase in perceived status have the potential to address the immediate concerns of poor staff morale and retention in early childhood programs (Sumison, 2007; 2005), but, by perceiving themselves as advocates, practitioners saw real possibilities for increasing community and policy-maker awareness of the foundational importance of infant-toddler years and the structures that are needed to support high quality programs.

In conclusion, the limitations of the practitioner inquiry project must be acknowledged as these highlight the need for further investigations into the benefits and challenges associated with practitioner inquiry professional learning models. Goodfellow (2005) notes that the effectiveness of practitioner inquiry is often reliant on the motivation and the reflective capacity of participants. This study, while identifying a number of positive outcomes occurring within the group, was not able to identify details of change in individual participants. The present cohort represented diverse social and cultural backgrounds as well as a broad range of experience and qualification levels. If the sector is to develop effective professional learning programs for all early childhood staff, future research is needed to explore the ways in which individuals or different groups of practitioners experience and respond to reflexive-based professional learning programs as well as the level of support that they need to incorporate new materials into their programs. Furthermore, the importance of working as a team with colleagues was highlighted throughout the project, yet most of the participants were the only members of their room or centre to attend the program. Many participants were challenged as they attempted to communicate their new insights to team members or to their management bodies, who, as reported, had different levels of commitment to this new material. This highlights the need for policy makers to fund, and researchers to assess, the effectiveness of team or centre-based professional learning programs.

Finally, as a 6-month funded project, it was impossible to gauge whether the short-term changes reported could be sustained over time. While a passion for creating sustained change, theories to guide pedagogy and a willingness for educators to move into unchartered terrain may address issues of quality within early years education (Sumsion 2007; Waniganayake et al. 2008), real and effective long term pedagogical changes within early childhood programs may require practitioners to engage in ongoing opportunities for reflexivity, either at a program level or facilitated by external facilitators. By raising perceptions of status and empowerment, long-term change may not so much be dependent on increasing individual practitioner knowledge and reflexivity, but instead may hinge on the leadership ability of practitioners to communicate with and guide team, management and community members towards a collective vision in their program.

Acknowledgements

Semann & Slattery in collaboration with Macquarie University were funded by Communities at Work, the Professional Support Co-ordinator for the ACT to deliver this practitioner inquiry project. The authors would like to thank Toby Honig from Semann & Slattery for his role in the delivery of this project and the collection of the interview data and all the participants who invested their time and effort into this 6-month practitioner inquiry project, and for sharing their wealth of knowledge over this period.

References

Ailwood, Joanne. 2008. "Mothers, Teachers, Maternalism and Early Childhood Education and Care: Some Historical Connections." *Contemporary Issues in Early Childhood* 8: 157-165. doi:10.2304/ciec.2007.8.2.157.

Australian Government Department of Education, Employment and Workplace Relations. 2009. *"Belonging, Being and Becoming: The Early Years Learning Framework for Australia."* Canberra, ACT: DEEWR.

Braun, Virginia, and Victoria Clark. 2006. "Using Thematic Analysis in Psychology." *Qualitative Research in Psychology* 3: 77-101. doi:10.1191/1478088706qp063oa.

Burchinal, Margaret R., Joanne E. Roberts, Rhodus Riggins, Susan A. Zeisel, Eloise Neebe, and Donna Briant. 2000. "Relating Quality of Center-Based Child Care to Early Cognitive and Language Development Longitudinally." *Child Development* 71: 339-357. doi:10.1111/1467-8624.00149.

Community Services Ministers' Advisory Council. 2006. "National Children's Services Workforce Project." Cited. Available from http://www.community.wa.gov.au/NR/rdonlyres/12169719-D18E-4E91-B1F0-7EEDF6BEFAC4/0/DCDREPNCSWsurveysandbulletins2006.pdf.

Dahlberg, Gunilla, and Peter Moss. 2005. *Ethics and Politics in Early Childhood Education.* London: RoutledgeFalmer.

de Schipper, Elles. J., J. Marianne Riksen-Walraven, Sabine. A. E. Geurts, and Carolina de Weerth. 2008. "Cortisol Levels of Caregivers in Child

Care Centers as Related to the Quality of their Caregiving." *Early Childhood Research Quarterly*: 1-9. doi:10.1016/j.ecresq.2008.10.004.

Degotardi, Sheila, and Belinda Davis. "Understanding Infants: Characteristics of Early Childhood Practitioners' Interpretations of Infants and their Behaviours." *Early Years: An International Journal of Research and Development* 28: 221-234. doi: 10.1080/09575140802393686.

Degotardi, Sheila, and Emma Pearson. 2010. "Knowing Me, Knowing You: The Relationship Dynamics of Infant Play." In *Play in Early Childhood Education: Learning in Diverse Contexts*, edited by Marjorie Ebbeck and Manjula Waniganayake, 46-66. Melbourne: Oxford University Press.

Deynoot-Schaub, Mirjam J. Gevers, and Marianne Risken-Walraven. 2006. "Peer Contacts of 15-month-olds in Childcare: Links with Child Temperament, Parent-Child Interaction and Quality of Childcare." *Social Development* 15: 709-729. doi: 10.1111/j.1467-9507.2006.00366.x.

Ebbeck, Marjory, and Manjula Waniganayake. 2003. *Early Childhood Professionals: Leading Today and Tomorrow*. Sydney: Maclennan and Petty.

Fein, Greta G. 1995. "Infants in Group Care: Patterns of Despair and Detachment." *Early Childhood Research Quarterly* 10: 261-275. doi:10.1016/0885-2006(95)90007-1.

Goelman, Hillel, Barry Forer, Paul Kershaw, Gillian Doherty, Donna Lero, and Annette LaGrange. 2006. "Towards a Predictive Model of Quality in Canadian Child Care Centers." *Early Childhood Research Quarterly* 21: 280-295. doi:10.1016/j.ecresq.2006.07.005.

Gonzalez-Mena, Janet, and Dianne Widmeyer Eyer. 2007. *Infants, Toddlers, and Caregivers : A Curriculum of Respectful, Responsive Care and Education*. 7th ed. Boston: McGraw-Hill.

Goodfellow, Joy, and Helen Hedges. 2007. "Practitioner Research 'Centre Stage': Contexts, Contributions and Challenges." In *Theorising Early Childhood Practice: Emerging Dialogues*, edited by Linda Keesing-Styles and Helen Hedges, 187-210. Castle Hill, NSW: Pademelon Press.

Goodfellow, Joy. 2005. "Researching With/For Whom? Stepping In and Out of Practitioner Research." *Australian Journal of Early Childhood* 30: 48-57.

Greenman, Jim, Anne Stonehouse, and Gigi Schweikert. 2008. *Prime Times: A Handbook for Excellence in Infant and Toddler Programs*. 2nd ed. St Paul, MN: Redleaf Press.

Harrison, Linda. 2003. *Attachment: Building Secure Relationships in Early Childhood.* Watson, ACT: Australian Early Childhood Association.

Honig, Alice. 2002. *Secure Relationships: Nurturing Infant/Toddler Attachment in Early Care Settings.* Washington DC: NAEYC.

Howes, Carollee, Claire C. Hamilton, and Catherine Matheson. 1994. "Children's Relationships with Peers: Differential Associations with Aspects of the Teacher-Child Relationship." *Child Development* 65: 253-263. doi: 10.1111/j.1467-8624.1994.tb00-48.x.

Howes, Carollee, Deborah A. Phillips, and Marcy Whitebook. 1992. "Thresholds of Quality: Implications for the Social Development of Children in Center-Based Child Care." *Child Development* 63: 449-460. doi: 10.1111/j.1467-8624.1992.tb01639.x.

Ireland, Lynda. 2007. "Life is Good for Babies: The Pedagogical and Management Decisions Enabling a Teacher to be Employed in a Rural Infant-Toddler Program." *Education in Rural Australia* 17: 21-36.

Kilgallon, Pam, Carmel Maloney, and Graeme Lock. 2008. "Early Childhood Teachers Coping with Educational Change." *Australian Journal of Early Childhood* 33: 23-29.

Maton, Karl. 2003. "Reflexivity, Relationism, and Research: Pierre Bourdieu and the Epistemic Conditions of Social Scientific Knowledge." *Space and Culture* 6: 52-65.
doi: 10.1177/1206331202238962.

Maykut, Pamela, and Richard Morehouse. 1994. *Beginning Qualitative Research : A Philosophic and Practical Guide.* Washington, D.C: Falmer Press.

NICHD Early Child Care Research Network. 1998. "Early Child Care and Self-Control, Compliance and Problem Behavior at 24 and 36 Months." *Child Development* 69: 1145-1170. doi: 0009-3920/98/6904-0014$01.00.

—. 2000."The Relation of Child Care to Cognitive and Language Development." *Child Development* 71: 958-978. doi: 10.1111/1467-8624.00202.

—. 2001. "Child care and Children's Peer Interaction at 24 and 36 Months: The NICHD Study of Early Child Care." *Child Development* 72: 1478-1500. doi: 0009-3920/2001/7205-0014.

—. 2002. "Child-Care Structure - Process - Outcome: Direct and Indirect Effects of Child-Care Quality on Young Children's Development." *Psychological Science* 13: 199-206. doi: 10.1111/1467-9280.00438.

O'Connor, Angela, and Cathy Diggins. 2001. *On Reflection: Reflective Practice for Early Childhood Educators.* Lower Hutt, NZ: Open Mind Publishing.

Office of Early Childhood, Education and Child Care. 2008. "2006 Australian Government Census of Child Care Services", Canberra: Department of Education, Employment and Workplace Relations.

Orland-Barak, Lily. 2009. "Unpacking Variety in Practitioner Inquiry on Teaching and Teacher Education." *Educational Action Research* 17: 111-119. doi: 10.1080/09650790802667485

Phillips, Deborah A., Debra Mekos, Sandra Scarr, Kathleen McCartney, and Martha Abbott-Shim. 2001. "Within and Beyond the Classroom Door: Assessing Quality in Child Care Centres." *Early Childhood Research Quarterly* 15: 475-496. doi: 10.1016/S0885-2006(01)00077.

Phillips, Deborah, and Gina Adams. 2001. "Child Care and Our Youngest Children." *The Future of Children* 11: 35-51.

Phillipsen, Leslie C., Margaret R. Burchinal, Carollee Howes, and Debby Cryer. 1997. "The Prediction of Process Quality from Structural Features of Child Care " *Early Childhood Research Quarterly* 12: 281-303. doi:10.1016/S0885-2008(97)90004-1.

Raikes, Helen. 1996. "A Secure Base for Babies: Applying Attachment Concepts to the Infant Care Setting." *Young Children* 51: 59-67.

Semann, Anthony, Cristyn Davies, Colin Slattery, and Lorrainne Madden. 2009. *Making Learning Count: Mapping Learning and Professional Development in Children's Services.* Victoria: Community Child Care Cooperative.

Semann, Anthony, and Margaret Sims. 2010. "Quality - What Does It Mean and What Do We Do About It?" *Contemporary Research Insights* 1: 19-22.

Sorin, Reesa. 2005. "Changing Images of Childhood: Reconceptualising Early Childhood Practice." *International Journal of Transitions in Childhood* 1: 12-21.

Strauss, Anselm, and Juliet Corbin. 1998. *Basics of Qualitative Research: Techniques and Procedures for Developing Grounded Theory.* London: Sage.

Sumsion, Jennifer. 2005. "Putting Postmodern Theories into Practice in Early Childhood Teacher Education." In *Practical Transformations and Transformational Practices: Globalization, Postmodernism, and Early Childhood Education*, edited by John A. Sutterby, 193-216. New York: Elsevier.

—. 2005. "Staff Shortages in Children's Services: Challenging Taken-For-Granted Discourses." *Australian Journal of Early Childhood* 30: 40-48.

—. 2007. "Sustaining the Employment of Early Childhood Teachers in Long Day Care: A Case For Robust Hope, Critical Imagination and

Critical Action." *Asia-Pacific Journal of Teacher Education* 35: 311-327. doi: 10.1080/13598660701447247.

United Nations Children's Fund. 2008. "The Child Care Transition: A League Table of Early Childhood Education and Care in Economically Advantaged Countries." http://www.unicef-irc.org/publications/pdf/rc8_eng.pdf.

Waniganayake, Manjula, Linda Harrison, Sandra Cheeseman, Katey De Gioia, Carol Burgess, and Fran Press. 2008. "Practice Potentials: Impact of Participation in Professional Development and Support on Quality Outcomes for Children in Childcare Centres." Canberra Professional Support Coordinators Alliance, Access Macquarie and Department of Education, Employment and Workplace Relations. http://www.pscalliance.org.au/Research/assets/Practice%20potentials%20-%20impact%20of%20PDS%20on%20quality%20outcomes.pdf

Warrilow, Prue, Karen Fisher, Katherine Cummings, Jennifer Sumsion, Cynthia a'Beckett, and Jacqueline Tudball. 2002. "Early Childhood Teachers and Qualified Staff. Report to the Office of Childcare, NSW Department of Community Services." Accessed November 9, 2010. http://www.sprc.unsw.edu.au/reports/EarlyChildhoodTeachersFinalApril09.pdf.

CHAPTER FOUR

MIND THE GAP: MATERNAL PERCEPTIONS OF SEGREGATED SCHOOL "CHOICE" FOR STUDENTS WITH AUTISM IN NEW SOUTH WALES PRIMARY SCHOOLS

ROZANNA LILLEY

Introduction: Towards Inclusion?

Making a decision about where to send a child with a disability to school in New South Wales (NSW) occurs within the context of a highly fractured education field, riven by debate and controversy regarding both what is best for a child with a disability and for society as a whole. Social justice arguments advocating inclusive schooling do battle with special education arguments advocating expertise and the promise of the partial remediation of deficits (Slee 1996, 22). Both are increasingly inflected by the neoliberal discourse of choice which demands a conscientious consumer parent who carefully weighs up all the options and takes responsibility for their own actions (Campbell, Proctor, and Sherington 2009, 164).

Currently in NSW, students with a disability can be enrolled in a regular class, in a Support Class in a regular school or in a Special School (Department of Education and Training 2008, 10). These options are available in the Government, Catholic and Independent education sectors. Thus the push towards inclusion exists within the context of a firmly established special education system.

This picture of an ideological battleground between inclusion and special education, as well as between parental versus professional views about appropriate educational provision for children with disabilities, is further complicated by an intensively competitive academic environment in which schools vie for status and funding based partly on standardised performance indicators and accompanying anxiety about league table performance. Schools are caught in an invidious situation where government reforms foster competitive and exclusionary educational practices, while simultaneously embracing policies committed to the inclusion of all students with disabilities (see Malacrida 2003, 100). In this situation, the choices available to parents of students with disabilities are often both constrained and difficult.

A state parliamentary inquiry in 2010 found that NSW had more than 46000 students with a disability enrolled across Government, Catholic and Independent schools (Dow 2010). In particular, there has been a sharp increase in the number of students with an autism spectrum disorder. This reflects the rising prevalence of autism both within Australia and internationally. The following figure from the then Department of Education and Training (DET) gives a graphic indication of these rising numbers. In 2011 DET was restructured becoming part of the Department of Education and Communities (DEC) following a change in the State Government.

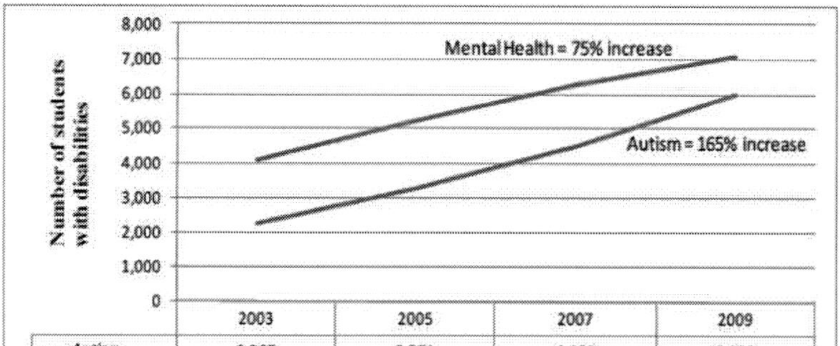

	2003	2005	2007	2009
Autism	2,267	3,271	4,492	5,995
Mental Health	4,080	5,233	6,285	7,082

Source: NSW DET data

Figure 1: Number of students with a mental health disorder or autism in NSW government schools, 2003-09. Available in NSW Government Submission (submission 715, 19), 18/03/2010, *Inquiry into the Provision of Education to Students with a Disability or Special Needs*

These increasing numbers, of course, bring increasing costs. The current disability education service budget for NSW for 2009/10 is $1.1 billion, which is almost 13% of the total NSW Government education budget of $8.577 billion (NSW Legislative Council General Purpose Standing Committee (GPSC) No.2 2010, xiv).

This chapter is concerned with the processes of primary school "choice" as experienced and narrated by mothers of children with autism in Sydney, NSW. Research has repeatedly found that women undertake most of the "emotional labour" of school choice (Campbell, Proctor, and Sherington 2009, 84-85). This is especially the case in the primary school years when mothers have most of the responsibility for caring for younger children. In particular, studies by Reay (2005), Ribbens (1993) and David (1993) in Britain have consistently pointed to the ways in which school choice is "engendered", with mothers across social class boundaries (Reay and Ball 1998) undertaking the hard work necessary to make informed decisions about schooling and to negotiate with various agents and agencies. This emphasis on engendered school choice has been confirmed in Australia in Aitchison's (2006) recent doctoral research.

Aitchison's (2006) study of 20 women in Sydney's inner west in 2002/2003 strongly underlined the fact that while current education rhetoric favours the term "parent", it is primarily mothers who undertake both the physical and emotional labour of school shopping (60, 236). Problematising Bourdieu's (1986) thesis that families, especially mothers, use schooling as part of an effort to advance their social position, Aitchison argues that in the Australian context the neoliberal promise of school choice is hollow, hedged about by structural constraints, including geographic and economic factors (223, 225). The two mothers of children with special needs included in her research found that their options were "severely restricted" and that they were "locked out of most schools" (226).

The following chapter extends Aitchison's interest in the experience of mothers of children with disabilities and the pronounced dilemmas they face in making decisions about schooling. These are dilemmas forged in the crucible of passionate disagreements about the value of inclusive versus special education, the fear of inadequate resources, sensitivities to social stigma and hopes for profound change. These dilemmas are sharpened by the added vulnerability of children with disabilities and the consequent need for heightened maternal care and vigilance.

This study bears a family resemblance to research by Carpenter and Emerald (2009; see also Carpenter and Austin 2007) in Australia. Usefully exploring the situation of women who mother children with Attention Deficit Hyperactivity Disorder (ADHD) and Autism Spectrum Disorder. Carpenter and her colleagues point to the ways in which these mothers feel both misunderstood and judged by medical and education professionals, as well as to the continuing potency of patriarchal constructs of motherhood, which effectively marginalise these women and their different maternal experiences. My work also has affinities with Malacrida's (2003) well-known book based on the narratives of Canadian and UK mothers of children diagnosed with AD(H)D.

While I am interested in the ways in which mothers engage with, or reject, education and disability discourses, I see these discourses as both complex and, often, contradictory. My aim is, in part, to focus on these complexities and contradictions embedded within maternal narratives constructed through a period of significant transition: sending a child with autism to primary school for the first time.

Choosing a Primary School for Children with Autism

This chapter is based on research done as part of a doctoral study titled *Maternal transitions: when children with autism start primary school.* The design of the project is qualitative and longitudinal with data derived from a series of semi-structured interviews with mothers of children with autism over a three-year period. Purposive sampling enabled access to mothers whose children were entering a variety of educational settings in Sydney, NSW, including regular classes, Support Classes and Schools for Specific Purposes (SSPs). The maternal narratives discussed in this paper derive from the first set of interviews conducted in late 2009 and early 2010 with 22 mothers whose children with autism were about to start primary school.

The majority of mothers across this sample talked in terms of being the parent responsible for choosing their child's primary school. Of the 22 women interviewed, 16 presented themselves as firmly in charge of this process, with five of these women indicating that in the case of conflict with their partner over primary schooling, the mothers' views took precedence. The remaining six mothers conveyed a greater sense of shared discussion and decision-making with their partners.

Alyce, the mother of two young children with autism and intellectual disability, said that, as her partner travels frequently for work, she had no option but to take charge:

> Just me. No help...it's all on me, chasing all the paperwork and ringing up all the schools, trying to find the appropriate places for them to go and, yeah, asking questions constantly to everyone you're meeting.

Here we begin to sense the extent to which educational institutions and other agencies and services all position mothers as the primary caregivers of children. When a child has a disability, these expectations of maternal care are intensified. This has much to do with the gender coding of early childhood as a "naturally" feminine space. Due to the entrenched nature of this gender coding, most of the work of navigating the complex autism service landscape, and of choosing schools, is undertaken by mothers (Lilley, in press).

Angela and Nathan, who were interviewed together, were very explicit about the intensified need to establish a sexual division of labour when a couple has a child with autism. Nathan commented:

> You can't have Angela at home, which really pumps therapies into Jarrod full time - just pumps him - and have her working at the same time. So that's meant that we've had to say: okay, well you take care of the therapies and the appointments, and I'll work.

Women emphasise not only the fact that they are responsible for most of the decisions to be made regarding both early intervention and primary school. They also frequently refer to the sheer hard work involved in making these decisions and acting on them. Indeed, four mothers in my sample actually visited more than five school settings, with one reporting that she went to eight different schools in search of a suitable placement for her son.

The extensive emotional labour of school choice has been documented by Reay (2005) and David (2005) in the context of parenting typically developing children in Britain. It is also clear that mothers in Australia invest considerable amounts of time and energy into school placement (see Aitchison 2006; Campbell, Proctor, and Sherington 2009). For mothers of children with autism, the high levels of pragmatic care and the emotional intensity of the process appears to be heightened both by the constraints around "choice" and the added vulnerability of children with autism.

When I asked one mother to describe the process of deciding which school her son should attend, she responded: "How painful was that!" Carmella, who was verbally threatened with prosecution by DET because her son had turned six and was not yet enrolled at school, stated that she was "desperate...so desperate". This desperation was underlined by Gemma: "I would spend many nights awake thinking about "where am I going to send him to school?""

When deciding on placement, mothers are making choices between Independent, Catholic and State (DET) schools. They are also making "choices", or being allocated places, in a variety of settings, both segregated and non-segregated, within these systems. Some of these settings are autism-specific, while others are either multi-categorical or largely intended for children with intellectual disabilities. Of the 22 women interviewed, 11 had enrolled their children in regular classes and nine in segregated classrooms (two in Support Classes and seven in SSPs). One woman was home-schooling her son and another had not yet enrolled her five year-old son, recently diagnosed with Asperger's, anywhere, as she was dissatisfied with her options thus far (see Figure 2).

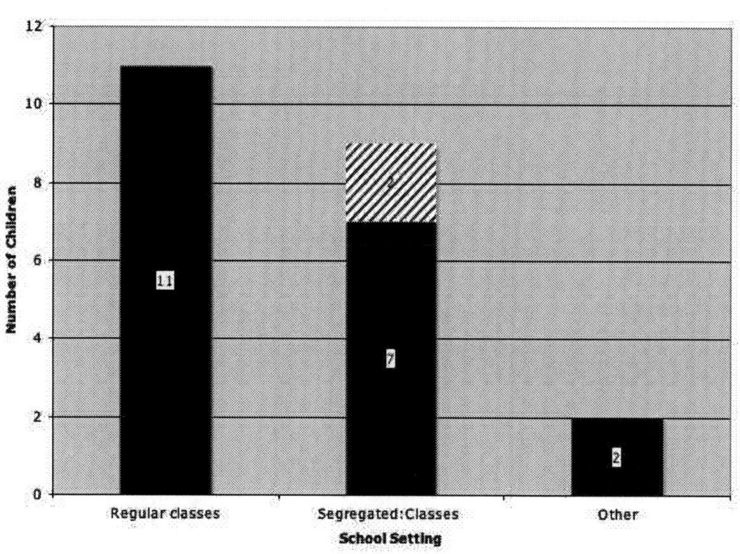

Figure 2: Number of children by class setting

None of the children attending regular classes was classified as having an intellectual disability (ID). Eight of the nine children attending segregated settings were described either as having been diagnosed with ID or developmental delay (DD). The child being home-schooled was said to have DD while the unplaced child had average intelligence, as indicated by his Asperger's diagnosis (see Figure 3). It is important to note here that there is heated debate regarding the appropriateness of intelligence testing for children with autism (Edelson 2006; Wolman 2008) and that children's classifications sometimes alter over time. My reason for reporting these classifications is that they can have a pivotal role in both allowing or disallowing access to some education settings, and in shaping other people's views of a child's academic potential.

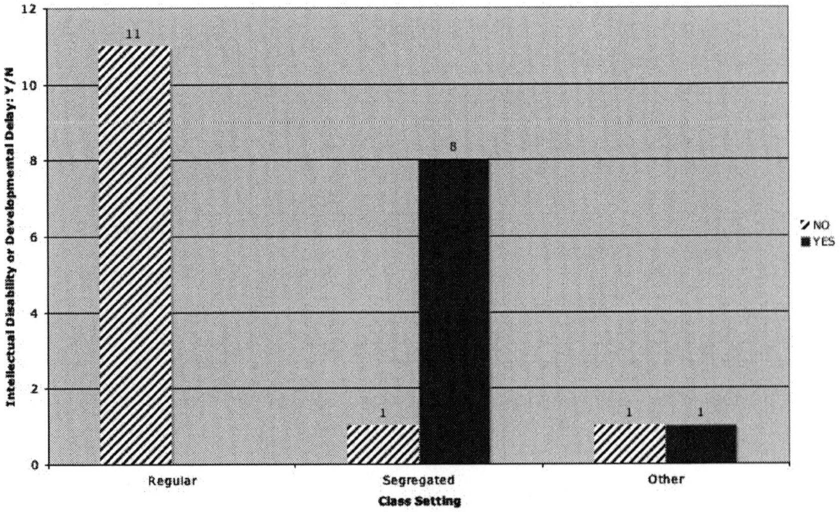

Figure 3: Intellectual disability by class setting

In the following chapter I confine my discussion to those families whose children with autism are attending segregated settings, either Support Classes or SSPs. In limiting myself to these nine cases, I aim to shed light on the reasons motivating mothers to choose segregated settings and on the dynamics of that "choice" process. I am especially interested in whether the philosophy of inclusive schooling has made any impact on this group of families and in whether legislative guarantees of inclusion in education have altered the landscape of school choice for parents of children with autism over the last decade or so.

Choosing Segregated Classrooms

Mothers reach the decision to send their child with autism to a segregated educational setting in NSW via a number of different routes. For some the decision seems self-evident, and their only concern is which segregated setting will provide the best support for their child.

Dung's son, Giang, is diagnosed with Autistic Disorder and a moderate ID. Giang is basically non-verbal. Dung never considered a regular class as an option for her son. Speaking to me through an interpreter, Dung explained that she saw her choice for Giang's first year of primary school as being either a government Support Class or an SSP. With her husband, she visited both of these settings. While her Vietnamese friends, worried about the lack of typically developing peer models in a SSP, advised her to choose a Support Class placement, Dung chose a Special School. She believes that in this environment, Giang will benefit from the special education expertise and the good facilities, including a swimming pool. Dung is very concerned about her son's "rough" behaviour towards his peers and, overall, she feels that her son will be both looked after and managed better in this segregated setting.

Alyce has two daughters with disability. Her oldest child, Annalisa, is diagnosed with autism and global developmental delay. She describes her decision to send Annalisa to a government SSP in the following terms:

> At first I must've been thinking way ahead of myself thinking that she would go to mainstream...and as soon as I got back, I filled out an enrolment information for her, down at the local school. Because I thought she might be able to go to a Support Class in a normal school...and I don't think I was in my right mind, because later on, when I got a Department of Education worker for me, I said, "Can we put in for an SSP? Because I really, really don't think she's ready for mainstream"... I put her in a Special School, because I really don't think she's ready. I must've just been thinking that she'd progress a lot more than she did. And as I through the year was doing everything, I just heard horror stories about kids going to mainstream and being left out. And it just got me thinking about it, you know. Was I thinking right about it, and what really did Annalisa need? Was it just my wish that she wanted to go to mainstream and be normal, as such? And I realised, no, she won't cope, she won't cope, and I want her

> to be happy. And that's more important to me, than whether she's normal. She's not normal, clearly not. She doesn't behave like a normal child.

In this potent retelling, Alyce conveys a poignant sense of her disappointment that Annalisa is enrolled in a SSP and of the logic that seemingly made such a choice inevitable. The trope of normality is deployed to accentuate a perceived dividing line between typical and atypical children. Within this logic, and the tale of insufficient developmental "progress" it highlights, typically developing children belong to regular classrooms and atypically developing children belong in segregated classrooms. For Annalisa, as for Dung, there is no choice between a regular class and a segregated class. There is, rather, a narrower decision to be made between a fully segregated setting and a partially segregated setting. The burden of belonging to these different settings falls on the child. Those who have failed to progress sufficiently require segregation, and the price of not accepting that perceived social fact would be her daughter's unhappiness and other unnamed potential horrors. Indeed, the initial idea of sending Annalisa to a "normal" school is presented as a form of maternal denial that stemmed from selfishness. Alyce believes the decision to send her daughter to SSP is a sign of her realistic coping, and therefore of good, and unselfish, mothering.

Not all mothers represent the decision to send their child with autism to a segregated setting as a form of maternal selflessness. Gemma thought long and hard about where to send her son Harry to school. Harry is five and reading well but is described by his mother as having significant behavioural difficulties. Initially, Gemma wanted Harry to attend a regular class with support in the year he was turning six. However, Autism Spectrum Australia (Aspect) offered Harry a place at one of their SSPs in the year he turned five. Gemma found herself, almost unexpectedly, enthusiastically accepting this offer.

Gemma described her decision in the following terms:

> If you'd have asked me before I was offered the Aspect spot, I would have told you that, really, I hope he goes to a mainstream school with a lot of aide support...maybe I'd prefer for him to start kindergarten at a mainstream school, with people who just know from day one, Harry's a bit odd...that's still what I think I guess, but I do also realise it's not the best place for him.

Here, once again, we see the discourse of sensible parenting, based on a realistic appraisal of her son's deficits, tied to a segregated schooling decision. Later in the interview I asked Gemma if having Harry at school would make a difference to her life. She replied:

> I think so. I hope so. I think that was part of the relief, I think, when I was offered the spot. I immediately thought, that's great for Harry, but I also thought, that's fabulous for me. I can get some of my life back.

Deciding Factors

While these nine mothers varied in their understandings of and attitudes towards segregated schooling, many mentioned the same factors as contributing to their choice of either a Support Class or a SSP. Many also held similar reservations about their choice.

The most commonly cited factor for choosing a segregated setting was the provision of special education expertise. This factor was explicitly mentioned by all of the parents. Often this first year of primary schooling was perceived as a continuation of early intervention therapies children had been receiving. This was especially the case where the school provided educational programs specifically tailored towards children with autism. Mothers whose children were enrolled in segregated settings on the basis of ID also stressed the advantages of special education, including teacher expertise, the flexibility offered by individual programs (IEPs) and small class sizes.

Four of the nine mothers whose children are enrolled in segregated settings mentioned "happiness" as one of their criterion for selecting a primary school. Two of the mothers interviewed believed their child would be happy in a segregated setting and two were concerned that their child would be unhappy due to the perceived social limitations and difficulties of peers with disabilities. The notion of segregation as promoting happiness was directly related to the idea that a segregated setting is more protective of the vulnerable.

The most commonly cited disadvantage of a segregated setting was the influence of peers with autism and/or intellectual disability. This was mentioned by seven of the nine mothers who chose a segregated setting. This was usually expressed as a concern with mimicking motor stereotypes, such as hand flapping, or being exposed to challenging behaviours. The lack of typically developing role models in a segregated setting was also mentioned.

Only two parents expressed concern about potentially low academic expectations in segregated classrooms. Most of the mothers whose children were enrolled in segregated settings had modest expectations for their child's future achievements at school, hoping they might gain some language or some independent living skills.

So far we have seen that special education expertise is the single most important factor attracting this group of mothers to segregated settings. We have also seen a strong concern with the happiness of children, with some parents hoping that a segregated setting will provide greater happiness and others fearing that it will not. A common parental misgiving about segregated settings among this group was the negative influence of disabled peers. Generally, expectations of academic achievement were low, with only one couple, whose son did not have an intellectual disability, seeming genuinely worried about this.

All of these factors need to be considered in the context of widespread dissatisfaction with the levels of funding and support available for children with autism (and other disabilities) in regular classrooms. A NSW Legislative Council Inquiry into the Provision of Education to Students with a Disability or Special Needs (IPESDSN), held in 2010, heard from scores of teachers that the level of support they are provided with in mainstream classes does not allow them to fulfil their responsibility to meet the learning needs of students with disabilities. Parents reiterated this view. This Inquiry found that the growth in demand for special education places was not only driven by an increase in the identification of students with disability. It is also a reflection, it was argued, of the lack of adequate support for students with disabilities in regular classes (NSW Legislative Council GPSC No.2 2010, xvi). The parents in this sample who were sending their children to Aspect base schools mentioned that they were partly driven to choose a segregated setting due to inadequate resourcing of children with disabilities in regular classes.

Overall, these mothers' experiences of finding a primary school setting for children with autism was not at all in harmony with either the neoliberal discourse of parental freedom to choose between a number of viable schooling options or the legislative rights to inclusive education for students with disabilities. Lack of resources in regular classes is a key structural constraint on such choice but so too were dominant ideologies of responsible mothering and disability, which made the choice of a segregated setting seem both more caring and selfless. In making this decision, mothers spent a great deal of time and energy balancing various considerations—an absence of typically developing role models versus special education expertise, for example. Mothers made their schooling "choice" within a context of structural and moral constraints that frequently left them feeling uncertain and guilty about whether or not they had made the correct decision. For some, the only choice they were actually making was between two types of segregated settings (a Support Class or an SSP) or between segregated settings in different sectors (such as DET or Independent).

It is worth noting that many mothers did not believe this was a permanent or, if you like, absolute choice. Six of the nine women being discussed here explicitly mentioned that they saw their child's segregated setting as a temporary option, believing, or hoping, they will eventually progress to a more inclusive classroom.

These narratives of potential transition rest on the idea that a child must have adequate skills to cope with a mainstream classroom setting. As has been pointed out by numerous commentators on ideologies of segregated education, the onus is on the child to change and not on the classroom to change to include all children. The stress on transition also reflects a growing trend across the education sectors to see special education placements as intensive short-term interventions, intended to accomplish the work of improvement or normalisation of children with autism so that they can attend mainstream schools without disrupting or unduly disturbing the classroom (see Douglas 2010 113).

Maternal Tactics

In 1998 Jenkinson conducted a study into the views of parents of children with disabilities in Victoria, Australia (Jenkinson 1998). Using a questionnaire, she aimed to identify the school characteristics that are most important in influencing parent choice of either mainstream or Special School settings. She concluded that parents who chose a segregated placement for their son or daughter were most often attracted to special education expertise and most often worried about their child's happiness. Factors rated more highly by parents who chose mainstream schooling were opportunities for socialisation and acquiring academic skills. Parents whose children were enrolled in both segregated and non-segregated settings were concerned about the provision of a safe and caring environment.

In some respects, despite the international push towards inclusive schooling of children with disabilities, and both federal and state legislation that supports this right, little seems to have changed since Jenkinson's study. What has altered is that many more students now have confirmed disabilities, with autism being one of the fastest growing categories. Further, overall the ratio of students with disability in NSW attending segregated classes compared to regular classes has decreased (Auditor-General 2006, 22). Students with autism are often perceived as having greater difficulties participating in regular school life than other students with disabilities. Unfortunately, there are no statistical pictures available of how many are attending segregated versus regular classrooms on a state-wide basis.

The sample of nine parents discussed here provides us with a nuanced understanding of the process of deciding on a primary school for a child with autism. We have seen in these maternal narratives the contours of an often distressing process in which mothers are faced with limited options. In the face of these limitations, mothers who "choose" segregated schooling are frequently pragmatic and resourceful, acting in what they perceive to be their child's best interests given inadequate resources for assisting children with autism in regular classes. We have also seen the tremendous weight of these maternal responsibilities and traced the ways in which ideologies of disability, of the firm line that purportedly separates the normal from the abnormal, continue to be played out in these womens' daily lives and feed into their conceptions of what it means to be a "good" mother. Mothers are constrained both by the problems of inadequate resourcing and by wider societal perceptions of their children's potential and their role in caring for those whose vulnerabilities are amplified by developmental difference.

When giving evidence to the 2010 IPESDSN, the then-Director General of the Department of Education and Training, Michael Coutts-Trotter, gave the following dry account of the tensions inherent in deciding on a school for students with disability. "There is, to a degree", he remarked, "somewhat of a tension between the convenience of the school system and the choices that parents want to make for their children" (IPESDSN Transcript 23 March 2010, 33). Others who gave evidence to the Inquiry were less circuitous in their depiction of a contentious process wherein education bureaucrats often discourage parents from insisting on regular classroom placements for children with disabilities. This is partly a matter of formal power ("child"s best interests", "unjustifiable hardship" etc.) but is more frequently achieved through strategies of persuasion that are an acceptable component of the veneer of quasi-participatory decision-making. Thus, the NSW Council for Intellectual Disability (CID) submission (No. 544, 10) stated: “Many parents have indicated to NSW CID that currently there is a limited choice in where their children can access school. Parents are advised that special units are the ‘best’ choice”.

The Legislative Council Committee in charge of the Inquiry received more than 700 submissions from parents, teachers and advocacy organisations. Recognising the inadequacy of resources devoted to these students in both segregated and non-segregated settings, they recommended that the NSW government substantially increase funding to all students with disabilities in NSW. The Committee defended the continued validity of the special education sector, arguing that while they support “the policy of inclusion for students with disabilities who can benefit from mainstream classes, at different times and for different reasons the most appropriate setting for a particular student may be in a SSP or support class in a regular school”. Not only was the legitimacy of the special education sector confirmed, the Committee also called on DET to increase the number of special education places and classes available in order to meet demand (NSW Legislative Council GPSC No. 2 Report 34 2010). Here we see parental “choice” being deployed to suggest that the continued provision of segregated school or class options is a valid consumer right. We are a long way, indeed, from the more radical views of the inclusion movement with its calls to abolish special education.

By focusing on nine mothers in NSW who have enrolled their children with autism in either SSPs or Support Classes, I hope to have shed some light on the maternal logics animating the so-called “choice” of segregated settings. At the heart of this process are mothers who attempt to make pragmatic decisions offering their children the best available care. Given the low levels of classroom support offered to many children with autism in regular classes, the decision to “choose” a segregated setting is, I suggest, a reasonable adjustment on the part of mothers. A realistic grasp of the constraints and moral dilemmas surrounding primary school choice frequently leads mothers to embrace a style of pragmatic decision-making involving flexible responses to changing circumstances, both within the education sector and in the perceived capacities or needs of their vulnerable children. There is a pronounced gap between the promises of inclusion and the realities of everyday education for the growing numbers of children diagnosed with autism. If we want to genuinely grasp something of the nature of these varied maternal choices in the face of available educational opportunities and wider political strategies, we need to mind the gap.

Acknowledgements

I thank the editors of this volume for assistance in preparing this chapter and my doctoral supervisor, Professor Jennifer Bowes, for her continued support. Neil Maclean also provided helpful comments. I am especially grateful to the mothers who generously shared their stories with me. The research project I draw on here has ethics approval, granted in 2009, from the Ethics Review Committee (Human Research), Macquarie University.

References

Aitchison, Claire. 2006. "Mothers and School Choice: Effects on the Home Front." PhD diss., University of Technology, Sydney. Retrieved from http://epress.lib.uts.edu.au/dspace/bitstream/handle/2100/351/02whole.pdf?sequence=2.

Auditor-General, New South Wales. 2006. "Performance Audit. Educating Primary School Students with Disabilities." Department of Education and Training. Retrieved from http://www.audit.nsw.gov.au/publications/reports/performance/2006/school_education/school_education.pdf

Bourdieu, Pierre. 1986. "The Forms of Capital." In *Handbook of Theory and Research for the Sociology of Education*, edited by John G. Richardson, 241-258. New York: Greenwood Press.

Campbell, Craig, Helen Proctor, and Geoffrey Sherington. 2009) *School Choice: How Parents Negotiate the New School Market in Australia.* Sydney: Allen & Unwin.

Carpenter, Lorelei, and Helena Austin. 2007. "Silenced, Silence, Silent: Motherhood in the Margins." *Qualitative Inquiry* 13:660-674. doi: 10.1177/1077800407301179.

Carpenter, Lorelei and Elke Emerald. 2009. *Stories from the Margin: Mothering a Child with ADHD or ASD.* Teneriffe, Queensland: Post Pressed.

David, Miriam. 1993. "Home-School Relations." In *Mothers and Education: Inside Out? Exploring Family-Education Policy and Experience*, edited by Miriam David, Rosalind Edwards, Mary Hughes, and Jane Ribbens. 31-58. New York, NY: St. Martin's Press.

—. 2005. "Activating Participation: A Personal Reflection on Research on Mothers and Education." In *Activating Participation: Parents and Teachers Working Towards Partnership*, edited by Gill Crozier, and Diane Reay. 3-21. Stoke on Trent, UK and Sterling, USA: Trentham Books.

Department of Education and Training. 2008. *Who's Going to Teach My Child? A Guide for Parents of Children with Special Learning Needs.* Sydney: New South Wales Department of Education and Training. Retrieved from http://www.schools.nsw.edu.au/media/downloads/schoolsweb/studentsupport/programs/lrngdificulties/whoteach.pdf.

Douglas, Patty. 2010. "'Problematising' Inclusion: Education and the Question of Autism." *Pedagogy, Culture & Society* 18:105-121. doi: 10.1080/14681366.2010.488039.

Dow, Steve. 2010. "Options for Special Needs Kids." *The Sydney Morning Herald*, August 9, Education:15.

Edelson, Meredyth G. 2006. "Are the Majority of Children with Autism Mentally Retarded? A Systematic Evaluation of the Data." *Focus on Autism and Other Developmental Disabilities* 21:66-83. doi: 10.1177/10883576060210020301.

"Inquiry into the Provision of Education to Students with a Disability or Special Needs." Transcript, 23 March 2010. Report of proceedings before General Purpose Standing Committee No. 2. Retrieved from http://www.parliament.nsw.gov.au/Prod/parlment/committee.nsf/0/328af88b0596edd7ca2576f0000dc4da/$FILE/100323%20Corrected%20transcript.pdf.

Jenkinson, Josephine C. 1998. "Parent Choice in the Education of Students with Disabilities." *International Journal of Disability, Development and Education* 45:189-202. doi: 10.1080/1034912980450205.

Lilley, Rozanna. In press. "Maternal Intimacies: Talking about Autism Diagnosis." *Australian Feminist Studies.*

Malacrida, Claudia. 2003. *Cold Comfort: Mothers, Professionals, and Attention Deficit Disorder.* Toronto, Buffalo, London: University of Toronto Press.

New South Wales Council for Intellectual Disability. 2010. "Inquiry into the Provision of Education to Students with a Disability or Special Needs." Submission No. 544, received 26 February. Retrieved from http://www.parliament.nsw.gov.au/Prod/parlment/committee.nsf/0/fb2470afac8f5d39ca2576e300007353/$FILE/Submission%20544.pdf.

New South Wales Government. 2010. "Inquiry into the Provision of Education to Students with a Disability or Special Needs." Submission No. 715, received 18 March. Retrieved from http://www.parliament.nsw.gov.au/Prod/parlment/committee.nsf/0/44d230fe6d9c1569ca2576ed007e6caf/$FILE/Submission%20715.pdf.

New South Wales Legislative Council General Purpose Standing Committee No.2. 2010. "The Provision of Education to Students with a Disability or Special Needs." Report 34, July. Retrieved from http://www.parliament.nsw.gov.au/Prod/parlment/committee.nsf/0/bd30607cceed0133ca25776200264698/$FILE/100716%20The%20provision%20of%20education%20to%20students%20with%20a%20disability.pdf.

Reay, Diane. 2005. "Mothers' Involvement in their Children's Schooling: Social Reproduction in Action?" In *Activating Participation: Parents and Teachers Working Towards Partnership*, edited by Gill Crozier, and Diane Reay, 23-37. Stoke on Trent, UK & Sterling, USA: Trentham Books.

Reay, Diane, and Stephen J. Ball. 1998. "'Making their Minds Up': Family Dynamics of School Choice." *British Educational Research Journal* 24:431-447. doi: 10.1080/0141192980240405.

Ribbens, Jane. 1993. "Standing by the School Gate — The Boundaries of Maternal Authority?" In *Mothers and Education: Inside Out? Exploring Family-Education Policy and Experience*, edited by Miriam David, Rosalind Edwards, Mary Hughes, and Jane Ribbens. 59-90. New York: St. Martin's Press.

Slee, Roger. 1996. "Inclusive Schooling in Australia? Not Yet!" *Cambridge Journal of Education* 26:19-32. doi: 10.1080/0305764960260102.

Wolman, David. 2008. "The Truth About Autism: Scientists Reconsider What They *Think* They Know." *Wired Magazine* 16.03:1-8. Accessed March 28, 2008. http://wired.com/print/medtech/health/magazine/16-03/ff_autism.

CHAPTER FIVE

PLACES

KATEY DE GIOIA AND PETER WHITEMAN

Spaces, walls, trestles and beams are synonymous with the notion of places for "learning" as they are likely representative in early childhood settings throughout the world. Within a developmental frame places have pre-existing purposes and the equipment within has a specific use. Early childhood settings were seen as a place of learning, in some ways disconnected from the world in which children and families lived; operating separately and taking control of providing developmentally appropriate practice for all children determined by their age and stage (Fleer 1995). Changes over time have enabled early childhood education and places for early childhood to take on a different form. In a post developmental frame, possibilities beyond walls and equipment exist. Early childhood settings have becomes hubs of change, providing services that are of cultural, social and economic significance to the community over and above care and education of children (Dahlberg, Moss, and Pence 1999; Moss 1995; Moss and Penn 1996; Hayden and Macdonald 2000; Doherty-Derkowski 1995; Lero 2000; Pence and Benner 2000; Hayden and Macdonald 2001).

Places and Early Childhood Education within a Developmental Frame

It's February, 1965, Lola leans forward and blows out the four candles on her candy pink *Dolly Varden* cake. Cheers punctuate the room in celebration of the significant milestone - the year before starting school. She smoothes down the back of her mini skirt, a mannerism she has seen her mother Sarah do many times, as she leaps from her chair to immerse herself among the presents and wrapping paper on the lounge room floor. She is in raptures over the new Barbie doll and her sister Skipper, and equally excited to notice the Hula Hoop, like the one twelve-year old

Jenny next door has. Lola rips into a rectangular shaped present and out tumble two commercially prepared phonics workbooks from her Aunty Sally. Aunty Sally is a primary teacher at the local school and is always sharing tips with Sarah for ensuring Lola will be ready for starting school in a year's time. Lola turns the pages and begins to look curiously at the carefully formed letters. She pulls out a colouring pencil (a gift from Grandma and Poppy) and holds it poised over the page. Sarah turns from the conversation about the Vietnam War at the kitchen table. The dread over conscription and Australia's involvement in the war is a constant which permeates conversations across the country. Noticing Lola with the books and pencils she places down her glass of orange Tang before hurrying over to Lola. She scoops up the books and checks them before declaring "Perfect, you didn't ruin them." She then continues, "Lola, these are for you and I to do together when your brother George is asleep. They will help you get ready for school!"

Sarah is up bright and early, it is Tuesday and she has many tasks to attend to before taking Lola to the local preschool at 9am. Sarah has been excited by the new wave of feminism in Australia, and with her husband Bob's support has been working two days a week at the local accountants' firm as a secretary. She feels this is an important role beyond wife and mother and will assist Lola in seeing the possibilities she has for her life ahead. Sarah and Bob firmly believe that preschool in the year before school offers many opportunities for Lola which she would not have had in the home environment or playing in the park with her friends. Sarah fits work in around the two days that Lola is at preschool, and George is dropped to her mother's on the way. She is happy to play with him and keep him occupied for that period of time.

Sarah and Lola arrive at the preschool at precisely 9am. The teacher is in conversation with another parent and Sarah hurries Lola in. She takes out of her bag the two lunch boxes carefully prepared for her daughter's day at preschool; one for morning tea and one containing her lunch. She places these in the high cupboards, each in the dedicated space above the sink. She turns back to her daughter and propels her towards the playdough table, glancing quickly at her watch to check she won't be late for work. Lola sits down and Sarah scans the room, "Everything in order for a perfect day of learning", she thinks to herself, seeing the familiar learning centres situated around the room and mentally ticking off in her head their importance for Lola's development prior to school. Mrs Shortwood had made these points clear at the beginning of the year at the very first parent meeting. Sarah knows that each of these activities has been carefully designed to promote specific skills:

- Playdough – essential for fine motor development to assist with writing
- Home corner – perfect for learning how to play with other children and role play about home
- Puzzles – A chance to use their mind and thinking skills
- Block play – many uses and benefits, all those mathematical skills in one place!

Sarah is trying to remember the value of easel painting when Mrs Shortwood interrupts her thoughts with a quick "Good morning" followed by, "So how is the birthday girl today?" Lola smiles up at Mrs Shortwood and continues working the green playdough with her fingers, having already lined up in front of her a snail and a snowman. Mrs Shortwood sits next to Lola and inspects her work asking her to explain how she had made the snail while jotting some notes into her notebook. She then looks up at Sarah and says, "So we shall see you at 3pm then." Refocusing her attention she continues her conversation with Lola about the construction of the snail. Sarah gives Lola a perfunctory kiss on the cheek and hurries out the door, checking her watch as she goes.

In this pre-developmental frame the choices Sarah and Bob have made for their daughter have been influenced by broader societal changes. Early childhood education is gaining respect in its own right. Previously, early childhood education had been deemed as "compensatory" programs for low-income families and children with additional needs. Studies in Australia and internationally are identifying the benefits of preschool education on later school achievement for all children, not just confined to those children from welfare backgrounds, and proclaim the role it plays in school readiness (Moss 1997; Lero 2000; Pence and Benner 2000; Dahlberg, Moss, and Pence 1999). This proves timely for women's entry into the workforce. Sarah is able to go to work within the hours of preschool knowing that she is advantaging her daughter with this choice.

The notion of location for learning is reinforced by this family the following day. It is Thursday, a non-preschool day. After Sarah has packed Bob off to work she dresses the children, wrestles George into the pram and they head off to the park; it is the perfect day for being outside. When they arrive Lola rushes to the swing and throws herself forward over the tyre seat using her feet to push her forward and outstretching her arms like a bird in flight. Sarah brings George over and straps him into the swing beside Lola. She instructs Lola, "Turn around and I will help you climb into the seat, you need to use your whole body to get the swing moving…now, kick out hard, forward, back, forward and back". Sarah sees one purpose for the swing and a specific way for Lola to use this. Lola slowly gets her body working in the rhythm her mother is repeating as she gently pushes George.

They retrace their steps home and George is placed into bed for his mid-morning nap. Sarah disappears into Bob's study and returns with one of the phonics workbooks which her Aunty had given Lola for her birthday. She opens it to the first page, runs the heel of her hand down the middle of the pages in an effort to keep the workbook open. "Right" she says in a businesslike manner, "Let's start with 'a'. Now can you see how you draw a circle and then a joining stick? You try now Lola." The next half an hour is spent with Lola laboriously forming circles joined to sticks while her mother looks on, occasionally repositioning the pencil within her fingers (as Aunty Sally had shown her) and offering words of encouragement. When George starts to cry from his room, her mother closes the book and returns it to the study declaring learning time over for the day. Sarah does not realise that the day has held many opportunities for learning for both George and Lola; conversations on the way to the park, pointing out the nest in the tree and how it had arrived there, the conversation about the shape of the sandwiches which Sarah had packed for morning tea for the children. Rather, the focus of learning in Sarah's eyes happened at the table and through didactic instruction. Sarah is not familiar with child-centred learning, or the knowledge that repeated didactic instruction may increase reliance on adults and has been seen to foster superficial learning (Stipek et al. 1995; Katz 1988). She is working with the knowledge of her time, and ensuring that her daughter makes a positive start to school so that she can have opportunities beyond which Sarah is able to comprehend in the current world within which she lives.

Places and Early Childhood Education within a Post-developmental Frame

Early childhood education has evolved since the 1990s. The notion of learning being confined to four walls and a classroom has been broadened to an understanding that the early years are rife with learning in differing context and situations. Early childhood education has been redefined to incorporate a community-centred approach. This broadened approach emphasises that learning occurs beyond the early childhood setting to incorporate the family and community (McBride 1999; Hayden 2000; Hayden and Macdonald 2000).

Chen is a four year old boy who lives in the outer city suburbs. He is second generation Chinese. His grandfather is a chef and came to Australia to find a better life for his family. He returned to China to marry his childhood sweetheart, bringing her with him to the county he fell in love with. Chen lives with his mother and three elder brothers Huang, Dong and Li. However, they prefer to use the Australian names they have each chosen for themselves; Andrew, Toby and Jaden. Andrew and Toby are in high school and Jaden in his final year at primary school. Chen's father died last year in a car accident. The family misses him terribly and talk about him often.

It's July 2002, Chen is woken by the sound of his two eldest brothers fighting over the radio in their bedroom. Chen can hear strains of Destiny's Child interspersed with Shikara's *Whenever, Wherever*, along with thumping against the wall he shares with his brother Jaden. Rubbing his eyes and stepping over the Hot Wheels cars complete with roads and bridges he had been working on, he heads towards his brothers' room to watch the morning spectacle. His mother, already up and dressed for the day has beaten him to the door and is loudly admonishing the boys for their behaviour. Andrew skulks towards the bathroom and Toby seizes the opportunity to change the station with a defiant push of a button. The final strains of Destiny's Child ring through the air. He smiles cheekily at his mother. Lien turns on her heel, deftly grabbing Chen by the hand and heads towards the kitchen. It's breakfast time. Lien places a bowl of cornflakes in front of Chen, reminding him that today is Monday and he is off to Ye Ye and Ma Ma's house (his father's parents). Lien has to leave for work in five minutes and it is Andrew's responsibility to walk Chen there on his way to school, after dropping Jaden at primary school. Chen smiles quietly to himself. He loves going to see Ye Ye; he always has a story about his dad, and has been teaching him to read Cantonese.

Lien checks in on the older boys, telling them that she is off to work now and quickly going through the checklist of responsibilities they have for the day. She kisses each child and heads out the door to the car. She knows the situation is not ideal for the boys, but then who could have predicted what has happened. She backs out the driveway thinking about the patchwork care arrangement she has for Chen. Two days with her in-laws, two days at long day care and one at home with her. She knows that this type of arrangement is quite common (Bowes et al. 2003) as she had spoken with the Director when the changes needed to be made. At the same time though, she worries about the impact it would have on Chen starting school in relation to his literacy and social skills (Bowes et al. 2009).

Chen has arrived at his grandparents' house. Andrew gives him a kiss on the forehead followed up with a brotherly punch on the arm. He greets his Ma Ma with a quick "Hello" and heads off down the driveway with Toby. Chen rushes past his Ma Ma calling for Ye Ye, as he moves through the house. This has become a morning ritual for Chen. He knows his grandfather will be in the kitchen either cutting vegetables or standing over a large pot on the stove, and he is not disappointed. Chen pulls a chair over to the bench and clambers up next to his grandfather who places his arm around him and gives him a quick squeeze while inquiring about his morning in Cantonese. Chen responds in English and reaches for the knife he knows will be there for him. His grandfather taught him last week how to cut spring onions for the restaurant and he proudly commences his task. His grandfather thinks that it is important for Chen to learn about his heritage and is glad that Lien also agrees with this (DeCapua and Wintergerst 2009). Ma Ma joins them in the kitchen and takes up her position at the kitchen table. She is checking over the menu and listing additional grocery needs for service this evening. Occasionally she comments to Ye Ye and Chen in Cantonese, and they both respond to her in Cantonese.

The next morning unfolds in a similar fashion to the day before, however over breakfast Lien reminds Chen that he is off to the children's centre. She places his cereal in front of him and asks if he is looking forward to his day. Chen can't wait to get there. Last week his teacher Natalia had spoken with his mum about his days at his grandparents' house and Chen is keen to tell her about what he had done yesterday. The older boys are left to get themselves to school and Lien and Chen head out the door. The short car ride to the children's centre has them walking in the door at 7.30am. The centre is a hive of activity even though it is still early. The children are all gathered in one room, scattered among the various experiences available. A small group of four children are eating breakfast and Chen can see Tracey helping Stefania to feed herself. Tracey turns and gives Chen a big smile and greets him and his mum with a "Good morning

Chen and Lien". Rebecca looks up from block corner where she is discussing an intricate structure with two of Chen's friends and motions for him to join them. Chen turns to his mum who leans down to kiss him and he is off to Rebecca, John and Deshi. John's father is a builder and recently Natalia had arranged an excursion for the older children to walk a few blocks to see the house he is in the middle of renovating. The teachers and educators at the centre value the partnerships with families and the local community and have been reflecting on ways to make these connections authentic for the children (Giovacco-Johnson 2009). A wall has been removed from the house in preparation for the extension and the children were able to see right into the house. There had been much conversation and capturing of the children's theories by the teachers (Edwards 1998) and it is this provocation which is inspiring the block corner discussion at the moment. Rebecca has a mini tape recorder placed near her and is extending the children's ideas through her questioning. She is also encouraging them to test their theories with the blocks. Deshi and John are in the middle of trying to work out how to remove some blocks from their structure without it all toppling down. They are poring over some photos of their building, and drawings they have done to try to work out the most successful way for this to happen.

Natalia arrives to commence her shift at 9.30am. By this time the majority of the children have arrived. The babies and toddlers have moved to settle into their own rooms and experiences that the day holds for them. Natalia greets all the children by name as she moves through the room, discussing with them what they are doing, offering some ideas or just listening. Just the other day she read an article about really listening to children and is trying to introduce this pedagogy of listening (Rinaldi 2001) into her way of teaching. She sees Chen deeply engaged in the block corner with Deshi and John. Rebecca stops her on the way over and fills her in on the morning and the three boys. Natalia is fascinated by the amount of time they have been in block corner and, thanking Rebecca, moves over to listen to the boys. They turn, excited to see her, and share the photos and drawings of what they have been doing. Once the conversation is finished, Deshi and John return to their deliberations and Chen looks expectantly at Natalia. She smiles at him and says, "Yes, I know what that look is for. I spoke to your grandfather yesterday after you left his place and he would be delighted to have us come to the restaurant for lunch. You will be able to share with us your new skills and information about being a chef. I am going to prepare the information to send home with children today." Chen shrieks in delight and turns to share his news with John and Deshi.

Natalia, the teacher in the child care centre, along with the Director Nicola has been taking a leadership role in changing pedagogy and practice. Having worked in early childhood for many years they have recently become invigorated by the new curriculum for their State (New South Wales Department of Community Services Office of Childcare 2002). It has challenged them to think about the way they work with children and connect with families and communities. They are starting to notice changes in the children and in their reflections on children's learning. There is an excitement in the centre, and the teachers and educators are keen to harness the excitement and build on their knowledge and new ways of thinking in an effort to really make a difference in the lives of the children and families through their connections and partnerships.

References

Bowes, Jennifer., Linda. Harrison, Naomi. Sweller, Alan. Taylor, and Cathrine Neilsen-Hewett. 2009. From child care to school: Influences on children's adjustment and achievement in the year before school and the first year of school. Findings from the child care choices longitudinal extension study. North Ryde: Macquarie University.

Bowes, Jennifer., Sarah. Wise, Linda. Harrison, Ann. Sanson, Judy. Ungerer, Johanna. Watson, and Tracey. S. Simpson. 2003. "Continuity of care in the early years? Multiple and changeable child care arrangements in Australia." *Family Matters* (64):30-35.

Dahlberg, Gunilla, Peter Moss, and Alan R. Pence. 1999. *Beyond quality in early childhood education and care: Postmodern perspectives.* London: Falmer Press.

DeCapua, Andrea, and Ann C. Wintergerst. 2009. "Second-generation language maintenance and identity: A case study." *Bilingual Research Journal* no. 1:5-24.

Doherty-Derkowski, G. 1995. *Quality matters: Excellence in early childhood programs.* Ontario: Addison Wesley.

Edwards, Carolyn. 1998. Partner, nurturer and guide: The role of the teacher. In *The hundred languages of children: The Reggio Emilia approach- advanced reflections*, edited by Carolyn. Edwards, Lella. Gandini and George. Forman. Westport CT: Ablex.

Fleer, Marilyn. 1995. *DAP centrism: Challenging developmentally appropriate practice.* Watson ACT: Australian Early Childhood Association.

Giovacco-Johnson, Tricia. 2009. "Portraits of partnership: The Hopes and Dreams Project." *Early Childhood Education Journal* no. 37 (2):127-135.

Hayden, J. 2000. *Landscapes in early childhood education: Cross national perspectives on empowerment.* New York: Peter lang Publishers.

Hayden, Jacqueline., and John Macdonald, J. 2001. "Community centred childcare: A new answer to 'who benefits'?" *Australian Research in Early Childhood Education* no. 8 (1):33-40.

Hayden, Jacqueline., and John. J. Macdonald. 2000. "Health promotion: A new leadership role for early childhood professionals." *Australian Journal of Early Childhood Education* no. 25 (1):32-38.

Katz, Lillian. 1988. "Engaging children's minds: The implications of research for early childhood education." In *A resource guide to public school early childhood programs*, edited by C. Warger, 32-52. Alexandria, VA: Association for Supervision and Curriculum Development.

Lero, Donna S. 2000. "Early childhood education - An empowering force for the 21st century?" In *Landscapes in early childhood education: Cross national perspectives on empowerment.*, edited by Jacqueline Hayden, 375-385. New York: Peter Lang Publishers.

McBride, S. L. 1999. "Family centred practices: Research in review." *Young Children* no. 54 (3):62-70.

Moss, Peter. 1995. Defining objectives in early childhood services. Paper read at European Conference on Quality of Early Childhood Education, at Paris.

—. 1997. "Early childhood services in Europe." *Policy Options* no. 18 (1):27-30.

Moss, Peter., and Helen. Penn. 1996. *Transforming nursery education.* London: Paul Chapman Publishing Ltd.

New South Wales Department of Community Services Office of Childcare, . 2002. NSW curriculum framework for children's services. The practice of relationships: Essential provisions for children's services. Sydney: New South Wales Department of Community Services.

Pence, Alan. R., and Allison. Benner. 2000. "British Columbia's ministry for children andfamilies: A case study in progress." In *Landscapes in early childhood education: Cross national perspectives on empowerment.*, edited by J. Hayden, 361-374. New York: Peter Lang Publishers.

Rinaldi, Carlina. 2001. "The pedagogy of listening: The listening perspective from Reggio Emilia." *Innovations in Early Education: The International Reggio Exchange* no. 8 (4):1-4.

Stipek, Deborah., Rachelle. Feiler, Denise. Daniels, and Sharon. Milburn. 1995. "Effects of different instructional approaches on young children's achievement and motivation." *Child Development* no. 66:209-223.

CHAPTER SIX

PLACES TO PLAY OUTDOORS: SEDENTARY AND SAFE OR ACTIVE AND RISKY?

SHIRLEY WYVER, PAUL TRANTER, ELLEN BEATE HANSEN SANDSETER, GERALDINE NAUGHTON, HELEN LITTLE, ANITA BUNDY, JO RAGEN AND LINA ENGELEN

For more than a decade there has been growing concern about global reductions in physical activity and increases in sedentary behaviours. Initially, it was unclear whether children would be protected from this trend. Perhaps children's playfulness and associated activity levels would act as a protective factor. There is now compelling evidence that children's activity levels are quite sensitive to environmental factors. For example, a recent US study of activity levels in preschoolers concluded that "…the characteristics of the school have a much greater influence on a child's activity level while in school than do the child's personal demographic characteristics" (Pate et al. 2004). There is also clear evidence that children's freedom to engage in active play, particularly outdoors, has diminished over the last generation (Clements, 2004). In this chapter, we examine some of the factors in young children's environments that influence levels of physical activity. Our main focus is on the physical characteristics of formal child care environments and to a lesser extent, school playgrounds. We examine the role of time, space, loose objects, risk-taking/safety and outdoor pedagogy in the context of children's play environments.

Until the latter part of the last century, research on play had focused on building a knowledge base of the unique role of play in the development of cognitive, linguistic, social abilities (see Bergen 2002, Pellegrini 2009;

Rubin, Fein, and Vandenberg 1983). The importance of play became recognised as a fundamental right for young children (UNICEF, 2006). Although researchers have continued these lines of investigation, attention has been redirected towards a battle to maintain adequate levels of play (e.g. Pellegrini 2006). Much of the recent interest in children's outdoor play has been motivated by alarming changes in children's health and predictions of their health status as adults. Chronic illnesses such as obesity and Type II diabetes are on the increase in many developed and developing countries (Stanley, Richardson, and Prior 2005; Jeffery and Sherwood 2008). Inactivity in early childhood is linked to poor outcomes in body fatness in late childhood (Moore et al. 2003) and early onset of childhood obesity is a strong predictor of obesity later in life (Magarey et al. 2003) It seems likely that these illnesses are the more obvious signs of an escalating constellation of physical and psychological problems affecting young children today, all of which could be at least partially reversed with adequate resourcing of outdoor play opportunities (see Ginsburg 2007).

Although our focus is on physical activity, it is important to note that the amount of time spent in sedentary behaviour is equally significant for health outcomes, and these behaviours seem to differ for boys and girls (te Velde et al. 2007). Variations in children's behaviours are of particular significance when interventions are introduced to enhance physical activity or reduce sedentary behaviour. It is essential that these interventions do not inadvertently interrupt other aspects of children's behaviour that may be developmentally important. For example, interventions that are highly directive may not offer the opportunities for social and cognitive problem-solving found in more "playful" contexts and may fail to capture children's intrinsic motivations. Schools and child care have been identified as important settings for children's physical activity (Story, Kaphingst, and French 2006a, 2006b; Reilly 2010; Ward et al. 2010). Although some have argued for greater regulatory requirements to increase time spent in physical activity in child care (Story et al. 2006a), teacher characteristics may be more important. Teacher education levels correlate positively with physical activity in child care and, as will be discussed below, pedagogy is important and can be diminished by regulatory requirements. It is also important that teachers have measures to for assessing environments for adequacy of provision of physical activity (see Ward et al. 2008).

Definitions, Measures and Methods

In this chapter, we define play as a transaction that is relatively intrinsically motivated, internally controlled and free from unnecessary constraints of reality (Skard & Bundy 2008). Physical activity is inclusive of all daily opportunities for movement, such as unstructured play, organised activities (swim class, dance), and active transport to and from destinations (walking, riding bicycles) and sedentary behaviour is characterised by times spent using minimal energy expenditure such as viewing television and other electronic screens, time in passive transport and prolonged amounts of time spent stationary rather than moving. Child health advocates call for a balance between active and not-so-active opportunities during a child's day. Intervention refers to any planned change that occurs in the child's environment. In most of the studies cited this has involved a change in the physical environment or programming. A recent review of the links between childcare policies, preschool environments, physical activity and sedentary behavior concluded intervention studies targeting these factors were warranted (Trost, Ward, and Senso 2010).

The studies we cite examine correlations or associations between factors in early childhood environments and physical activity, with some involving experimental designs. None of the studies cited meets criteria to make claims about causality (see Bauman et al. 2002). Although we draw a distinction between play and physical activity, it is important to note that most of the studies discussed below do not make this distinction. Most studies assume that when children are engaged in physical activity, they are playing. This assumption is often made because, while it is conceptually easy to differentiate play and physical activity, empirically it is an onerous task for which currently available measurement and coding schemes are not well designed. Children are more likely to be physically active when outdoors (see Hinkley et al. 2008) and physical activity typically occurs during outdoor play (Sallis, Prochaska, and Taylor 2000) particularly natural environments (see Fjørtoft 2001). Outdoor play has a significant role in all areas of development: physical, cognitive, social and emotional (e.g. see Pellegrini 2006).

Throughout this chapter, we refer to children's physical activity levels including the way in which physical activity was measured in each study. Some of the common measures involve use of devices (accelerometers, pedometers) or observation. As can be seen from the photo of a child wearing an accelerometer (Figure 1), the devices used in measuring children's activity levels are often small and relatively non-intrusive. Children participating in research can play freely without being directly observed. Nonetheless, most researchers do not rely solely on these instruments and include some direct observations, questionnaires for children, parents and teachers, and other instruments to provide a more comprehensive picture of the quality and context of physical activity. When reading these studies, it is important to keep in mind that measurement of young children's physical activity levels is still in its early stages. All measures have limitations. For example, accelerometry, which is often considered the best form of currently available measurement, is a measure of quantity, not quality of movement. Accelerometry has poor detection of some movements, such as those that are non-weight bearing (Pfeiffer et al. 2006) and has been found to have large error rates occur for some outdoor activities such as swinging (Storli and Hagen 2010). Despite these difficulties, it has been found to be a valid measure of children's physical activity and correlates positively with more accurate, but more intrusive measures of metabolic measures (Pfeiffer et al).

Figure 1: An accelerometer worn by a child

Outdoor Play as a Context for Physical Activity

Our focus is on opportunities for outdoor play in child care and school contexts. However, it is important to note that erosions of opportunities for children to engage in outdoor play has occurred in all contexts in which children regularly participate (Clements 2004; Wyver et al. 2010). Elsewhere, we have discussed the multiple contexts in which erosions to opportunities for play have occurred (Bundy et al. 2009; Tranter and Malone 2004). We have contrasted the play environments in Australia, UK and US with Scandinavian countries such as Norway, in which high levels of outdoor play continue, to demonstrate that sacrifices in quality and quantity of play are not just an unfortunate by-product of life in a modern Western society (Wyver et al. 2010). Reduction in opportunities for play relate directly to a devaluing of play in society as reflected particularly in school curricula, aggressive marketing to parents of educational toys and programs (Ginsburg 2007), excessive concerns about safety (Franklin and Cromby 2009; Gill, 2007) and urban planning that is not child friendly (Sharpe and Tranter 2010).

Significant adults, such as parents and teachers, have an important role in ensuring children have access to environments that enable adequate daily physical activity and do not encourage excessive sedentary behaviours. Unfortunately, adults do not necessarily recognise problems when they exist. For example, a significant proportion of mothers fail to notice that their child is overweight (Baughcum et al. 2000). There is also evidence of low levels of awareness of physical activity guidelines among parents of young children and early childhood teachers (Dwyer et al. 2008) and there seems to be poor community understanding of the importance of physical activity in young children's lives. A recent community survey conducted in Melbourne (Australia) revealed that most adults did not rate environmental factors (e.g. places to walk and cycle) as important in prevention of obesity in children. Respondents recognised the role of multiple factors in childhood obesity and demonstrated awareness of problems associated with consumption of certain food types and exposure to related advertising, yet only 27% of adults rated out-of-school physical activity as having an extremely important role in obesity prevention, and even less (19%) considered in-school physical activity to be important (Hardus et al. 2003).

Space, Time, Objects and Affordances

Much of the research examining the relationships between space, time, objects and physical activity or play has contributed to an understanding of the statistical relationships between environmental features and children's behaviour (e.g. examining increases or decreases in children's activity in relation to square metres of space available). This type of research is the main evidence used in this chapter to discuss the relationship between outdoor play environments and physical activity. Investigation of statistical relationships has been essential in revealing how modifications in the environment are associated with changes in physical activity. In some studies, these environmental factors have been manipulated in experimental designs. These studies not only provide a high standard of scientific evidence, but also demonstrate that small, inexpensive changes in outdoor play environments can often lead to significant changes in physical activity.

Although we consider the statistical evidence to bc foundational in understanding the relationship between outdoor play and physical activity, it does not capture all aspects of the relationship. Researchers have also attempted to examine the environment from the child's perspective. These studies have included a range of methods from quasi-experimental to ethnographic designs. Some of the most interesting work has come from European countries in which children's outdoor play in formal schooling involves engaging with nature. In these contexts, children encounter a wide range of terrains, natural loose objects and animals (e.g. see Waller 2010; Waters and Maynard 2010).

A theoretical approach currently used by many Scandinavian researchers investigating outdoor play is based on Gibsonian perceptual theory – particularly the idea of affordances. Affordances were originally described by Gibson (1977) as the combined properties of surface and substance relative to an individual. Affordances differ depending on an individual's characteristics such as height, age and experience in the environment. For example, a small tree may afford climbing for a young child, but not for an infant or large adult. Developments of Gibson's work by Kyttä (2002, 2004) and Heft's (1988) taxonomy have been important in enabling these researchers to test hypotheses relating to affordances and the natural environment (e.g. Sandseter 2009). Kyttä (2004) distinguished between *potential* and *actualised affordances*. Potential affordances are those that are available to the individual, while actualised affordances are those that the individual perceives, acts on and modifies. Although potential affordances may remain the same, actualised affordance will vary depending on children's individual characteristics (Niklasson and Sandberg 2010). Actualised affordances change with children's physical development and experience in the environment. Potential affordances also change, such as when ground conditions alter during different seasons (Storli and Hagen 2010).

Time

It seems self-evident that time spent outdoors is critical in ensuring children can engage in levels of physical activity. Recommendations for *minimum* amounts of moderate (equivalent to brisk walking level) and vigorous (huff-puff level) physical activities (MVPA) and sedentary periods are usually presented as amount of time per day. For example, in Australia the current recommendations for daily MVPA are for three hours per day for children between 1 to 5 years and one hour per day for children aged 5 to 12 years (Australian Government, Department of Health and Ageing, 2010). Sedentary episodes should not exceed 60 minutes of preschoolers non-sleep time (National Association of Sport and Physical Education). Cardon et al. (2008) used pedometers to investigate physical activity during outdoor play of 4 to 5 year olds from 39 Belgian public preschools (783 participants in total). Step counts per minute were higher for shorter durations of outdoor play, but overall physical activity was greater for longer durations of outdoor play. The authors note that there can be an initial burst of activity when children go outdoors, but this is followed by activity reduction, possibly due to fatigue or boredom. Findings such as these highlight that the amount of time offered for outdoor play to preschoolers should exceed the minimum recommended time for play. Young children engage in short bursts of MVPA rather than sustained periods of MVPA which are characteristic of adults and older children (Burdette, Whitaker, and Daniels 2004).

Space

A range of recent studies have examined the relationship between amount of space available and physical activity. Some studies also include analyses of the relationship between space and sedentary behaviour. In these studies, space is usually defined as the total square metres of outdoor playground space available to all children and/or the number of square metres available per child (an estimate based on the total square metres of outdoor playground divided by the number of children present at the time of observation). However, the estimate is based on horizontal space, not vertical space (e.g. does not include availability of trees to climb).

Numerous studies have found a relationship between the amount of physical activity and space (usually measured by square metres of available ground surface) available per child or overall (Trost, Ward, and Senso 2010). Space remains an important predictor of physical activity and sedentary behaviour in 9-10 year-olds. Ridgers, Fairclough, and Stratton (2010) conducted observations of recess play behaviour in English schools. They used accelerometry to record physical activity. Space available in playgrounds was between 1637.1 and 2392.9 m^2 (4.6-13.8 m^2 per child). Space available per child was found to be positively associated with physical activity and negatively associated with sedentary behaviour. Other predictors in this study were gender (girls engaged in more sedentary behaviours, boys in more vigorous activity), equipment (presence of playground equipment was positively associated with vigorous activity) and temperature (higher temperatures were negatively associated with vigorous activity). Bolderman et al. (2006) classified 11 Swedish preschool outdoor play areas as small (<2000 m^2), medium (2000-6000 m^2) and large (>6000 m^2). They also examined other features of the environment, such as presence of vegetation, to classify sites as either high or low. Pedometers were used to measure activity levels (step counts). Step counts in environments with a rating of "high" were approximately 20% greater than in environments with a low rating. Cardon et al. (2008) found a significant relationship between the number of children per square metre and step count (a higher step count was recorded in centres where there were fewer children per square metre).

Studies of space in outdoor play environments cannot be considered conclusive. While the outdoor play areas studied vary in terms of size, there were other factors that varied (e.g. vegetation as noted in the Bolderman et al. research). It is also possible that there are differences in the characteristics of people selecting these environments. For example, larger environments may be more likely to be selected by parents and/or staff who value physical activity. More research is needed to determine the extent to which other factors might contribute to the relationship between activity level and space. The current evidence, however, does indicate that space is of importance when planning outdoor environments for children.

In New South Wales (Australia), the current minimum space permitted per child in 0-5 settings is $7m^2$ (Community Services). Other Australian states have also adopted the same minimum permitted outdoor space (see for example, Department of Education and Early Childhood Development). Currently, there are no published data on the actual size of outdoor playgrounds in New South Wales centres. The minimum size is well below the average of 47 m^2 in Norwegian preschools (average outdoor area 2600 m^2) (Moser and Martinsen 2010a). When asked about the Norwegian specification for minimum space per child, Thomas Moser responded that the Ministry decided against specifying a minimum as this may lead to reduction in outdoor playground sizes (Moser and Martinsen 2010b).

Increasing outdoor space in established child care centres may be a difficult proposition due to lack of availability of additional space and cost of purchasing space if it is available. Excursions offer one possibility for extending space and can have an important role in connecting children with communities. Higher activity levels have been found in children attending centres that offer four or more excursions per month (Dowdaet al. 2004) although it should be noted that teacher qualification related positively to child activity levels and number of excursions in this study. In NSW, regulations for personnel and other requirements for excursions seem, anecdotally, to inhibit willingness of many child care staff to include regular excursions. The issue of onerous regulatory requirements as a barrier to excursions was also raised in the van Zandvoort et al. (2010) Canadian study. Revisions of these regulations should take into consideration the importance of excursions in extending children's access to outdoor space. Likewise, revisions to restrictions of heights for climbing (currently 1.5m for supervised early childhood settings - Standards Australia) could contribute to the overall space available to children. As noted in our later section on *risk-taking, regulation and surplus safety* there are significant pressures to maintain "safe" environments for children.

Loose Objects

Studies that have used number of objects as an independent variable have not found such objects to be an important influence in children's physical activity (Baughcum et al. 2000). When the characteristics of objects are examined, different findings emerge.

Hannon and Brown (2008) found that loose objects, identifiable as play equipment (e.g. hoops, bean bags, tunnels), when introduced to a preschool playground, led to an increase in light, moderate and vigorous physical activity. These objects were introduced in a free play context and the authors noted that a change in the play environment could be introduced with minimum expense. A Sydney-based playground intervention involved introduction of large loose objects, not readily identifiable as play objects (e.g. car tyres, hay bales, barrels) to school playgrounds. Significant increases in physical activity and playfulness were observed after the introduction of the equipment (Bundy et al 2009a; Bundy et al. 2009b). Both studies used a single group pretest-posttest design to examine changes associated with the introduction of loose parts, and used accelerometry to assess physical activity. While these findings are promising, lack of a control group in the designs means that it is not possible to exclude a range of competing explanations for the changes observed in physical activity and play (e.g. these changes may have occurred due to changes in children's maturity or changes in season). The authors of the Sydney study are currently engaged in a cluster randomised control trial (known as the Sydney Playground Project) to further investigate the influence of the introduction of loose parts to physical activity and play in school playgrounds.

One interesting observation from the Sydney Playground Project is the selection of light and heavy loose materials. The researchers intentionally selected a range of weights to be used in the playground. Some teachers rejected objects that were too heavy for young children to lift, ignoring the potential for children to recruit involvement of peers. Fortunately teachers were persuaded by the researchers to try these objects and monitor children's responses. Initial observations indicate that the heavier objects have been popular with children and have encouraged cooperative play, as children need to recruit peers in order to play with the heavier objects. Figure 2 shows an example of the cooperative play with loose materials in the Sydney Playground Project.

Competition for objects and maintenance has been reported as a problem in childcare. This can include insufficient numbers of preferred objects, or some objects being underutilised due to dilapidation can act as a barrier to physical play (van Zandvoort et al. 2010). There is some evidence that such barriers are unlikely to exist in natural playgrounds. For example, a recent German study compared the behaviours of the same group of preschoolers in contemporary (childcare) and natural play areas.

Observational records of children's behaviour revealed that children spent time queuing for equipment in the contemporary playground, but did not engage in this type of idle time when in the natural outdoor setting (Luchs and Fikus 2010). Similarly, Cardon et al. (2008) speculated that their finding of a lack of relationship between availability of equipment (loose and fixed) and physical activity was due to children often standing in line waiting to use equipment.

Figure 2: An example of play with loose materials from the Sydney Playground Project

Risk-taking, Regulation and Surplus Safety

Adults can generally choose between activities that are perceived as high or low risk. There are also opportunities for adults to access qualified instructors to help them learn new physical skills that might enhance career or recreation opportunities. For many children, the analogous option in child care or schools is denied. Although outdoor playgrounds in child care and schools are supervised by staff trained in helping children learn new skills (and have first aid training if something goes wrong) and include peers who can also offer support, in many countries risky activities are prohibited in these contexts. Children have the options of giving up on the idea of engaging in risky behaviour or taking covert risks (risk compensation). Three Australian studies are informative in this respect. Each of these studies reports on interviews or focus groups conducted with teachers based in Sydney. The first was based in middle SES childcare centres. A key finding was the regulatory environment of the early childhood centres inhibited teachers' provision of sufficiently challenging outdoor play experiences for the children in their care. The teachers reported that this resulted in children seeking challenge, and at times inappropriate risk-taking in other areas of the physical environment (climbing fences, stacking large blocks to climb on) which then led to a greater need for monitoring and intervention to ensure children's safety (Little 2010). The second study recruited participants from lower SES childcare centres. The parents of children attending these centres were generally from non-English speaking backgrounds (mainly Middle Eastern and Chinese). The authors note that these groups were targeted because children from these backgrounds are at greater risk of obesity. Teachers reported regulatory requirements to be a barrier to physical activity, but also a generally overprotective attitude of parents. The latter point was reinforced in the parent focus groups which were also conducted in this study (Dwyer et al. 2008). The third is the school-based study by Bundy et al. (2008, 2009a) discussed in the previous section on loose and fixed objects. Teachers in this study noted that they had seen many positive changes in children's outdoor play behaviours following the play intervention. In particular, they commented on increased creativity and social interaction in outdoor play. Nonetheless, these teachers raised concerns about safety. Despite the fact that the number of reported injuries did not increase, the playground was perceived as less safe for children. In each of these studies, teachers considered their approaches to risk and safety as consistent with a societal trend towards increased (over)protection of children and/or related to regulatory requirements. They did not see their approaches as being based on pedagogical decision making. Indeed, teachers commented on concerns that low tolerance of risk taking has reduced valuable opportunities for early learning and reduced children's resilience. Although Australian studies have been used to highlight excessive concerns about safety in children's outdoor play, this phenomenon is not unique to Australia (e.g. see Gill 2007).

In recent decades a critical tension has developed between two essential considerations for children's health and well-being: physically active play and safety CCarver, Timperio, and Crawford 2008). "Risk anxiety" or "surplus safety" (Stephenson 2003; Buchanan 1999) has placed these two goals in conflict; the balance has tipped squarely toward safety. "Risk anxious adults" seem to feel that any risk is too much risk and that unstructured physical play is unsafe (Thomson 2007; Thomson 2003). Surplus safety (Buchanan 1999), in the guise of risk assessment, has reduced the level of exciting, challenging and stimulating play in school grounds. Play spaces are now more commonly a reflection of what adults perceive as a safe environment than of the innate desires of children to have a stimulating and challenging play space.

> "If we work to keep the playground bland, safe and ring-fenced by rules, are we restricting children's opportunities to indulge in, and extend their understanding and appreciation of the world around them?" (Thomson 2007, 497).

Adults who restrict children's active play to keep them safe focus on one narrow set of dangers, to the exclusion of risks that arise *because of* restricted activity (Stephenson 2003). The long-term health benefits of play have been sacrificed in favor of the short-term health benefits of safety. This has created a number of social traps and a "downward spiral of fear" (Mullan 2003, 352). Yet, there will always be some risk of injury when children play.

Organised school activities potentially provide opportunities for children to be physically active (Jago and Baranowski 2004). However, many children fail to achieve energy expenditure targets because organised activities fail to yield the benefits of "risky", and hence "fun" and "challenging" active outdoor play. One to two hours can be a long time for young children. Very few structured activities are sufficiently motivating to engage them that long. A feedback loop is established, in which decreased motivation leads to decreased duration, which in turn leads to decreased activity and decreased energy expenditure. Structured activities may also reduce activity levels of some children. For example, Storli and Hagen (2010) reported low standard deviations on accelerometry measures when adult directed activities occurred. They interpreted this as indicative of increased activity levels for the less active children and reduced activity levels for the more active children. Teachers in Dwyer et al. (2010) expressed concern that too much emphasis on structured physical activity may diminish the creativity that should be part of children's play. A Norwegian study also found that play in challenging nature areas, opposed to play on structured playgrounds, showed clear differences in children's (5-7 years of age) physical- and motor competence after a 6 months intervention. The children playing in challenging nature areas made a statistical significant progress on physical and motor competences such as balance, muscle strength, coordination, agility, and flexibility compared to the children playing on the structured playground (Fjørtoft, 2000). This is in accordance with a similar study among Swedish preschool children (Grahn et al. 1997). Another Norwegian study has also documented that play in challenging nature areas has a significant effect on children's spatial-orientation skills compared to play on ordinary structured playgrounds (Fiskum 2004).

There is a growing awareness of the importance of everyday risk-taking for children (Mayes and Chittenden 2001). In some areas, particularly in Norway and Japan, school grounds are being designed in ways that encourage risk-taking and challenging play. In some Japanese kindergartens, playgrounds have high wooden beams and walls for climbing. In Norway, there is a realisation that being afraid to use the body actively poses a much greater risk than play equipment (Steinsvik 2004). Sandseter's (2009, 2010) research demonstrates the importance of context and pedagogy in young children's risky play. Many of the play categories developed by Sandseter (2007a, 2007b) are unlikely to be observed in childcare in countries such as Australia. These categories are: play at great heights, play at high speed, play with dangerous elements, rough-and-tumble, and play in which children disappear from adult view. Examples of outdoor play in a Norwegian preschool is shown in Figures 3 and 4. It is important to note that the Norwegian approach to risk-taking is part of a broader pedagogical approach to children's learning. The approach to learning that occurs in the outdoor preschools involves a different approach to interacting with the environment and attracts different types of staff. For example, Emilsen and Lysklett (2008) report that more males are attracted to teaching in these preschools than in traditional preschools.

In a Norwegian study on childhood accidents, Boyesen (1997) found that an exaggerated focus on safety regulations and prohibition of risky play and activities among children were not useful as injury prevention strategies. Rather, Boyesen states that only through children learning how to master risks themselves will injury prevention be successful. This means that in order for a child to "learn" how to master a risk situation, s/he will necessarily need to somehow approach the situation, and thereby increase the risk.

Figure 3: Norwegian preschool children climbing a rock wall on one of their weekly hikes out in nature areas

Figure 4: Norwegian preschool children taking part in building a climbing tower of logs and branches

Resources

Researchers and practitioners interested in outdoor play have developed a range of resources to disseminate research findings and ideas. The following is a list of some of the internet resources and organisations recommended by the authors of this chapter.

- Sydney Playground Project
http://sydney.edu.au/health_sciences/sydney_playground_project
- EECERA Outdoor Play and Learning Special Interest Group
http://sites.google.com/site/outdoorplaylearning/Home/archive
- PRAV http://www.prav.asn.au/
- International Play Association (IPA) http://ipaworld.org/
- IPA/USA http://www.ipausa.org/

References

Australian Government, Department of Health and Ageing. "Physical Activity." Last modified October 01, 2010. http://www.health.gov.au/internet/main/publishing.nsf/content/health-pubhlth-strateg-phys-act-guidelines#rec_0_5

Baughcum, Amy E., Leigh A. Chamberlin, Cindy M. Deeks, Scott W. Powers and Robert C. Whitaker. 2000. "Maternal Perceptions of Overweight Preschool Children." *Pediatrics* 106: 1380-1386. doi 10.1542/peds.106.6.1380

Bauman, Adrian E., James F Sallis, David A Dzewaltowski, and Neville Owen. 2002. "Toward a Better Understanding of the Influences on Physical Activity: The Role of Determinants, Correlates, Causal Variables, Mediators, Moderators, and Confounders." *American Journal of Preventive Medicine* 23(2S): 5-14. doi: 10.1016/S0749-3797(02)00469-5

Bergen, Doris. 2002. The role of pretend play in children's cognitive development, *Early Childhood Research & Practice,* 12: http://ecrp.uiuc.edu/v4n1/bergen.html

Bolderman, Cecilia, Margareta Blennow, Henrik Dal, Fredrika Mårtensson, Anders Raustorp, Katarina Yuen, and Ulf Wester. 2006. "Impact of Preschool Environment Upon Children's Physical Activity and Sun Exposure." *Preventive Medicine,* 42: 301-308. doi:10.1016/j.ypmed.2005.12.006

Boyesen, M. 1997. "Den Truende Tryggheten." PhD diss., Norwegian University of Science and Technology Norway, Trondheim.

Buchanan, Charles. 1999. “Building Better Playgrounds: A Project for Parents?” *UAB Magazine*, http://main.uab.edu/show.asp?durki=25353

Bundy, Anita, Tim Luckett, Paul Tranter, Geraldine Naughton, Shirley Wyver, Jo Ragen, and Greta Spies. 2009a. “The Risk is That There is “No Risk”: A Simple Innovative Intervention to Increase Children’s Activity Levels.” *International Journal of Early Years Education,* 17: 33-45. doi: 10.1080/09669760802699878

Bundy, Anita, Paul Tranter, Tim Luckett, Geraldine Naughton, Shirley Wyver, Greta Spies and Jo Ragen. 2008. Playful Interaction: Occupational Therapy For ‘All’ Children on the Playground. *American Journal of Occupational Therapy* 62: 522-527.

Bundy, Anita, Paul Tranter, Geraldine Naughton, Shirley Wyver and Tim Luckett. 2009b. “Playfulness: Interactions Between Play Contexts and Child Development.” In *Children, Families and Communities: Contexts and Consequences,* edited by Jennifer Bowes and Rebekah Grace, 76-87. Melbourne: Oxford University Press.

Burdette, Hillary L., Robert C. Whitaker, and Stephen R. Daniels. 2004. “Parental Report of Outdoor Playtime as a Measure of Physical Activity in Preschool-Aged Children.” *Archives of Pediatrics & Adolescent Medicine* 158: 353-357.

Cardon, Greet, Eveline Van Cauwenberghe, Valery Labarque, Leen Haerens, and Ilse De Bourdeaudhuij. 2008. “The Contribution of Preschool Playground Factors in Explaining Children’s Physical Activity During Recess.” *International Journal of Behavioral Nutrition and Physical Activity*, 5: doi:10.1186/1479-5868-5-11

Carver, Alison, Anna Timperio and David Crawford. 2008. “Playing it Safe: The Influence of Neighbourhood Safety on Children’s Physical Activity - A Review.” *Health and Place,* 14**:** 217-227. doi:10.1016/j.healthplace.2007.06.004

Clements, Rhonda. 2004. “An Investigation of the Status of Outdoor Play.” *Contemporary Issues in Early Childhood* 5: 68-80, http://www.wwwords.co.uk/pdf/validate.asp?j=ciec&vol=5&issue=1&year=2004&article=7_Clements_CIEC_5_1_web

Community Services. *Children’s Services Regulation 2004.* Accessed August 26, 2010. http://www.community.nsw.gov.au/for_agencies_that_work_with_us/children’s_services.html

Department of Education and Early Childhood Development. *Children’s Services Regulations 2009.* Accessed December 20, 2010. http://www.eduweb.vic.gov.au/edulibrary/public/earlychildhood/CSRegulations2009-53sr001.pdf

Dowda, Marsha, Russell R. Pate, Stewart G. Trost, M. Joao C.A. Almeida, and John R. Sirard. 2004. "Influences of Preschool Policies and Practices on Children's Physical Activity." *Journal of Community Health* 29: 183-196.

Dwyer, Genevieve M, Joy Higgs, Louise Hardy, and Louise Baur. 2008. "What Do Parents and Preschool Staff Tell Us About Young Children's Physical Activity: A Qualitative Study." *International Journal of Behavioral Nutrition and Physical Activity,* 5: doi:10.1186/1479-5868-5-66

Emilsen, Kari, and Olav Bjarne Lysklett. 2008. "Nature and outdoor preschools in Norway are attractive to men." Poster paper presented at the European Early Childhood Education Research Association Conference, Stavanger, Norway, September 3-6. Retrieved from http://www.dmmh.no/index.php?ID=789&lang=eng

Fiskum, T. 2004. "Effekt av Barnehagemiljø på Motorisk og Spatial Kompetanse hos Barn. En Tverrsnittstudie av den Motoriske og Spatiale Kompetansen hos Barn i en Friluftsbarnehage og Farn i en Tradisjonell Barnehage." Master diss., Nord-Trøndelag University College, Norway, Levanger, 2004.

Fjørtoft, Ingunn. 2000. "Landscape and Playscape. Learning Effects from Playing in a Natural Environment on Motor Development in Children." PhD diss, Norwegian School of Sport Science, Norway, Oslo.

Fjørtoft, Ingunn. 2001. "The Natural Environment as a Playground for Children: The Impact of Outdoor Play Activities in Pre-Primary School Children." *Early Childhood Education Journal* 29: 111-117.

Franklin, Leanne and John Cromby. 2009. "Everyday Fear: Parenting and Childhood in a Culture of Fear." In *The Many Forms of Fear, Horror and Terror,* edited by Leanne Franklin and Ravenel Richardson, 161-174. Oxford: Inter-Disciplinary Press. http://www.inter-disciplinary.net/wp-content/uploads/2010/01/FHT-3.pdf

Gibson, James J. 1977. "The Theory of Affordances." In *Perceiving, Acting, and Knowing: Toward an Ecological Psychology,* edited by Robert Shaw and John Bransford, 67-82. New York: Lawrence Erlbaum.

Gill, Tim. 2007. *No Fear: Growing up in a Risk Averse Society.* London: Calouste Gulbenkian Foundation. http://www.gulbenkian.org.uk/media/item/1266/223/No-fear-19.12.07.pdf

Ginsburg, Kenneth R. and the Committee on Communications and the Committee on Psychosocial Aspects of Child and Family Health. 2007. "The Importance of Play in Promoting Healthy Child Development and

Maintaining Strong Parent-Child Bonds." *Pediatrics* 119: 182-191. doi:10.1542/peds.2006-2697

Grahn, P., F. Mårtensson, P. Lindblad, P. Nilsson, and A. Ekman, A. 1997. *Ute på Dagis.* Alnarp: The University of Agriculture in Sweden.

Hannon, James C. and Barbara B. Brown. 2008. "Increasing Preschoolers' Physical Activity Intensities: An Activity-Friendly Preschool Playground Intervention." *Preventive Medicine* 46: 532-536. doi:10.1016/j.ypmed.2008.01.006

Hardus, P.M., C.L. van Vuuren, D. Crawford, and A. Worsley. 2003. "Public Perceptions of the Causes and Prevention of Obesity among Primary School Children." *International Journal of Obesity,* 27: 1465-1471. doi:10.1038/sj.ijo.0802463

Hinkley, Trina, David Crawford, Jo Salmon, Anthony D. Okely, and Kylie Hesketh. 2008. "Preschool Children and Physical Activity: A Review of Correlates." *American Journal of Preventive Medicine* 34: 435-44. doi:10.1016/j.amepre.2008.02.001

Heft, Harry. 1988. "Affordances of Children's Environments: A Functional Approach to Environmental Description." *Children's Environments Quarterly* 5: 29-37.

Jago, Russell and Tom Baranowski. 2004. "Non-Curricular Approaches for Increasing Physical Activity in Youth: A Review." *Preventive Medicine* 39**:** 157-163. doi:10.1016/j.ypmed.2004.01.014

Jeffery, R. and N. Sherwood, N. 2008. "Is the Obesity Epidemic Exaggerated? No", *BMJ* 336: 245. doi: 10.1136/bmj.39458.495127.AD

Kyttä, Marketta. 2004. "The Extent of Children's Independent Mobility and the Number of Actualized Affordances as Criteria for Child-Friendly Environments." *Journal of Environmental Psychology*, 24: 179-198. doi:10.1016/S0272-4944(03)00073-2

Little, Helen. 2010. "Risk, Challenge and Safety in Outdoor Play: Pedagogical and Regulatory Tensions." *Asia-Pacific Journal of Research in Early Childhood Education* 4: 3-24. Accessed January 10, 2011. http://www.pecerajournal.com/Pecera_Journal/Journal_2010_files/1.pdf

Luchs, Antje and Monika Fikus. 2010. "Playscapes and Playscape Activities Speaking – A Methodological Analysis." Paper presented at the 20th European Early Childhood Education Research Association Conference, Birmingham, UK. 6-8 September.

Magarey, A.M, Daniels, L.A, Boulton, T.J, and Cockington, R.A. 2003. "Predicting Obesity in Early Adulthood from Childhood and Parental Obesity." *International Journal of Obesity* 27: 505-13.

doi:10.1038/sj.ijo.0802251

Moore, Lynn L., Di Gao, M Loring Bradlee, L. Adrienne Cupples, Anuradha Sundarajan-Ramamurti, Munro H. Proctor, Maggie Y. Hood, Martha R. Singer, and Curtis Ellison. 2003. "Does Early Physical Activity Predict Body Fat Change Throughout Childhood?" *Preventive Medicine* 37: 10–17. doi:10.1016/S0091-7435(03)00048-3

Moser, Thomas and Marianne T. Martinsen. 2010a. "The Outdoor Environment in Norwegian Kindergartens as Pedagogical space for Toddlers' Play, Learning and Development." *European Early Childhood Education Research Journal* 18: 457-471. doi 10.1080/1350293X.2010.525923

Moser, Thomas and Marianne Torve Martinsen. 2010b. "The Outdoor Environment in Norwegian Kindergartens as Pedagogical space for Toddlers' Play, Learning and Development." Paper presented at the 20th European Early Childhood Education Research Association Conference, Birmingham, UK. 6-8 September.

Mullan, Elaine. 2003. "Do You Think Your Local Area is a Good Place for Young People to Grow Up? The Effects of Traffic and Car Parking on Young People's Views." *Health and Place* 9: 351-360. doi:10.1016/S1353-8292(02)00069-2

National Association of Sport and Physical Education. "Active Start: A Statement of Physical Activity Guidelines for Children from Birth to Age 5, 2nd Edition. Accessed January 10, 2011. http://www.aahperd.org/naspe/standards/nationalGuidelines/ActiveStart.cfm

Niklasson, Laila and Anette Sandberg. 2010. "Children and the Outdoor Environment." *European Early Childhood Research Journal* 18: 485-496. doi 10.1080/1350293X.2010.525945

Pate, Russell R, Karin A. Pfeiffer, Stewart G. Trost, Paula Ziegler, and Marsha Dowda. 2004. "Physical Activity Among Children Attending Preschools." *Pediatrics* 115: 1258-1263, doi:10.1542/peds.2003-1088-L

Pellegrini, Anthony D. and Robyn M Holmes. 2006. "The Role of Recess in Primary School." In *Play=Learning: How Play Motivates and Enhances Children's Cognitive and Social-Emotional Growth,* edited by Dorothy G Singer, Roberta Michnick Golinkoff and Kathy Hirsh-Pasek, 36-53. Oxford, Oxford University Press.

Pellegrini, Anthony D. 2009. "Research and Policy on Children's Play." *Child Development Perspectives* 3: 131-136. doi: 10.1111/j.1750-8606.2009.00092.x

Pfeiffer, Karin A., Kerry L. McIver, Marsha Dowda, Maria J.C.A. Almeida and Russell R. Pate. 2006. "Validation and Calibration of the Actical Accelerometer in Preschool Children." *Medicine & Science in Sports and Exercise* 38: 152-157. doi 10.1249/01.mss.0000183219.44127.e7

Reilly, John J. 2010. "Low Levels of Objectively Measured Physical Activity in Preschoolers in Child Care." *Medicine & Science in Sports & Exercise* 42: 502-507. doi 10.1249/MSS.0b013e3181cea100

Ridgers, Nicola D., Stuart J. Fairclough and Gareth Stratton. 2010. "Variables Associated with Children's Physical Activity Levels During Recess: The A-CLASS Project." *International Journal of Behavioral Nutrition and Physical Activity* 7: 74. doi: 10.1186/1479-5868-7-74.

Rubin, Kenneth H, Greta Fein and Brian Vandenberg. 1983. "Play." In *Handbook of Child Psychology: Vol. 4. Socialization, Personality and Social Development,* edited by E. Mavis Hetherington, 693-774. New York: Wiley.

Sallis, James F., Judith J. Prochaska, and Wendell C. Taylor. 2000. "A Review of Correlates of Physical Activity of Children and Adolescents." *Medicine & Science in Sports & Exercise* 32: 963-975.

Sandseter, Ellen Beate Hansen. 2009. "Affordances for Risky Play in Preschool: The Importance of Features in the Play Environment." *Early Childhood Education Journal* 36: 439-446. doi 10.1007/s10643-009-0307-2

Sharpe, Scott and PaulTranter. The Hope For Oil Crisis: Children, Oil Vulnerability and (In)Dependent Mobility." *Australian Planner* 47 (2010): 284-292.

Skard, Geva and Anita C. Bundy. 2008. "Test of Playfulness." In *Play in Occupational Therapy for Children, 2nd edition,* edited by L. Diane Parham and Linda S. Fazio, 71- 93. Missouri, Mosby Elsevier.

Standards Australia. *Playground equipment. Part 1: General safety requirements and test methods. AS4685:2004.* Sydney: Standards Australia.

Stanley, Fiona, Sue Richardson, and Margot Prior, M. 2005. *Children of the Lucky Country? How Australian Society Has Turned Its Back on Children and Why Children Matter.* Sydney: Macmillan.

Steinsvik, R. M. 2004. "Playgrounds in kindergartens schools and residential areas." Paper presented at Challenging Winter Frontiers", Anchorage, Alaska, February. http://www.wintercities.com/Resources/playgrounds.pdf

Stephenson, Alison. 2003. "Physical Risk-Taking: Dangerous or endangered." *Early Years: An International Journal of Research and Development,* 23: 35-43. doi 10.1080/0957514032000045573

Storli, Rune and Trond Løge Hagen. 2010. "Affordances in Outdoor Environments and Children's Physically Active Play in Pre-School." *European Early childhood Education Research Journal* 18: 445-456. doi: 10.1080/1350293X.2010.525923

Story, Mary, Karen M. Kaphingst and Simone French. 2006a. "The Role of Child Care Settings in Obesity Prevention." *The Future of Children* 16: 143-168. Accessed January 5, 2011 http://muse.jhu.edu/journals/future_of_children/v016/16.1story02.html

Story, Mary, Karen M. Kaphingst and Simone French. 2006b. "The Role of Schools in Obesity Prevention." *The Future of Children* 16: 109-142. Accessed January 5, 2011 http://muse.jhu.edu/journals/future_of_children/v016/16.1story01.html

te Velde, Saskia J., Ilse De Bourdeaudhuij, Inga Thorsdottir, Mette Rasmussen, Maria Hagströmer, Knut-Inge Klepp and Johannes Brug. 2007. "Patterns in Sedentary and Exercise Behaviors and Associations with Overweight in 9-14-Year-Old Boys and Girls – A Cross-Sectional Study. *BMC Public Health* 7. doi:10.1186/1471-2458-7-16

Thomson, Sarah. 2003. A Well-Equipped Hamster Cage: The Rationalisation of Primary School Playtime. *Education 3-13* 31**:** 54-59. doi:10.1080/03004270385200231

—. 2007. "Do's and Don'ts: Children's Experiences of the Primary School Playground." *Environmental Education Research* 13**:** 487-500. doi 10.1080/13504620701581588

Tranter, Paul J. and Karen Malone. 2004. "Geographies of Environmental Learning: An Exploration of Children's Use of School Grounds." *Children's Geographies* 2: 131-155. doi 10.1080/1473328032000168813

Trost, Stewart, G., Dianne S. Ward and Meghan Senso. 2010. "Effects of Child Care Policy and Environment on Physical Activity." *Medicine and Science in Sports and Exercise* 42: 520-525. doi 10.1249/MSS.0b013e3181cea3ef

UNICEF. "Convention on the Rights of the Child." Accessed January 11, 2011. http://www.unicef.org/crc/

van Zandvoort, Melissa, Tucker, Patricia, Irwin, Jennifer D, and Burke, Shauna M. 2010. "Physical Activity at Daycare: Issues, Challenges and Perspectives." *Early Years* 30: 175-188. doi 10.1080/09575141003667282

Waller, Tim. 2010. "'Let's Throw That Big Stick in the River': An Exploration of Gender in the Construction of Shared Narratives Around Outdoor Spaces." *European Early Childhood Research Journal* 18: 527-542. doi 10.1080/1350293X.2010.525953

Ward, Dianne S., Derek Hales, Katie Haverly, Julie Marks, Sara Benjamin, Sarah Ball and Stewart Trost. 2008. "An Instrument to Assess the Obesogenic Environment of Child Care Centres." *American Journal of Health Behavior* 32: 380-396. doi 10.1249/MSS.0b013e3181cea406

Ward, Dianne S., Amber Vaughn, Christine McWilliams and Derek Hales. 2010. "Interventions for Increasing Physical Activity at Child Care." *Medicine & Science in Sports & Exercise* 42: 526-534. doi: 10.1249/MSS.0b013e3181cea406

Waters, Jane and Trisha Maynard. 2010. "What's so interesting outside? A Study of Child-Initiated Interaction with Teachers in the Natural Outdoor Environment." *European Early Childhood Research Journal* 18: 473-483. doi: 10.1080/1350293X.2010.525939

Wyver, Shirley, Paul Tranter, Geraldine Naughton, Helen Little, Ellen Beate Hansen Sandseter, and Anita Bundy. 2010. "Ten ways to restrict children's freedom to play: The problem of surplus safety." *Contemporary Issues in Early Childhood,* 11: 263-277. doi:10.2304/ciec.2010.11.3.263

CHAPTER SEVEN

PARENTS', HEALTHCARE PROFESSIONALS' AND PLAY THERAPISTS' PERCEPTIONS ON THE FUNCTION OF HOSPITAL PLAY THERAPY AND THE ROLE OF A HOSPITAL PLAY THERAPIST

CHRISTINE ZUVELA AND FRANCES GIBSON

Play, Play Therapy and Children

Play has long been known to be a natural communication medium for children as it allows use of their "creativity while developing their imagination, dexterity, and physical, cognitive and emotional strength" (Ginsburg 2007, 183). Through play, a child explores the world around them and during a stressful event a child may use play as a means to understand the circumstances (Watson 1994), reveal their anxieties or preferred ways of coping (Camastral 2008).

Play therapy uses this natural communication as a "helping interaction between a trained adult and a child that seeks to relieve the child's emotional distress through the symbolic communication of play" (Webb 1999, 30). Given the varied approaches adopted, however, play therapy's function with children remains hard to define. The foundation of play therapy was within psychoanalytic theory (Freud 1938, quoted in Frost, Worthham, and Reifel 2005). Many approaches to play therapy have been developed which can essentially be grouped as either structured, including psychoanalytic (Freud 1946; Klien 1955, quoted in Landreth 2002) and release therapy developed by David Levy (Astramovich 1999) or non-directive approaches such as child centred (Rogers 1942; Axline 1947, quoted in Frost et al. 2005) and filial therapy (Hutton 2005; Tew et al. 2002; Yuqing 2005). Play therapy is also used in a range of contexts, including for children who are traumatised as a result of abuse, war or natural disasters (Griffith 1997; Ogawa 2004), experiencing distress as a result of divorce, marital or family dysfunctions (Camastral 2008; Wittenborn et al. 2006), and children with special needs. This diversity of approaches, differing contexts and the lack of consistency in treatment settings makes it hard to examine the functions of play therapy as a whole (LeBlanc and Ritchie 2001; Bratton, Ray, and Rhine 2005).

Child Hospitalisation and Play Therapy

Hospitalisation and chronic illness have been "recognised as stressful events since children and adults are vulnerable to the psychological strains imposed by illness" (Bolig, Fernie, and Klien 1986, 101). Research has shown that children who are hospitalised and suffer from chronic illnesses experience a range of negative emotional feelings (Landreth 2002), psychological disruption and distress (Boekaerts and Roder 1999; Popovich 2003), including anxiousness due to fear of separation and medical procedures, loss of control, unfamiliar instruments and environments, and the invasive nature of some procedures (Breweret al. 2006; Frost et al. 2005). The potential for play to enhance children's psychological well-being in a hospital setting has contributed to the development of hospital-based play therapy by reducing any hospital-related anxiety (Brewer et al. 2006; Landreth 2002), preparing them for medical procedures (Brewer et al. 2006; Hallowell et al. 2008; Zahr 1998), and helping them develop strategies to cope and manage their illness (Boekaerts and Roder 1999; Christiano and Russ 1996).

Zahr (1998), for example, tested the effectiveness of play therapy in reducing anxiety in preparation for medical procedures and found that children who participated had significantly lower blood pressure and were calmer during actual procedures. However, equivocal results were reported by Jones and Landreth (2002) who examined the effectiveness of play therapy with children who had insulin-dependent diabetes mellitus (IDDM). Using an experimental design within the context of a camp for IDDM patients, these researchers found that all the children's anxiety levels decreased during the 10 weeks program regardless of play therapy participation, indicating that the camp itself may have reduced stress. However, a play therapist's account of events with two participating children showed that the use of play therapy helped reduce anxiety specifically towards their illness (Jones and Landreth 2002).

Other research has indicated that play therapy may be beneficial in reducing children's anxiety and distress before, during and after a medical procedure in such contexts as an emergency department (Goymour et al. 2002), and through "practice" in preparation for magnetic resonance imaging (MRI) evidenced by a considerable number of children subsequently undergoing an MRI without general anaesthetic (78%) (Hallowell, et al. 2008). While Hallowell et al.'s results were significant they acknowledged that the lack of a control group limited generalisation. Nonetheless, with a controlled experimental design Li and Lopez (2008) examined the effectiveness of therapeutic doll play in preparing children for an anaesthesia induction and reported reduced anxiety levels in the experimental group during the real procedure.

Children with chronic illnesses are confronted with challenges of achieving optimal growth and development while learning to manage their illness (Boekaerts and Roder 1999). Their imagination can lead to fears about hospitalisation and affect coping, thus it is important to find out what the child believes will happen in hospital (Abbott 1990). In a single case study, Abbott used therapeutic play to explore the child's imagination, fears and knowledge about his upcoming cardiac surgery and his coping mechanisms to then assist him both before and after the event. Others have also found a positive relationship between children playing out their emotions and coping (Christiano and Russ 1996).

While studies have proposed certain benefits of play therapy for hospitalised and chronically ill children, limitations within the research are apparent, since most of the research has not been able to generalise beyond specific contexts (LeBlanc and Ritchie 2001) due to relatively small sample sizes and the inclusion of groups of children undergoing only one type of medical procedure or with one type of illness. Furthermore, other variables within the settings were not accounted for or controlled, including the child's temperament, the presence of their mother, the relationship between the nurse and the child and the co-occurrence of counselling or other allied health interventions (Johnston 1993; Zahr 1998). Although the inclusion of experimental designs to establish effectiveness is a strength in the research area, a more exploratory approach might capture other "independent" factors that contribute to the function of play therapy.

The Hospital Play Therapist's Role

Hospital play therapists focus on the potential effects hospitalisation and illness may have on a child. They work towards normalising the environment (Webster 2000), developing a trustworthy relationship for communication (Wilmot 2007), and encouraging children to express themselves, all with play as the medium (Landreth 2002). Most literature in this area, however, is anecdotal or contained in professional and procedural documents with a lack of empirical research targeting the specific roles and responsibilities.

Gaynard, Hausslem and Demarsh (1989) examined the role of a child life specialist, the American term for a hospital play therapist and observed that while they spend at least half of their time (50%) with patients, a significant amount of their time was involved in other work activities or roles. In a more recent study, Cole, Diener, Wright and Gaynard, (2001) found that a key part of a child life specialist's work was preparation and orientation of patients as well as facilitating growth and development, patient support, advocacy and family support. It is hard, however, to generalise these findings to the profession as a whole as both studies involved small samples with one representing a single site (Cole et al. 2001) or intermittent observations over two weeks that may not have captured the change and varied responsibilities during a full week, nor over a monthly or longer cycle (Gaynard, et al).

In Australia, there has been no research on the roles or responsibilities of a hospital play therapist, and little research on play therapy within a hospital. The Association for the Wellbeing of Child Health (AWCH) funded by NSW Health released a policy in relation to the care of children in a hospital setting. Statement two of the policy briefly describes the role of a hospital play therapist as:

> Hospitals that accept children should employ appropriately qualified play specialists: to plan play programmes for children of all ages; to provide appropriate play activities for children with special needs; to encourage and assist children to benefit from play activities; and to increase the understanding of parents and other members of the health care team in all aspects of play for children. (AWCH 2002, 4)

Even though this is a recommended policy, it is not known whether the majority of Australian Paediatric Hospitals and specialist units employ play therapists or whether they follow these proposals and the general roles and responsibilities of a hospital play therapist suggested by AWCH.

This study aimed to gain a broader understanding within the Australian context of the role and function of play therapists and play therapy for children in hospital. The two primary aims were to explore parent, health care professional and hospital play therapist's perceptions concerning, i) the function and importance of play therapy in a hospital setting, and ii) the role of a hospital play therapist.

Method

For this study, a mixed method model was adopted comprising an initial questionnaire-based survey (Phase One) concerning beliefs about the function of play therapy, its importance within a hospital context and the role of a hospital play therapist. This was followed by semi–structured interviews with a subset of participants (Phase Two) to explore in more depth their specific observations, experiences and knowledge of play therapy and therapists.

The target population was parents, healthcare professionals (allied health, nurses, and medical staff) and hospital play therapists. Recruitment eligibility criteria for health professionals and parents were that they had some direct experience with hospital play therapists and play therapy. For Phase One, professionals and parents were invited to participate through a series of targeted advertisements placed with relevant national professional and health associations and local media. Overall, 26 participants were recruited for Phase One: 7 parents, 9 health care professionals, and 10 play therapists. On completion of Phase One they were invited to participate in the Phase Two interviews, and 9 participants, 3 from each group were recruited.

A questionnaire was developed based on a study conduct by Cole et al. (2001) and was modified to suit an Australian context. It comprised both open-ended and closed questions within three sections. Section one covered background factors that might influence beliefs. Health care professionals were asked how often they were exposed to hospital play therapy and about their role within the hospital. Parent questions addressed their child's illness and how often their child saw a play therapist. Play therapists were asked how long they had been in the field, their role within the hospital and their contact with other health care professionals.

Sections two and three concerned beliefs about play therapy and play therapists. Parallel forms of the questionnaire were developed for parents, health professionals and play therapists to capture each group's unique perspective. Questions addressed play therapy's main function, the main role of a hospital play therapist and a specific checklist concerning the roles of a play therapist, (Cole et al. 2002). Participants also rated the importance of play therapy compared to medical and surgical treatments and other treatment, therapies and support services on a 5-point Likert Scale.

The semi–structured interviews explored participants' perceptions and knowledge of play therapy and play therapists through their experiences and observations. Interviews were recorded using an MP3 recorder and full de-identified transcripts were returned to the participants to validate content. Participants were asked about their experience of hospital play therapy, how it worked or did not work and what it was about the play therapy that helped. They were also asked to describe the role of a hospital play therapist in more detail, including the unique characteristics of the role.

Quantitative questionnaire data were analysed using the Statistical Package for Social Sciences (SPSS Version 17). Descriptive statistics, including the frequency, roles and functions of play therapy and therapists, and correlational analyses examining the relationships between roles and functions were conducted. Mean comparisons were made to examine the potential influence of background experience on findings of play therapy as a parent, a therapist or health professional,. Non-parametric tests including Spearman correlations and Kruskal Wallis mean comparisons were employed, due to the small sample size and negatively skewed results.

Open-ended questions were analysed through content analysis using QSR NVivo 8 (QSR International, 2009) and emerging themes and patterns were collated according to the frequency of words and phrases. Interview transcripts were also entered into NVivo and thematic analysis was applied. One third of the interview transcripts were analysed by an independent coder using the themes suggested by initial analysis through NVivo. Content that was not mapped onto themes was conferenced and either re-classified to an existing category or a new category was generated. The data were also referenced to the literature examining evidence in support of, or contrary to identified themes.

Results

Perceptions on the Function of Hospital Play Therapy

Content analysis of open-ended questionnaire data revealed the two most common functions of play therapy to be "entertain" (n=10, 38.4%) and "distract" or "distraction" (n=10, 38.4%). These were mentioned more so by parents and health care professionals than by play therapists. The next most common function was around helping children "cope with hospital" (n=8, 30.8%), which was mostly mentioned by play therapists. Other functions identified were to "decrease stress and anxiety" (n=7, 26.9%) or "increase the health and wellbeing" (n=6, 23%) of the child and to provide "procedural support" or assist in "preparing children for medical procedures" (n=6, 23%).

Perceptions on the Importance of Hospital Play Therapy

An examination of mean importance ratings shown in Table 1 indicated that over half of the participants believed play therapy to be just as important as medical and surgical procedures (n=14, 53.8%). Nonetheless, while some participants believed play therapy to be more important (n=6, 23.1%) than medical and surgical procedures, some believed it to be less or not important (n=6, 23.1%). Likewise, some rated play therapy to be more important (n=7, 26.9%) compared to other therapies, treatment and support services. However, only one participant believed it to be not important. Overall, participants tended to rate both IMPTMSP and IMPTTSS similarly, as correlational analysis revealed a significant positive relationship ($r=0.699$, $p<0.01$).

Table 1: Importance ratings of play therapy compared to medical and surgical procedures (IMPMSP) and play therapy compared to other treatments, therapies and support services (IMPTTSS).

	M	SD
IMPMSP (n=26)	3.12	1.033
IMPTTSS (n=26)	3.27	0.778

Note. Rating scale was as follows: 1 = not important; 2 = less important; 3 = just as important; 4 = slightly more important; 5 = more important

Perceptions of the Role of a Hospital Play Therapist

The most commonly-nominated role was to "provide activities for children" (n=16, 61.5%). A number of participants believed that the role of a hospital play therapist was to help with "procedural support" or "preparing children for medical procedures" (n=10, 38.4%) and "occupying" or "entertaining" children was nominated by over a quarter (n=7, 26.9%). Further analysis revealed similar results to the perceived function of play therapy in that no play therapist believed "entertain", was part of their role. Also, similarly to perceptions of the function of play therapy, eight (30.8%) participants, mostly play therapists, referred to part of the role as "helping children cope with hospital". Roles that were mentioned with less frequency included "reducing children's stress" (n=5, 19.2%), encouraging "self expression" (n=4, 15.4%) and "developing a relationship with children" (n=1, 3.8%) or being a non-threatening friend (n=2, 7.8%).

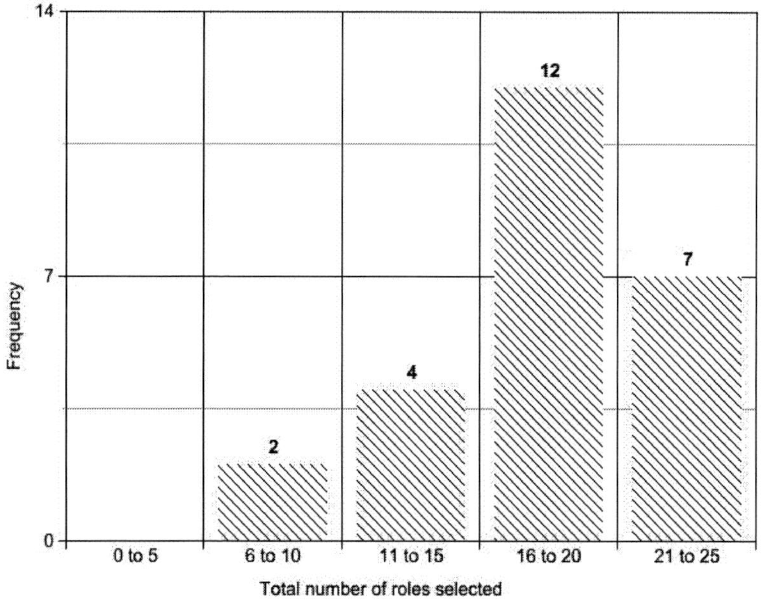

Figure 1: Distribution of total number of roles for combined participant groups

A score for total number of roles nominated was calculated, and analysis revealed that the majority selected most of the roles, as the distribution of scores were negatively skewed (-0.875) (see Figure 1).

Table 2: Total Percentages of Roles Ticked

Role	Total
Feelings & sense of mastery	92.3%
Decrease children's stress levels	96.2%
Heighten feelings of competency	92.3%
Group sessions for patients	80.8%
Provide programs for play rooms	84.6%
Foster growth development & minimize adverse reactions to hospital	96.2%
Play equipment	96.2%
Policy & procedural development	84.6%
Document child's psychological health	53.8%
Document child's physical health	23.1%
Pre admission orientation visits	57.7%
Explain medical procedures to families	30.8%
Consult with parents about patients physical health	15.4%
Consult with parents about patients psychological wellbeing	50%
Distract patients during invasive medical routines	88.5%
Entertain children	57.7%
Familiarise children with new surroundings	73.1%
Warm & welcoming environment	92.3%
Parent support	76.9%
Participate in conferences, seminars etc	92.3%
Clean play equipment	80.8%

Sharing information concerning children with other HCP	88.5%
Goals for emotional & social needs for children	76.9%
Set up play rooms	73.1%

Note: HCP-Health Care Professionals

Further analysis revealed that 16 of the 24 potential play therapist roles were selected by at least 70% of participants (see Table 2). A Kruskal-Wallis test of number of roles nominated across the discrete participant groups revealed a non-significant trend for play therapists to nominate more roles than both parents and health care professionals, $\chi 2$ (2, n=26) = 5.953, p=0.051.

Experience and Observations of Play Therapy and Play Therapists

Six main themes emerged from analysis of interview data, which encompassed the unique role of play therapy and play therapists. Quotes from interviews are included to exemplify themes. Codes for quotes were as follows, P-parents, PT-play therapists, HCP-health care professionals.

Play Therapy as a Tool to Help Children Cope with Hospital. Participant experiences and observations were quite positive in that they believed play therapy helped children cope with hospitalisation. Three central sub-themes were apparent in regard to how play helped children cope; assisting with procedures, distracting the children and engaging or occupying children.

Procedural Support. Participant experiences of play therapy helping children cope were largely around procedural support. For example:

> …medical play, where you're letting the children explore the medical equipment, and role play hospital experiences and procedures…using the medical kits and dolls…preparing them for upcoming treatments (PT309).

Furthermore, play therapists used medical play as a way of recognising children's fears and anxieties, for example, "sometimes you can gauge their anxiety or stress levels" (PT309). Additionally, the use of dolls or teddy bears was a common strategy commented on to help prepare children for medical procedures:

> …so every time he got attached to the drip, the bear got attached as well. Every time he had injections the bear got injections as well. It was a really helpful way of having him work through all the procedures (P106).

Distraction. The way in which play therapy distracted children from the hospital experience was also apparent, whether it was a strategy used during a medical procedure or just on the wards. For example a parent recalled a time when a play therapist helped by distracting their child:

> The play therapist was playing with her while she was getting a cannula put in. She did not twinge… normally she's screaming when she's getting a cannula put in and I have to hold her down. (P103, lines).

Another parent commented that it allowed the child to forget, "…it just makes her forget of all the crap she has to deal with" (P104, lines).

Engaging / Occupying Children. The belief that play therapy engaged children to help take their minds off their illness was another sub-theme around assisting children to cope. Views from health care professionals and parents were largely around keeping the children occupied while in hospital, for example, "It kept her pre-occupied" (P103) and "…it helped them to be engaged and have something to do, not be bored" (HCP207).

Play therapist perceptions of engaging children was more around building relationships, procedural support and distraction, as seen in the following

> …for this child it was a matter of somebody engaging with him with something that he was actually interested in" (PT301). This particular play therapist engaged with this child to build the relationship with him and eventually helped him through a medical procedure. In addition, engaging children in play therapy also helped children with pain management, …it was more appropriate to have her more engaged in her pain management than medication (PT308).

The Many Roles of a Hospital Play Therapist

Many different kinds of roles that the hospital play therapist was responsible for were revealed. Play therapists' days were seen to be broken up into providing play therapy to children as well as documentation, administrative tasks, attending conferences or meetings, cleaning and ordering equipment:

> …so one of them will go and do a lot of the office work, making sure their stats are up to date, making sure that the toys are clean. (HCP203)

Providing play activities that were developmentally appropriate was seen as an important role, "…interact with the children and help with the development and play" (P103). Furthermore, providing procedural support was specifically identified, "…their job was to help kids get through procedures and help them deal with being in hospital". (P106)

Play Therapist and Child: "It's a different relationship". (P106)

It was commonly noted that the role of a play therapist was unique in many ways. As one play therapist observed, they focused solely on the child; they saw the child, not their illness:

> I think the thing we do well is that we see the child holistically. I don't think that happens across the board…I think they tend to see the condition and the illness as opposed to seeing the child (PT301).

Another theme to emerge was that the play therapist was not seen as a threat to the child:

> It's purely (play therapist name) is not there to hurt her or make her feel uncomfortable in any way…(play therapist name) doesn't have any threatening things about her at all. (P104)

Discussion

Both questionnaire data and interviews revealed several key functions of play therapy and roles of a play therapist within a hospital setting. Functions included helping children cope, assisting them through medical procedures, distraction, to entertain or occupy and to reduce anxiety. Participants in this study largely saw play therapist roles similarly to the functions of play therapy. Other specific roles that emerged were, providing activities that encourage development and developing a non-threatening relationship with children.

Overall, helping children cope with hospital was seen as the main purpose of play therapy. Furthermore, the play therapist's role was seen to assist children understand their illness and medical treatments and to give them strategies to cope. Several elements emerged, including the use of procedural support, distraction and reducing children's fear and anxiety, that supported the notion that play therapy helped children cope in hospital. This finding is consistent with previous research indicating the therapeutic value of play in helping children cope with their illnesses (Abbott 1990; Gariepy and Howe 2003; Goymour et al. 2002; Li and Lopez 2008).

Concerning the more specific functions of hospital play therapy and therapist roles, participants believed procedural support to be important. Procedural support is an approach that hospital play therapists use to help prepare and assist children in medical procedures (Abbott 1990). Support for these perceptions is apparent in the literature, as several studies have found preparing children for medical procedures helps them cope by reducing their stress and anxiety (Hallowell et al. 2008; Li and Lopez 2008). Furthermore, preparation and orientation have been identified as a common role of a hospital play therapist (Cole et al. 2001; Gaynard et al. 1989). One strategy discussed by participants was the use of dolls in procedural support. Support for these perceptions of this specific play therapy strategy's effectiveness was evident in Li and Lopez's (2008) experimental study finding that the use of dolls reduced children's anxiety levels during medical procedures. Another strategy mentioned and also identified in previous research, was the use of medical play to recognise any fears or anxieties within the children and help them understand the procedures and their illness (Abbott 1990; Gariepy and Howe 2003; Goymour et al. 2002).

The term distraction was also used in terms of procedural support. As a strategy, however, some participants, in particular health care professionals referred to distraction more often and somewhat differently than play therapists. While it was not the intention of this study to compare groups in relation to their perceptions, the findings concerning distraction proved interesting. Goymour, et al. (2000, 11) characterised distraction as "a positive action that diverts the child's attention from the process and potentially allow blocking of unpleasant sensations". Yet according to Webstar (2000, 27) distraction is not "a diversion that seeks to occupy or entertain children away from the realities of the situation". Instead, it is "used to engage and raise coping strategies with the child, families and staff". In the current study, health care professionals tended to discuss distraction in terms of a diversion, whereas play therapists, while believing in distraction as a diversion, expressed that their role in this regard was more than just entertaining children. Furthermore, they believed the use of distraction engaged children and helped them develop coping strategies.

Parents' views were similar to that of health care professionals concerning distraction; while they made notably fewer direct references to it, they did provide examples of what could be characterised as distraction. These differing perceptions of distraction combined with the diverse definitions within the literature indicate a need for clarification of the function of distraction within hospital play therapy.

Most participants believed that the play therapist has a responsibility to provide age-appropriate play experiences that encourage children's developmental skills. Similar results were found to that of Gaynard et al. (1989) and Cole et al. (2001), who reported that a hospital play therapist's primary role was mainly to do with providing activities for children. While children were in hospital, play therapists were to minimise the disruption to their development (Cole et al. 2001). Therefore, the role of hospital play therapists is not only to provide play activities that help them cope with hospitalisation, there is also a responsibility to use play as a means to encourage and further children's development.

Further functions and roles of a play therapist identified were to entertain, occupy and engage children. Again, it was not the intention of this study to compare groups, but it is worth noting that parents and health care professionals believed that the function of hospital play therapy and the role of a play therapist were to either occupy or entertain children, whereas play therapists mentioned these infrequently. Cole et al. (2001) also found such a disparity and concluded that health care professionals may not recognise the importance and purpose of play. It is possible that this discrepancy is around the notion of play itself. While research has discovered how important play is for children in regard to their development and learning (Frost et al. 2005), perceptions that play is simply fun and entertaining for children still exist (Ginsburg 2007; Kim 2002). Therefore, parents and health care professionals may be viewing the provision of play experiences for hospitalised children as simply entertainment, when in fact, play therapists are aiming to provide experiences to encourage children's development, give them a means to communicate and help them cope with their hospitalisation (Cole et al. 2001). It is likely there are times when hospital play therapy may appear to be entertaining children, and indeed is experienced that in way, while achieving other less visible functions, such as reducing their anxiety or helping them cope by allowing them to express themselves through play. Nonetheless, play therapists' unwillingness to refer to their work as entertaining was notable and could possibly be linked to the idea that this description diminishes the importance of hospital play therapy and their role.

Throughout the literature, hospital play therapy is seen as an agent to help reduce children's anxiety and stress levels, and assist children's psychological wellbeing (Brewer et al. 2006; Jones and Landreth 2002; Zahr 1998). While this may be the case, participants in the current study focussed more on the strategies used in hospital play therapy and the broader outcome of helping children cope. Despite this, most participants indicated on the checklist of potential roles that reducing stress and anxiety was the responsibility of the hospital play therapist, and some mentioned it in response to open-ended questions. More broadly, however, the functions and roles discussed thus far have been found to result in lower anxiety and stress levels (Hallowell et al. 2008; Li and Lopez 2008; Zahr 1998), thus assisting children's psychological wellbeing.

The current results corresponded with previous research that has found developing strong and trustworthy relationships with their patients is a key part of the play therapist's role (Landreth 2002; Nalavany et al. 2005). However, the uniqueness of this relationship between a hospital play therapist and child was also highlighted in the current research. Most participants commented that the relationship that develops between the play therapist and child was different, since the therapist is there for the child and not their illness. While all health care professionals within a hospital have important roles in regard to patient care, most are focused on treating the illness, injury or impairment. Play therapists however, are there to engage with the child as they undergo treatment. Furthermore, play therapists are not directly involved in administering procedures that might result in pain or discomfort to the child, and are thus less likely to be threatening to children. It could be argued that the play therapist is in a unique position to see the child first and foremost, regardless of their condition, and that through play they create a trustworthy relationship where children can express themselves, and develop a non-threatening friendship with the child.

Finally, the findings indicated that most participants believed play therapy to be just as important as medical and surgical procedures as well as other treatments, therapies and support services within a hospital. This suggests that hospital play therapy is not seen as an extra, but as an integral part of the health care provided within a hospital. As one play therapist expressed "we're not icing in the cake…we're the actual ingredient" (PT308).

Limitations and Implications for Future Research

Despite the unique contributions of this study to the literature concerning perceptions of play therapy and the roles of play therapists by those directly involved, there are limitations. A small sample size for the survey phase of the study reduced the statistical power and the potential validity of the study's results. More participants would be beneficial in gaining a broader perspective that could have led to findings that could be generalised with more confidence. Recruitment procedures resulted in mainly parents who had children with cancer-related illnesses being involved in the study. Therefore, perceptions from parents with diverse experiences within a hospital setting were not represented in the sample. In addition, the influence of cultural factors on perceptions was not incorporated as a focus in this research. Finally, discrepancies between groups of participants and the terms used for the function of hospital play therapy, in particular such terms as distraction, procedural support, engaging children or occupying / entertaining children, made it difficult to conclude whether these were primary functions or not. Further research into what aspects of play therapy are seen as strategies, as distinct from functions and professional roles, or responsibilities is warranted.

Implications for Practice

The aim of this research was to examine the perceptions of parents, health care professionals and play therapists on the function of hospital play therapy and the role of a play therapist. The results of the study found a range of functions of hospital play therapy, and provided an insight into the role of hospital play therapists and their responsibilities towards children who are ill or have a serious injury or disability. However, discrepancies between perceptions of parents and health care professionals, and play therapy professionals were also evident. More specifically, health care professionals and parents believed the function of hospital play therapy and the role of a hospital play therapist was more to do with entertaining or occupying the children. In addition, different perceptions concerning distraction in hospital play therapy between parents and health care professionals, compared to play therapists, were apparent. This suggests that parents of hospitalised children, hospital health care professionals and play therapists are likely to have different expectations in regard to what the focus of therapy might be, and the outcomes. Such discrepancies in expectations may compromise communication between professionals and parents alike. A key part of teamwork requires all employees to understand roles within the workplace (Cole et al. 2001). Furthermore, as the AWCH statement reads, play therapists need to increase the understanding of play therapy by other health care professionals and parents. Consequently, it would seem that more could be done by the play therapy profession within the healthcare sector to raise awareness on the function of hospital play therapy. In the meantime, raising the awareness of hospital play therapists, through such findings as those reported here, might go some small way to contributing to improved communication between those involved in the healthcare of children in hospital.

References

Abbott, Karen. 2009. "Therapeutic use of play in the psychological preparation of preschool children undergoing cardiac surgery". *Issues in Comprehensive Pediatric Nursing* 13: 265-277.

AWCH (Association for the Welfare of Child Health). 2002. *A recommended policy relating to the provision of play for children in hospital.* NSW: National Office. Accessed 3rd January, 2009, http://www.awch.org.au/pdfs/AWCH_Play_Provision_Policy.pdf

Astramovich, Randell, L. 1999. "Play therapy theories: a comparison of three approaches". Paper presented at the National Conference of the Association for Counselor Education and Supervision, New Orleans LA.

Boekaerts, Irma. and Monigue Roder. 1999. "Stress, coping and adjustment in children withchronic disease: a review of the literature". *Disability and Rehabilitation,* 21:311-337.

Bolig, Rosemary, David E. Fernie and Elisa L. Klien. 1986. "Unstructured play in hospital settings: an internal locus of control rationale". *Child Health,* 15: 101-107.

Bratton, Sue C., Dee Ray, and Tammy Rhine. 2005. "The efficacy of play therapy with children: A meta-analytic review of treatment outcomes". *Professional Psychology: Research and Practice* 36: 376-390.

Brewer, Stephanie. Shannon L. Gleditsch, Dorothy Syblik, Mary E. Tietjens, and Heidi W. Vacik. 2006. "Pediatric Anxiety: Child life intervention in day surgery". *Journal of Pediatric Nursing* 21: 13-22.

Camastral, Silvia. 2008. "No small change: Process-oriented play therapy for children of separating parents". *Australian and New Zealand Journal of Family Therapy* 29:100-106.

Christiano, Beth A., and Sandra W. Russ. 1996. Play as a predictor of coping and distress in children during an invasive dental procedure. *Journal of Clinical Child Psychology* 25:130-138.

Cole, Wendy, Marissa Diener, Cheryl Wright, and Laura Gaynard. 2001. "Healthcare professionals' perceptions of a Child Life Specialist". *Children's Health Care* 30:1-15.

Frost, Joe L., Sue Wortham, and Stuart Reifel, Stuart. 2005. *Play and child development* (2nd ed.). New Jersey: Pearson Education, 2005.

Gariepy, Nadine. and N. Howe. 2003. "The therapeutic power of play: examining the play of young children with leukaemia". *Child Care, Health and Development* 29: 523-537.

Gaynard, Laura, Evelyn Hausslem, and Joseph P. DeMarsh. 1989. "Child life specialists: a report of an observational study". *Child Health Care* 18:75-81.

Ginsburg, Kenneth R. 2007. "The importance of play in promoting healthy child development and maintaining strong parent-child bonds". *Pediatrics* 119 (2007): 182-191.

Goymour, Kirsty L., Claire Stephenson, Belinda Goodenough, and Clare Boulton. 2002. "Evaluating the role of play therapy in the paediatric emergency department". *Australian Emergency Nursing Journal,* 3:10-12.

Griffith, Mariellen. 1997. "Empowering techniques of play therapy: A method for working with sexually abused children". *Journal of Mental Health Counselling* 19:130-143.

Hallowell, Leanne M., Shari E. Stewart, Cicero Silva, and Michael R. Ditchfield. 2008. "Reviewing the process of preparing children for MRI". *Pediatr Radiol* 38:271-279.

Hutton, Deborah. 2005. "Filial Therapy: shifting the balance". *Clinical Child Psychology and Psychiatry* 9:260-271.

Johnson, Cameron. 1993. "Art, play therapy programs help children whose parents are dying of Cancer". *Canadian Medical Association Journal* 149:1528-1530.

Jones, Elizabeth M., and Garry Landreth. 2002. "The efficacy of intensive individual play therapy for chronically ill children". *International Journal of Play Therapy* 11:117-140.

Kim, Myoungsoon. 2002. "Parents' perceptions and behaviours regarding toys for young children's play in Korea". *Education* 122:793-808.

Landreth, Garry. 2002. *Play therapy: The art of the relationship* (2nd ed.). New York: Brunner-Routledge.

LeBlanc, Michael, and Martin Ritchie Martin. 2001. "A meta-analysis of play therapy outcomes". *Counselling Psychology Quarterly* 14:149-163.

Li, Ho Cheung W., and Violeta Lopez. 2008. "Effectiveness and appropriateness of therapeutic play intervention in preparing children for surgery: a randomized controlled trial study". *Journal of Specialists in Pediatric Nursing* 13:63-73.

Nalavany, Blace A., Tomi Gomory, Scott D. Ryan, and Jeffrey R. Lacasse. 2005. "Mapping the characteristics of a 'good' play therapist". *International Journal of Play Therapy* 14:27-50.

Ogawa, Yumiko. 2004. "Childhood trauma and play therapy intervention for traumatised children". *Journal of Professional Counselling: Practice, Theory and Research* 32:19-29.

Popovich, Deborah M. 2003. "Preserving dignity in the young hospitalised child". *Nursing Forum* 38:12-17.

QSR International. 2009. *NVivo 8* Computer Software. Doncaster, Vic: QSR International.

Tcw, Krisit., Garry Landrcth, Kimbcrly Joincr, and Misty Solt. 2002. "Filial therapy with parents of chronically ill children". *International Journal of Play Therapy* 11:79-100.

Watson, M. W. 1994. "The relationship between anxiety and pretend play". In *Children and Play: Clinical and developmental approaches to meaning and representation.* Edited by Arietta Slade and Dennie P. Wolf, 33-47. New York: Oxford University Press.

Webb, Nancy B. 1999. "Play therapy crisis intervention with children". In *Play therapy with children in crisis: individual, group and family treatment.* Edited by Nancy B. Webb, 29-48. (2nd ed.). New York: The Guildford Press.

Webster, Alison. 2000. "The facilitating role of the play specialist". *Paediatric Nursing* 12: 24-27.

Wilmot, Michelle. 2007. "The specialised play specialist". *Paediatric Nursing* 10:33.

Wittenborn, Andrea K., Anthony J. Faber, Ashley M. Harvey, and Volker Thomas. 2006. "Emotionally focused family therapy and play therapy techniques". *The American Journal of Family Therapy* 34:333-342.

Yuqing, Guo. 2005. "Filial therapy for children's behavioural and emotional problems in mainland China". *Journal of Child and Adolescent Psychiatric Nursing* 18:171-180.

Zahr, Lina K. 1998. "Therapeutic play for hospitalsed preschoolers in Lebanon." *Pediatric Nursing* 23:449-455.

CHAPTER EIGHT

PRACTICES

PETER WHITEMAN, KATEY DE GIOIA AND ROSEMARY DUNN

Observation has been and remains a lynchpin of early childhood practice. As far back as the mid-nineteenth century (e.g. Darwin 1877), understandings of children were formed on the basis of observation. As our field has transcended the boundaries of logical positivism, observation, in various guises has endured as an important tool. The rise of discourses such as the new sociologies (e.g. Corsaro 2010), feminism (e.g. Cockburn 2005; Thorne 1987) and children's rights (e.g. Moss and Petrie 2002) positions children as active agents in their own learning and development, and acknowledges that this occurs within complex social contexts. In so doing, the notions of observation and, in turn, teaching, have been similarly transformed. Objective observation no longer suffices as the sole basis for pedagogical decision-making. Instead, we look to nuanced interpretations of a multitude of data that are gathered by a range of people in a range of contexts. We look to children, teachers, parents and other stakeholders as researchers who contribute to our understanding of children and their learning. The myopic lens has become a kaleidoscope of prisms and mirrors, an intricate system of information and reflection, interwoven to inform the complex pedagogies that characterise early childhood education in the twenty-first century. The following four stories, from four early childhood settings, trace the shifts from observation to research, and top-down and predetermined, to bottom-up and generative platforms on which pedagogical decisions and professional practice have been based.

Pre-Developmental Pedagogy

At precisely 7.00 am, a hand reaches from under the bedclothes to silence the alarm that has just begun to sound from the pale green Bakelite clock on the bedside table. It is a Monday in 1953, and 21-year-old Barbara is alive with excitement as today is her first day in her new role as a preschool teacher. Thirty minutes later, Barbara demurely exits the bathroom resplendent in a navy blue nylon shirt-waisted dress, beads and flat shoes. With some makeup and her fashionably curly hair up, she heads for the kitchen where she quickly prepares and consumes a breakfast of porridge made with oats, and hot tea. Gathering an apple for morning tea and slicing some white bread to make a tomato and cheese sandwich for lunch follows. With her books and papers packed the night before, Barbara begins the half-hour walk to her new job.

An 8.10 am arrival at preschool sees Barbara with ample time to prepare the environment before the children (three-five years old) appear in another ninety minutes or so. After stowing her lunch in the refrigerator, she dons her apron in readiness for a short, intense burst of physical exertion that sees shelves wheeled into place, chairs matched with tables, paints and puzzles set out and a balance beam returned to its rightful place in the playground. Barbara's new position is in a preschool located in a church hall. Consequently, every Friday afternoon, staff dismantle the room in order that church activities can occur unimpeded on the weekend, and Monday morning always sees the return of the preschool furniture and equipment.

Barbara's pedagogical decisions are centred on what she knows children need to know. Her teaching is content driven, and her knowledge comes from other people's observations. These people are not her colleagues; in fact she never even met them when they were alive. Barbara acquired her knowledge from the likes of Gesell (1928, 1940) and Hall (1904). She was particularly intrigued by Gesell's observations of children in his photographic dome (Gesell 1928) and knowing that her knowledge of children was based on detailed observations, the lineage of which could be traced back to Darwin, she felt that she was in a prime position to decide what her charges needed to learn and how they needed to learn it.

By 9.30 am, a steady stream of children has begun to trickle into the room. Goodbyes to mothers are often declared at the door and as the adults turn on their heels to head home, children busily stow their belongings in small, wooden door-less lockers, repair to the classroom and commence the activities to which Barbara directs them. Some muffled discontent can be heard from children as they see that yet again, the new *Mr Potato Head* toy has not made it onto the shelves in their classroom. Barbara knows her activities are the best for the children because she has used the results of Gesell's observations as the primary source for her planning decisions. Barbara spends her time with the children showing them what to do with the equipment she has set out and how to do it. She looks forward to the early afternoon because that's when the children sleep and she has some time to relax before the short afternoon period devoted to using the outdoor equipment.

Developmental Times

Although becoming somewhat commonplace in the business world, personal computers do not have a tremendous presence in Patricia's preschool room. *Green Gables* is a not-for-profit community-based preschool, managed by a parent committee that employs a Director, a trained early childhood teacher (Patricia) and two untrained assistants. The Director and Patricia are each in charge of one of the rooms at the preschool and each has one assistant to help them. The children's free play is punctuated by moments of precise re-enactment of television dramas such as *The Smurfs* and *Dallas.* At times, the powerfully swaggered shoulder pads of the girls' dress-up clothes give way to mothering role-play with a *Cabbage Patch* doll or two, while at the same time, boys shed their blue and white Smurf "kit" to sport purple, blue, orange or red bandanas as they morph into Donatello, Leonardo, Michelangelo or Raphael, the *Teenage Mutant Ninja Turtles.* It is 1989, and while Patricia is enthusiastic about the children's role-play, she draws the line at their use of real implements to represent the swords, nunchucks, bo staffs and other weapons of turtledom.

Observing the children at play is something that takes a lot of 28-year-old Patricia's day. She can often be seen discreetly armed with a checklist of expected behaviours ticking off significant elements of specific developmental domains. When she is not scouring for entries on the checklist, she has a small notepad in her pocket, ready to jot down any critical or otherwise important events that she notices. Mindful of keeping her distance and ensuring that her observations go as un-noticed as possible, she writes down only enough notes to jog her memory later in the day, when she spends time filling in all the details of her observations and systematically preparing her own interpretations of what she has seen, relative to the normative pictures of children's development provided by such famous names as Piaget.

Since Barbara's teaching days three decades earlier, Patricia and her contemporaries take a much more active role in planning for individual children. Observation remains at the core of their practice, but the role of observer has undergone somewhat of a transformation. Whereas Barbara decided what and how to teach based on what Gesell knew about children's development, Patricia and her colleagues take charge of the observation process, carefully and objectively identifying behaviours deemed significant to observe. Once a full record is made, intact with unabbreviated detail, conclusions are drawn about the child and decisions made about what needs to be taught. These interpretations of the observed behaviours are made according to known developmental norms. Steeped in a developmental tradition, Patricia can explain children's apparent inability to conserve liquid until around 5 years of age according to Piaget and often sets out water-play equipment, resplendent with a range of appropriately shaped vessels for children to explore, when she notices that a child almost ready to begin formal school begins to pour water from one container to another. Parents are always pleased to hear about their children's progress from Patricia, especially as they are able to compare their child to "normal" progress.

Patricia always has her college human development textbooks at hand to guide her in interpreting observations and planning for teaching. Her need to constantly refer to these has become less over the years. She has internalised much of this knowledge because she spends so much of her time observing the children and thinking about the implications of what she sees. Her knowledge in this area is deep-seated and secure and she often recalls technical detail, particularly in relation to pre-operational thought (Piaget and Inhelder 1974) because most of the children for whom she is responsible are in this stage of development. A quick glance around Patricia's room confirms her commitment to learning based on the work of Piaget and Inhelder. One sees a raft of opportunities for children to explore in a workshop-like environment. Patricia has abandoned knowledge transmission in favour of the children constructing knowledge by acting on the environment; an environment arranged according to needs identified via careful, objective observation and interpretation.

Patricia's thirst for on-going professional knowledge is sated in part, by joining a group of early childhood teachers who have begun to meet monthly after working hours to discuss individual and group readings of current professional literature. It is at a meeting of this group that Patricia met Lisa, a teacher from across town with just a few more years experience, and a different, although related approach to early childhood practice. Speaking with Lisa about her approach to observation and her classroom gave Patricia some food for thought.

Lisa has been teaching for four years longer than Patricia. Although graduating from a regular birth-8 years program, she took a few classes in Montessori education while at University and recently developed an interest in the application in early childhood realms of some of Vygotsky's ideas (e.g. Vygotsky 1986). The children and families of Lisa's group at *Stepping Stones Children's Centre* share many similarities with those at *Green Gables.* Unsurprisingly, play is characterised by similar scripts, based on popular culture. The difference is the ways in which Lisa responds to the children's play. Just like Patricia, observation of children is the core pillar of her planning strategy, but her observations are markedly different to Patricia's in one particular way. Where Patricia's observation of children enacting ninja turtles might highlight the types of locomotion and control the children exhibit, the way they prepared their costumes or the manner in which they manipulated their pretend swords, Lisa homes in on the language that surrounds the children's play. Her reasoning for this is not so much to determine the extent of the children's vocabulary, for example, but because her interest is in how the children use language with each other and their teachers to mediate learning. Lisa's notion of observation is strongly influenced by her Montessori experience and growing interest in reading about Vygotsky's ideas. She believes that children's learning is socially located and that it is often in the form of collective action, with ever-decreasing support from the more experienced, such as teachers or other children. Her mantra is the oft-quoted Montessori saying that she first encountered during discussions at University: "The greatest sign of success for a teacher is to be able to say, the children are now working as if I did not exist."

Lisa has come to know that as with most things, culture plays an important role in learning and development, and that simply realising Vygotsky's ideals in her current environment would be fruitless. After all, the West in the 1980s is hardly Russia in the 1930s. She acknowledges the growing critique stemming from western interest in Vygotky's work (e.g. Wertsch 1985), but sees great potential in her practice for notions such as the Zone of Proximal Development (Vygotsky 1986) and scaffolding (Wood, Bruner, and Ross 1976) as she works towards Montessori's abovementioned adage. In turn, this has a profound influence on how she observes children.

Lisa's observations are generally anecdotal, still undertaken objectively and from a distance, but close enough to hear what the children say to each other and the teacher, and to facilitate later examination of the relationships that are building in the room. While her undergraduate education was steeped in developmental tradition, she doesn't look so much for perceived gaps in developmental profiles like Patricia, but is more concerned with finding out how children learn, the conditions in which they do so and who they learn with. This allows her to plan for individuals, but individuals as members of groups. Lisa's teaching positions her or another (including other adults and/or children) as the more knowledgeable other, contributing to children's learning by ensuring that where possible, learning experiences are facilitated within the child's zone of proximal development, with scaffolding (often in the form of language) gradually removed as knowledge and skills are internalised by the learner(s). So when a child first decides to solve a rather complex three-dimensional wooden puzzle for example, Lisa sits with her and may question, offer solutions, or make thinking "visible" by talking through the puzzle solution process with the child. At all times, Lisa's intervention is carefully planned to ensure that the child's interest is continually aroused and the challenge at hand challenging enough for the child to remain engaged, but not so challenging that the child abandons her endeavours in favour of something more achievable. This is why Lisa places so much importance on how she undertakes observations. As a good teacher, she knows her charges well, but she can't achieve this without careful acknowledgment of them as social beings.

After speaking with Lisa and visiting *Stepping Stones*, Patricia is keen to garner some new tools to observe children. She remains attached to the importance of content, but at the same time is beginning to shift her thinking a little to also acknowledge the multiple ways that children of the same age may engage with that content. She has started to widen her observational techniques, not so much in the way she observes, but in the choices she makes about what to observe and certainly in the manner in which she interprets those observations. At times, she finds it challenging to relinquish the importance she previously bestowed on content, but she is committed to modifying her approach to acknowledge the social nature of children.

A Post-Developmental Era

Fast-forward to 2007. Eric and Stephanie are both in their mid-thirties and have had experience teaching birth to 5-year-old children in prior-to-school settings as well as 5-8 year olds in the early years of school. They currently team teach in a fairly new preschool that has a computer in each room for children's use, each connected to an interactive whiteboard. Eric's day commences in stark contrast to Barbara's 1953 morning. By 8.00 am, he has been to the gym, breakfasted on a balanced protein shake and drives his hybrid car to *Planet Learn, Preschool Learning Centre* in the inner suburbs of a large city. Eric and Stephanie's workday begins at 8.00 am with a half-hour meeting to ensure their plans for the day are in place. Equipment required for the morning session was carefully placed before leaving the previous afternoon. Decisions about what learning engagements would be on offer were based on careful consideration of quite complex developmental records. These include observations, snippets of video taken over the previous week, notes of conversations with parents and children, "work' that children have selected to include in their learning portfolio, and so on. Eric and Stephanie's records are complex, multimodal affairs, with a range of voices evident. Children, teachers, other professionals and parents are all heard here. In fact, the whole notion of observation has been turned on its head and transformed into something quite different.

Calm, gentle music emanates from an iPod docked in the corner of the room. The children begin to arrive, each accompanied by a parent. They greet Eric and Stephanie and after a short conversation with parents and children, the parents leave for work. The iPod is shutdown and the children gravitate towards things that interest and excite them. As several children begin to explore the new paint that has recently been purchased, Stephanie goes to the storeroom and returns with a small, unobtrusive video camera. She has noticed that two of the boys are talking about what they are doing, and using technical terms to talk about their art-making. She is excited at the prospect of the children using words like "line," "shape," "colour" and wants record their actions on video for later perusal. She spends about 10 minutes making the video while the children engage exhaustively with the brushes and paints. At first, they look up and smile at Stephanie and ask her what she is doing. Stephanie's honest and frank reply reminds them that she is recording what they are doing so that they can look at it together sometime later. The children are very accepting of this response and return to the task at hand. Stephanie stops recording and about forty-five minutes later, returns to the table where the children's interest is beginning to wane, and they have started to clean the brushes and return them to the storage area. Stephanie notices that each has "signed" his name on the front of his painting, just as an adult artist would. She grins in quiet satisfaction to herself, knowing that the children's work is valued as a work of art in its own right, and proud of the fact that teachers don't take control by turning the paintings over and writing the children's name on the back. She makes a mental note to herself that she should follow up on the children's discussion of brown, green and grey colour with a walk around the local area, discussing the colour of foliage that can be found nearby, and perhaps extending the children's technical skills to encompass ways of representing texture in two-dimensional art forms. Meanwhile, she takes the boys to the computer and they search online galleries for access to artworks from varying eras that have similarities with their creations.

Meanwhile, Eric and another child are preparing a learning story (see Carr 2001, for an full explanation of learning stories) with her father, using a photomontage consisting of images from the preschool, from home and from outings in the community. All three have important information to contribute as Eric writes descriptions and interpretations of events depicted in the photographs. When complete, the child takes the learning story and carefully attaches it to the wall, just inside the front door. She proudly announces that everyone will be able to see what she has been learning when they enter the preschool. She waves goodbye to her father and joins some other children perusing picture books. Later in the day, Stephanie will revisit the video she recorded with the children. They will sit down together and in discussion, Stephanie will skilfully draw out information about what the children were doing, why they were doing it and what it means. She will be privy to the children's innermost thoughts about their art, and begin to know about their facility with the technical language that underpins their art making. For this process, Stephanie draws on Forman's (1999) Instant Video Revisiting (IVR) tool, which allows children to move beyond description of action, and begin to unpack intent. As part of these discussions, the children's talk begins to centre on whether it might be possible to transform a shape (a two dimensional construct) into a form (a three dimensional construct). They wonder about turning a circle into a cylinder ("a stick" in their terms), so Stephanie undertakes to bring in some clay and practise all manner of extrusion techniques with the children.

Learning stories and IVR are but some of the tools in Eric and Stephanie's observational tool kit; a tool kit that renders the label "observation" ineffective in capturing the true details of the process. Eric and Stephanie, along with the children, other professionals and parents are more than observers: they are researchers. For some time, they have been dedicated to critiquing the objective, distant observation that was so important in the past because they acknowledge that they (and a whole host of other stakeholders) are actually right in the middle of what they are "observing." This is the first important departure from previous versions of observation – considered, subjective interpretations of events contribute to rich understandings of complex behaviours and issues. The second difference is based on contemporary understandings of how children develop. A range of disciplines now affirms that a unilateral trajectory is insufficient to describe how children develop and learn (see, for example, Corsaro 2010; Dahlberg and Moss 2005; Fosnot 2005; Thelan and Smith 1994). While studying for her master's degree, Stephanie began to delve beyond Bronfenbrenner's (2004) bioecological approach and has encouraged Eric to join her. To inform their pedagogical decisions, they gather data in tandem with various partners, ensuring that they maximise the ecological validity of what underpins the children's everyday experiences at preschool. Such actions auger well, as observation continues to be transformed by people, circumstances and events that we are yet to encounter.

References

Bronfenbrenner, Urie. 2004. *Making human beings human: Bioecological perspectives on human development*. Thousand Oaks, CA: Sage Publications.

Carr, Margaret. 2001. *Assessment in early childhood settings : learning stories*. London: Sage.

Cockburn, Tom. 2005. "Children and the feminist ethic of care." *Childhood* no. 12 (1):71-89.

Corsaro, William A. 2010. *The sociology of childhood*. 3rd ed. Thousand Oaks, CA: Pine Forge Press.

Dahlberg, Gunilla, and Peter Moss. 2005. *Ethics and politics in early childhood education*. London: Routlegde Falmer.

Darwin, Charles. 1877. "A biographical sketch of an infant." *Mind* no. 2 (7):285-294.

Forman, George E. 1999. Instant video revisiting: The video camera as a "tool of the mind" for young children. *Early Childhood Research and Practice* 1 (2), http://ecrp.uiuc.edu/v1n2/forman.html.

Fosnot, Catherine Twomey. 2005. Constructivism revisited: Implications and reflections. *The Constructivist* 16 (1), https://sites.google.com/site/assocforconstructteaching/journal/the-constructivist-archive.

Gesell, Arnold. 1928. *infancy and human growth.* New York: Macmillan.

—. 1940. *The first five years of life: A guide to the study of the preschool child.* New York: Harper & Brothers.

Hall, G Stanley. 1904. *Adolescence: Its psychology and its relations to physiology, snthropology, sociology, sex, crime, religion and education.* New York: D. Appleton and Company.

Moss, Peter, and Pat Petrie. 2002. *From children's services to children's apces: Public policy, children and childhood.* New York: Routledge Falmer.

Piaget, Jean, and Bärbel Inhelder. 1974. *The child's construction of quantities.* London: Routledge & Kegan Paul Ltd.

Thelan, Esther, and Linda B. Smith. 1994. *A dynamic systems approach to the development of cognition and action.* Cambridge, MA: MIT Press.

Thorne, Barrie. 1987. "Re-visioning women and social change: Where are the children?" *Gender and Society* no. 1:85-109.

Vygotsky, Lev Semyonovich. 1986. *Thought and language.* Translated by Alex Kozulin. Cambridge, MA: MIT Press.

Wertsch, James. 1985. *Vygotsky and the social formation of mind.* Cambridge, MA: Harvard University Press.

Wood, David, Jerome E. Bruner, and Gail Ross. 1976. "The role of tutoring in problem solving." *Journal of Child Psychology and Psychiatry* no. 17:89-100.

CHAPTER NINE

YOUNG CHILDREN'S VOICES: DEVELOPING INNOVATIVE RESEARCH METHODS

ELSPETH STEPHENSON

Introduction

Since the release of United Nations Convention on the Rights of the child in 1987 there has been a gradual recognition of the need to incorporate the voices of children into educational research. The Convention clearly states that children have the right to express their views on matters that relate directly to them (article 12). Acknowledgement of this in recent years has called for The Convention to be used as a framework for research with young children (Smith 2007).

Alongside this developing recognition, is the growth of Childhood Studies as a disciplinary area (Hallet and Prout 2003; Christensen & James 2000) which has challenged traditional ways in which young children are viewed by offering a more contemporary approach to the construction of childhood. Rather than seeing them as helpless and needy, young children are increasingly being recognised as competent individuals who are "experts in their own lives" and capable of having agency, given the right opportunities. The growing question for researchers working with young children then, no longer focuses on "why" the voice of the child is important in educational research, but "how" it is to be legitimately captured.

Capturing the Voices of Children with Legitimacy

When embarking on research, design and method need to be carefully considered, since they will have a significant impact on successful outcomes. When designing research to be undertaken with young children, consideration of their age is important. If young children are to be given an opportunity to offer their views, what is asked of them needs to be relevant and appealing, to allow effective engagement with the concepts being explored. Similarly, developmental appropriateness needs to be ensured. If children do not possess the skills required to engage in a specific communicative activity, then the resulting data will fail to capture their authentic views. This is a particular challenge while young children's language skills are emerging, when research conducted to gain others' perspectives is linguistically based. Alternative ways of providing effective communication for children need to be explored if methods are to be successful. Malaguzzi, in his work with the Reggio Emilia approach to early childhood education and the "100 languages of children" (Edwards, Gandini, and Forman 1998), acknowledges that children use many forms of communication. Children use a wide variety of visual media "to explore understandings, to reconstruct previous ones, to construct and co-construct revisited understandings of phenomena investigated" (p28). This approach to working with young children may be useful to researchers, as they pursue effective communication methods with young children.

Design and methods are significant in achieving authentic outcomes of research carried out with young children, but they are not the only aspects that need to be considered if research in this area is to be conducted legitimately. The process of implementation of the chosen method needs to be carefully considered, as does the response to the data, as both of these aspects are integral to the way in which data are made.

The notion of "making" data is an important one here. In qualitative research the interpretation of findings and co-construction of knowledge are central to legitimate outcomes (Richards 2005). This is unlike quantitative data where information is already available, as "Autumn leaves lying around waiting to be swept up, ready to be collected and then numerically represented" (Richards 2005, 37). The processes involved with qualitative data are more complex. Meaning is not "lying around in nature waiting to be scooped up by the senses" but "is constructed, (which) in this context means produced in acts of interpretations" (Steedman 1991, 54).

The task of creating an appropriate situation, sensitively recording participants' perceptions and handling the data well become much more than pure collection and require sensitivity in the way that the chosen method shapes the data (Richards 2005). "How the researcher defines the domain of the problem and constructs the method, how she presents herself to her informants, and how she receives the responses and judges their relevance to her research focus, all are elements which shape the nature of the data being elicited." (Jorgenson 1991, 211). The process of selection of aspects of data involves interpretation. Thus, making data is "highly purposive, where the researcher will make data relevant for the purposes of the project and refer to participants for clarity and guidance" (Richards 2005, 41).

The Jigsaw Approach

One method currently being developed by the author of this chapter in response to the challenges of capturing the authentic voice of the young child is the Jigsaw approach. This works, in principle, like a child's jigsaw. In a child's jigsaw, there may be only a few pieces, with each piece having some meaning. When all the pieces are put together however, a picture is made which has much more meaning than each of the parts on their own.

For example, imagine a jigsaw of a face. It has four pieces: two pieces showing eyes, one piece showing a nose, and one piece showing a mouth. Each piece has some meaning by itself. The piece that has a picture of a mouth tells us it is a person's mouth, and it may be a "smiley" mouth. The eye piece tells us it is an eye, of a particular colour. When the jigsaw is put together we can gain much more information about the face as a whole. Clues to greater information noticed in an individual piece (facial lines around the eye, or skin colour, for example), may be more obvious once the jigsaw is complete (telling us approximate age and cultural background of the person). Together the pieces give us a depth of understanding that the individual pieces alone may only hint at, or may not show at all.

The Jigsaw approach then, involves the making of a jigsaw. The pieces of the jigsaw are created from individual activities undertaken by the child, and then pieced together by the child during discussion with the researcher to form a large picture. The Jigsaw approach begins with children's engagement in a range of different arts-related activities. These are offered to children as communication tools to respond to questions related to the topic of the research. The outcome of each activity becomes a piece of the jigsaw and a vehicle through which the child communicates his thoughts. Each piece gives us some information towards understanding the phenomenon under inquiry. It is when all the pieces come together to make the jigsaw that a deeper understanding of the phenomenon under investigation is developed between the child and researcher.

Building the Jigsaw Together

The jigsaw building process occurs with the child and researcher working together. The child and the researcher look at each jigsaw piece together and revisit previous communication. This enables the researcher to confirm or refine her translations of the child's work. Once this discussion has finished, the child is invited to place the piece on the floor. He is asked to consider where it may "fit" in relation to the other pieces already placed. This process is repeated with each jigsaw piece. Once all the pieces have been revisited and placed as part of the jigsaw, the child and researcher view the completed picture. It is at this point that co-construction of meaning occurs. The researcher shares what she sees while trying to make sense of the picture as a whole. The child is invited to do the same and respond to the comments made by the researcher. It is through this discussion that a shared understanding is reached and meaning is co-constructed. Themes relating to the research are explored as they emerge.

This method is based on the Mosaic Approach developed by Clark and Moss (2005). The Mosaic Approach is also used in an attempt to gain greater understanding of a concept from the perspective of the child. As with the Jigsaw approach, the Mosaic approach offers children a variety of ways to communicate their views. These are then brought together, along with the views of the practitioners working with them, and those of their parents, in order to build a "mosaic" from which meaning is co-constructed. The main difference between these two approaches is that the data in the Jigsaw approach are made only between the researcher and the child. While the views of parents and practitioners may be sought in other ways, they do not form any part of the final product – the Jigsaw.

The Jigsaw Approach in Practice

An example of how this works in practice comes from a study, undertaken with 4 and 5 year olds (Stephenson 2010) which sought to gain the children's perspective of their wellbeing as they transitioned from preschool to school. The study involved 5 episodes of data making (data sets) over a 12-month period.

In each data set, the children were asked to respond to a number of questions. For example, in the first data making session, the children were asked questions relating to what made them feel well. Each question was introduced in an age-appropriate way, for example with a story. The children were then offered a range of activities through which to respond. Activities offered over the course of the data sets included felt board stories, painting, drawing, play dough, puppetry, music, collage and the use of digital cameras.

Once each activity had been completed, the product of that activity was discussed so that the researcher could translate into spoken words what the child had communicated through visual media. It then became a piece of that child's jigsaw. Once all the activities had been completed, the jigsaw pieces (products of the activities) were brought together. The overall product (Jigsaw) was then used to co-construct meaning between the child and the researcher. The outcome of this work was the development of a greater understanding of the child's perspective of his/her wellbeing at that time.

An example of a jigsaw in reality is taken from the first data set. The jigsaw was constructed with a child called Jessica. In response to the question posed by the researcher, "What kinds of things make you feel well?" Jessica completed the following:

Figure 1: Jessica's felt board story

This visual story (Figure 1) shows her brother with a sad face and Jessica with a happy face. He was feeling very sad because he had been scolded by his mother, but Jessica was feeling good because she could play with him, care for him and make him feel better.

Figure 2: Jessica's painting

Figure 2 is a visual representation of Jessica playing outside with her brother. They are both painted with big smiles, depicting the wellness that Jessica feels as a result of this experience.

Jessica also took more than sixty digital photographs in the preschool, every one of which was of her friends and her teachers. While each "piece" of the jigsaw told a story of her involvement with friends and family, as can be seen in the completed jigsaw (Figure 3), when all the pieces of the jigsaw were put together by Jessica, the completed picture showed, overwhelmingly, the significance of people to her wellbeing.

Figure 3: Jessica's completed Jigsaw

As Figure 3 shows, people were the only thing represented by Jessica in response to the question "What kinds of things make you feel well?" When the jigsaw was completed, the researcher commented that people were in all her pieces. This was acknowledged by Jessica. The question was then posed "does this mean that people are important to making you feel well?" The response was an animated "YES"! The researcher interpreted this to mean that relationships are significant to Jessica's wellbeing.

As adults, we may assume that relationships would be important to a young child, but other children's jigsaws from this study offered very different views. Another example of a jigsaw created by a child in response to the question, "What kinds of things make you feel well?" gave a very different response, as can be seen in Figure 4. Each of the pieces created by this child showed open spaces, sky and trees. No people were represented. Interestingly, this child chose not to sit in a small room and take part in felt board or painting activities, he chose only to take photographs.

Figure 4: Another child's completed jigsaw.

Through engagement in this process, a greater understanding of wellbeing was developed for each child at that time.

The Jigsaw approach involves three main interactive processes. The first is translation. This involves the researcher translating into spoken words, the child's responses to individual activities (jigsaw pieces) offered through various visual media. The second is the process of co-construction. This occurs once the jigsaw has been made. It involves the researcher verbally exploring what she sees in the completed jigsaw, listening to the child's responses to these ideas and negotiating shared understanding to make meaning together. The final procedure is interpretation. This occurs at the end of the process, when the researcher interprets the meaning that has been co-constructed within the theoretical framework of the study. Such interpretation is used to build theory, in this case about children's wellbeing.

All of these processes, while being significant to the success of the approach, have attached to them potential issues to be resolved when striving to ensure legitimate outcomes. Three main issues identified here are relationships, active listening and reflexivity.

Relationships

Relationship building is a challenging area when working with young children, since time constraints placed on researchers may not permit strong relationships to be established prior to the making of data. Yet, relationships are critical to building rapport with qualitative research participants where the need for them to relax supports their ability to disclose. This is critical to the quality of data (Grieg and Taylor 1999). The relationship status with a young child, however, may have a different impact on his desire to share his views.

While relationships are critical to the security of the young child, the value placed on the relationship by the child can have a significant impact on the way he responds to the adult. The child may have invested a great deal into building a relationship and will aspire to be seen by the adult in a positive light. Answering a question correctly may be seen to increase the strength of a relationship. Therefore, this may have an impact on the way in which the child responds to questions. In a situation where the child has little or no vested interest in the relationship, he may be more inclined to speak his mind. Here, concern for the potential impact a response may have to the developing relationship may not be so great. This certainly seemed to be the case in the current study (Stephenson 2010).

Relationships are also significant for the way in which the interviewee constructs the interviewer. This has an effect upon the responses given and also to the relationship as it forms. There are multiple levels of this as the knowledge producers move in and out of their perceived roles (Jorgenson

1991). The idea of the "expert" asking the questions has implications for the responses to those questions. This is particularly relevant when working with young children, as the way childhood is constructed within the research context is important to the responses received. If children are treated as competent human beings, whose opinions are sought and valued, they are more likely to see themselves as having agency and voice their opinions with confidence. If, on the other hand, they are used to being questioned in a context where the answer is already known and the reason for the question is to check knowledge, then the potential to answer "correctly or incorrectly" may have an effect on the responses offered. The child's perception of how they are perceived and how they perceive the researcher will have implications for legitimate outcomes. To address this issue in the current study, the researcher carefully framed the children as experts and the researcher as learner (Stephenson 2010). This was done by asking the children to teach the researcher about how it felt to be going to school, as it was a long time since the researcher had done this and could no longer remember how it felt! This language was used consistently and the idea of the children teaching was regularly revisited throughout the study.

Movement within the relationship as it develops is also important to consider, as it will begin to transform the data. Judgments are made about the parts of the response that are considered relevant for the research and those which are not. Those not directly related to the question are seen from a different relationship perspective and therefore not included in the data, i.e. comments offered to the researcher in "teacher" role, as opposed to "researcher "role (Jorgenson 1991).

Thus, these complexities of relationship become significant to the process of implementation and will have an impact on how the data are shaped.

Active Listening

The skill of active listening is an essential tool for researchers working with young children if they are to capture the children's voices with authenticity. Just as children communicate with all their senses, the researcher needs to listen with all her senses, so that not only the words are heard, but the intonation with which the words are used, as well as the body language that accompanies the words are "heard". According to Egan (1994, 96), "Non-verbal communication can punctuate or modify interpersonal communication". Such non-verbal communication can confirm or deny what is being said. In fact "the face and body are extremely communicative" (Egan 1994, 95). When facial expressions are inconsistent with spoken words, they "are believed more than words" Egan (1994, 95). Non-verbal communication can also strengthen or emphasise what is being said (Egan, 1994). Thus, such aspects of listening enable the researcher to check the accuracy with which a translation may occur, or tell the researcher that their understanding of something is not shared by the child, requiring further exploration before shared meaning can be found. Without active listening, what the child really wants to say may not be fully heard.

Reflexivity

Reflexivity is a significant consideration, as reflections that occur during making and responding to data will have an impact on the conclusions drawn. Opportunities for understanding are coloured by the ways in which the researcher reflects on what she knows and what she wants to know in the research context. Reflexivity involves multiple levels of reflection working in conjunction with one another. Those levels build on and feed off one another as meaning is developed. Reflection in this context means:

> thinking about the conditions for what one is doing, investigating the way in which the theoretical, cultural and political context of individual and intellectual involvement affects the interaction with whatever is being researched. (Alvesson and Skoldberg 2000, 245).

Reflective research, according to Alvesson and Skoldberg (2000) has two characteristics. These are careful interpretation, and reflection. The first acknowledges that all empirical data are the results of interpretation. What we choose to see as data, the "bits" that are taken from interactions, are chosen because of pre-conceived ideas or theories that the researcher brings to the research process. This calls, say Alvesson and Skoldberg (2000, 5)

> … for the utmost awareness of the theoretical assumptions, the importance of language and pre-understanding, all of which constitute major determinants of the interpretation.

The second characteristic is that of reflection which can be defined as "interpretation of interpretation" (Alvesson and Skoldberg 2000, 6). This causes the researcher to be cognisant of the many elements that are brought together that influence the interpretation process, along with the problematic nature of language in the research context. The researcher needs to be mindful of these significant interpretations that occur on every level, if legitimate outcomes are to result.

In the current study (Stephenson 2010), there were two knowledge producers: the researcher and the child. Each was working reflectively throughout the process of knowledge production. The researcher was reflecting on: her knowledge of relevant theories of wellbeing; her understanding of relationships; the various communication tools used, and how each of these would influence the making of the data. Meanwhile, the child was reflecting on: his perception of the researcher; his understanding of the research process; his understanding of the world, and how this related to the questions asked by the researcher. As each question was asked and each data set developed, the responses of both knowledge producers offered more avenues for reflection. The outcomes of these reflections further impacted on the data making process. All of this happened within a context that created certain understandings, the results of which were born from initial reflections of both knowledge producers. This multi-layering and integration of reflection needs to be acknowledged as it had a significant part to play in the way the data were shaped, and thus on the eventual findings of the study.

There was only one place within this process where reflection could not occur in the first instance. This was between the researcher and the child in the first data set. While the reflections of the researcher regarding 4-5 year old children in general influenced the process of data making, the researcher could not reflect on individual children, since they were unknown to her at that stage. This is significant for this study, as the researcher needed to rely heavily on actively listening to what the child shared in order to facilitate the data making process. This meant that when translating for the child, the only thing brought to the process by the researcher was what was heard directly from the child. As the data sets developed, the relationship between child and researcher built and knowledge of the individual grew. This had the potential to increase the level of reflection brought to the process by the researcher. It is important to be mindful of this and its potential impact on the data. While it is difficult to be aware of every underlying assumption that is brought to the process, working towards finding "blind spots" of culture, theoretical and political contexts needs to occur if legitimate outcomes are to be achieved (Alvesson and Skoldberg 2000). Our reflexivity, says Steier (1991, 7)

> reveals itself as an awareness of the recognition that we allow ourselves to hear what our subjects are telling us, not by imposing our categories on them, but by trying to see how our categories may not fit.

If the focus is too narrow on any one particular theory, then the empirical material is more likely to confirm the beliefs held by the researcher. This can reduce the legitimacy of the completed work.

To avoid this, during the process of data making, the researcher needs to reflect on why meaning has been made in the way it has, and whether other "meanings" exist and are valid. In the current study (Stephenson 2010), the researcher constantly referred to the child to make sure that translations were accurate and that there was agreement with meaning that had been co-constructed.

Thus, reflexivity is important to the way in which such a method develops and to the emerging data as they are created. Without acknowledging the significance of this, researchers are at risk of offering findings that may not represent the authentic voice of the child.

Conclusion

There are many areas to consider, when attempting to capture the authentic voice of the young child. Design and methods need to be carefully considered in line with the age and development of the children whose perspectives are being sought. The researcher needs to consider issues connected to relationships with children and their potential impact on the data. Active listening needs to be employed to ensure that the child's voice is heard with accuracy. Finally, the acknowledgement of reflexivity and the role it has to play in shaping the data, along with how they are analysed is significant for legitimate outcomes in this area. Most importantly, the method employed needs to offer children opportunities to use the skills they have available to them, so that they are able to freely communicate their views and feelings.

With these things in place, research can offer children opportunities to express themselves on matters that are of importance to them, while giving legitimate access to what is finally being recognised as a valid and much sought-after voice.

References

Alvesson, Mats, and Kaj Skoldberg. 2000. *Reflexive Methodology: New Vistas for Qualitative Research.* London: Sage.

Christensen, Pia M., and Allison James. 2000. *Research with Children: Perspectives and Practices.* London: Falmer Press.

Clark, Alison, and Peter Moss. 2005. *Listening to Young Children: The Mosaic Approach.* Bath: National Children's Bureau.

Edwards, Carolyn, Lella Gandini, and George Forman, eds. 1998. *The Hundred Languages of Children. The Reggio Emilia Approach – Advanced Reflections.* London: Ablex Publishing Corporation.

Egan, Gerard. 1994. *The Skilled Helper.* California: Brooks/Cole Publishing Company.

Hallet, Christine, and Alan Prout, eds. 2003. *Hearing the Voices of Children: Social Policy for a new century.* London: Routledge Farmer.

Greig, Anne and Jayne Taylor. 1999. *Doing Research with Young Children.* London: Sage Publications.

Jorgensen, Jane. 1991. "Co-constructing the Interviewer/Co-constructing Family." In *Research and Reflexivity*, edited by Frederick Steier, 210-225. London: Sage.

Richards, Lyn. 2005. *Handling Qualitative Data: A practical guide.* London: Sage.

Smith, Anne. 2007. "Children's rights and early childhood education. Links to theory and advocacy." Australian Journal of Early Childhood 32, 3: 1-8. Accessed November 10, 2010. http://search.informit.com.au/fullText;dn=161851;res=AEIPT>

Steedman, Peter. 1991. "On the relations between seeing, interpreting and knowing." In *Research and Reflexivity*, edited by Frederick Steier, 53-61. London: Sage.

Steier, Frederick, ed. 1991. *Research and Reflexivity.* London: Sage.

Stephenson, Elspeth. "An investigation into young children's perceptions of their wellbeing during transition from pre-school to school." PhD dissertation., University of South Australia, 2010.

Thomson, Pat. ed. 2008. *Doing Visual Research with Children and Young People.* London: Routledge.

CHAPTER TEN

A VISION OF HISTORY: YOUNG CHILDREN'S PERSPECTIVES ON A MUSEUM

ROSEMARY DUNN

Introduction

Adults take children to museums in the belief that they will enjoy the experience and learn. Perspectives on children and childhood have changed; it is not enough to assume a museum visit will be "good for them". What *do* children get out of a museum visit? What are they drawn to? This study sought to explore the under-researched perspective of young children in the context of a small social history museum; which aspects of a museum experience seem most relevant or interesting to young children, aged 3-8 years? What relationships might exist between the known interests of each child and their response to a museum?

Background

Studies of Children and Museums

Children are an important visitor group for museums from at least two perspectives. Museums are seen as educational institutions by museums themselves as well as museum visitors, making children a target audience (Falk and Dierking 2000, 71-74; Farmery 2001, 38; International Council of Museums (ICOM) 2007, Article 3 par 1; Sterry and Beaumont 2006, 223). Children's experiences of museums are formative. Enjoyment of a museum experience in childhood makes it far more likely that, as an adult, the child will become a museum visitor. A positive museum experience for children, *and their families and teachers,* becomes crucial in the long term viability of museums as museums are forced to attract, retain and justify funding

(Falk and Dierking 2000, 74; Kelly et al. 2007, 2; MacRae 2007, 159; Mayfield 2005, 188-189; Mulligan and Brayfield 2004, 275-277; Rennie and Williams 2002, S7). It is of interest, then, to museums, families and schools to discover what creates a positive museum experience from the child's perspective.

One group of researchers commented nearly a decade ago that:

> With a few notable exceptions there is an absence in the literature of studies which examine very young children's perspectives and museum experiences …the voices of children in expressing and articulating their experiences are astonishingly absent.
>
> (Piscitelli and Anderson 2001, 270).

Kelly, with colleagues, at the Australian Museum in Sydney, is one of the few researchers other than Piscitelli and her colleagues to do so since then (Groundwater-Smith and Kelly 2003; Kelly et al. 2007; Anderson et al. 2002). The focus of museum research with children has tended to be on discovering what children have learned from museum visits, and how that learning has been situated within the context of interactions with adults, especially parents (see for example Crowley et al. 2001; Melber 2007; Patterson 2007; Sanford, Knutson, and Crowley 2007; Shine and Acosta 2000). A consistent finding in the research is that adults play a key role in the museum learning of children. Observational studies of both preschool and primary school-aged children have found that children who are supported by enthusiastic adults spend more time with exhibits and become more involved with the content and learning they offer (Bowker 2002, 132; Kisiel 2003, 13-14; Watson et al. 2002, 133-135). Children themselves (aged between five and eighteen) have indicated that the enthusiasm of an accompanying adult or member of museum staff enhances their enjoyment and learning (Groundwater-Smith and Kelly 2003, 6).

Imbalances in the Research

Fifty research studies and program evaluations that consider children as visitors and learners in museums were reviewed, dating from 1982 to 2008, from Australia, the United Kingdom, the United States, Germany, Denmark, Israel and New Zealand. The literature search conducted was deliberately broad, in an attempt to capture as many academic citations as possible, using "museum" and "young children" or "children" as a starting point. Significant imbalances were found.

The first trend to appear was that young children, under eight years of age, have received little research attention (Appendix 1). It is evident that primary school-aged children (eight to eleven years of age) have received greater attention than any other age group (25 studies). Young children aged five years and under were subjects in seventeen studies, and children aged five to seven years were subjects in sixteen studies. There are twenty multiple age group studies, however, only eight studies specifically focus on the museum experience of the under-eight years age group.

Secondly, it became apparent that there was a predominance of natural history and science museums as settings for museum research with and about children (Appendix 2). While they may seem to be doing essentially the same thing, under the definition developed by ICOM (2007, Section 3 par 1), museums can be grouped by the types of collections they house and exhibit, and the way those exhibits are presented. (Kirchberg 1996, 240; Mayfield 2005, 179-180). Sixty-eight different museum settings were identified within the reviewed articles. Together, natural history and science museum types account for 69.1% of the settings for research. Art museums and history museums are researched far less frequently, at 17.6% and 11.8% respectively. As this pattern started to become evident, studies set in art and history museums were actively sought, but with little success. A similar pattern was noted in Donald's (1991, 379-380) review of museum learning research. The reasons for this seem to lie primarily with a concern for the levels and quality of scientific learning in contemporary society, and the possibly more definable knowledge base of these museum types (Cox-Petersen et al. 2003, 201-202; Kawashima 1999, 30-31; Paris, Yambor, and Packard 1998, 267-268; Sterry and Beaumont 2006, 223).

Children's Perspectives on Museum Visits

Children's perspectives of museum visits are generally positive. Children's roles in family decision-making to visit museums has received little attention (Sterry and Beaumont 2006, 233). A recent study suggests that children do have significant direct influence over joint family decisions to visit (and re-visit) museums (Wu, Holmes, and Tribe 2010, 723). One of the few studies to explore the preferences of children (70 children aged four to five years) for museum types found a preference for natural history and social history museums, over art or science museums (Piscitelli and Anderson 2001, 278-279). In a larger follow-up study of approximately 100 four to seven-year old children by the same group of researchers, the natural history and social history museums prompted richer, more contextualised recollections as children made direct links between what they had seen and their own lives (Anderson et al. 2002, 228-229).

Across age groups, children express enthusiasm for seeing "real" things and opportunities for "hands on" experience in museums (Cox-Petersen et al. 2003, 205-206; Groundwater-Smith and Kelly 2003, 8-9; Jackson and Leahy 2005, 303-304; Kelly et al. 2007, 6; Kisiel 2003, 943). Interactive exhibits are perceived by child and adult visitors to both enhance their experience and to change their perceptions of museums as *old and dusty* (Falk et al. 2004, 188). Piscitelli and Anderson (2001, 279) concluded, however, that the relationship between children's experiences and understandings were still far more influential than interactivity on its own.

Young children have been found to respond to aspects of the museum experience other than the exhibits they contain. The preschool aged children in Fasoli's (2001, 6-8) study, centred on an art museum excursion, became absorbed in the "rules" of the museum at the expense of focus on the art. For most young children, the museum is a new environment and one that in some instances is not particularly "child-friendly". Children and their adult companions are frequently very aware of this (Farmery 2001, 39; Fasoli 2001, 8; 2003, 35) as are some museum educators who have created specific children's spaces and programs, or made adjustments to assist children's viewing of exhibits, but this is not uniform (Kelly et al. 2007, 2-3; Mulligan and Brayfield 2004, 291-292). Young children do need to learn how "to be" in a museum, but they can adapt to the social demands and rules with support (MacRae 2007, 163-164) .

Young Children's Interests

The relationship between children's personally-contextualised response to museums and their personal interests would seem then to be worth considering. Interests form a core of the personal context identified by Falk and Dierking that heavily influences both motivation and learning in museums (2000, 22-26). Young children's interests are, surprisingly, little studied. Interests are classified by researchers as either individual (tending to be persistent over time) or situational (reflecting more transient interests related to experience) Intense individual interests are common among young children and have been found to have a significant effect on young children's responses to experiences (Krapp 2002, 387-388)

There are age and gender-related patterns. The younger children in one library study focused on objects, showing a preference for animals or transportation, for example, over more abstract concepts like history. In the 6-7 years age group, interest in animals was perhaps higher than any other interest area, for both genders. Boys in this age group also showed a strong interest in transportation (Sturm 2003, 43). Similarly, very young boys have been found to develop both more intense interests and a greater interest in dinosaurs and transport than girls of the same age (DeLoache, Simcock, and Macari 2007, 1581,1583; Johnson et al. 2004, 332-333, 338). There has been no longitudinal research into the development and sustainment of children's interests into adulthood. Adults do play a role in supporting the interests of young children, museum visits being a resource to do this (Johnson et al. 2004, 338; DeLoache, Simcock, and Macari 2007, 1583-1584).

Method

The methodology of the current study focused on documenting the perspective of young children in a social history museum, through the use of digital photography and interviews with the children about their photographs, partly emulating previous work with young children in other museum-type settings (Cook and Hess 2007, 38-39; Kelly et al. 2007, 5). The use of digital photography was chosen because it is engaging, and a way to give children control over the data (Cook and Hess 2007, 32; Einarsdottir 2005, 526-527; Kelly et al. 2007, 4). The study used an adapted form of Photovoice®, where research participants take and annotate photographs for researchers to articulate the intention and meaning of the image (Wang et al. 1998, 75; Meyer and Kroeger 2005, 187-190). In this instance, the children did not control the data to that extent but their images, supported by their articulation of intention and meaning, form the core data of the study. Data collected about the photographs from the interview was crucial to providing the "voice" of the child (Einarsdottir 2005, 527). Parents answered pre and post-visit questionnaires developed from the types of questions raised by Falk and Dierking's (2000, 135-140) contextual model of learning. This developed a picture of the activities and experiences the child and his/her family and their motivations for museum visiting that, with observations of the child's response and interactions recorded at the museum, form a contextual background for that core.

The use of multiple methods when researching with children has been found to deliver a richer level of data and can supply a valuable level of triangulation (Christenson and James 2008, 160; Darbyshire, MacDougall, and Schiller 2005, 423-424; Scaife 2004, 72). The complexity of a museum visit and its many contexts demands multiple methods of data collection from different perspectives (Falk and Dierking 2000, 136-140; Rennie and Johnston 2004, S10-S11). The study was designed to capture data from a range of perspectives over a period of time.

Research Context

Figure 1: Experiment Farm Cottage, Harris Park, New South Wales.

Experiment Farm Cottage (EFC), Harris Park, NSW (Figure 1) was chosen as the setting for the study for specific reasons. It is a house museum, owned and operated by the National Trust of Australia (NSW) (NTA NSW). The museum consists of a bungalow and its reconstructed garden. The museum combines the familiar, a house and garden, with the differences that reflect the period of its construction. This familiarity provided a schema to support children's organisation and extension of information and knowledge (de Gorgas 2001, 10; Falk and Dierking 2000, 79-83). Hereafter any reference to Experiment Farm Cottage will be made as *the museum* (italicised).

Participants

Participants fell into one of two age groups, (a) 3-4 years (preschool aged) or (b) 6-7 years (school aged). A total of 24 children participated in the study, 14 aged 3-4 years (boys n=7, girls n=7) and 10 aged 6-8 years (boys n=4, girls n=6). Parents/carers of the children responded to advertisements placed in early childhood centres and via snowballing in the researcher's networks, so this represents a convenience sample. This sample size was selected as large enough to reveal diversity within the responses but was designed to allow for generalisations to be made. Written parental/carer consent and the child's verbal consent was given before data collection occurred.

Procedure

Each child participated in a guided tour of the museum with their parent or carer. The researcher accompanied the group as a non-participating observer. The tour is approximately one hour in length. This tour did not differ in any way from what might normally happen if the family visited *the museum* independently, except that the child was permitted to take photographs. Photography by visitors is not normally permitted but *the museum* extended permission for this to occur. Guides are trained by the National Trust (NSW) to conduct a standard tour through *the museum,* highlighting particular features, but they are encouraged to be flexible and meet the needs and interests of their tour group (National Trust (NSW) 2008, 4).

Each child was shown how to use the camera and told they could use the camera to take pictures of things they really liked or found interesting at *the museum*. The child's parent/carer was asked at the outset to support the child's exploration, taking into account that there is a policy of no touching or sitting on museum exhibits. The emphasis was on allowing the child to explore *the museum* and its grounds, within the protocols of the museum environment.

Following the tour the child was interviewed about the photographs, so that their commentary was recorded as a lens for interpretation. This interview was audio-recorded and subsequently transcribed.

The children's photographs were made into a journal and mailed, with the post visit parent/carer reflection questions, to the child and family. The journal gave the child and his/her family some opportunity to reflect on the experience at *the museum* and provide some insight into subsequent possible reinforcing events outside the museum (Kelly et al. 2007, 4; Falk and Dierking 2000, 130-132). The journal and reflection questions were returned to the researcher. The journal was copied, with the child's consent, and returned to the child.

Data Analysis

The children took a total of 1608 photographs (range 5-216, mean = 68). Photographs taken by adults that were not initiated by children, "unknowns", duplicates, or pictures for which there was no accompanying commentary (a total of 11%) were excluded from coding.

The museum staff provided a classification of museum features that formed the basic hierarchy developed for coding which features of the museum children photographed in Nvivo8 (QSR International 1999-2008). Additional nodes were subsequently developed to encompass other subjects for photographs, and explanations provided by children for the photographs. This was to showhe reasons why they had photographed features, and a range of other comments, including comments about the process of photography, through a process of constant comparison (Boeije 2002, 393).

Results

Frequently Photographed Features

Table 1 describes the most frequently photographed features of the museum within the groupings used for analysis for each age group. The frequencies with which museum features were photographed were tallied, but these gave only a partial insight into what the children found relevant or interesting. The degree to which the children took an interest in these items, independently or in response to adult cues, may indicate how engaged children were in the tour commentary given by the guide. It seems that children were, on the whole, engaged in the tour commentary, but were also giving attention to other features not directly dealt with in that commentary. While some of the most popular items, for example the birds and the well, are tour highlights, most floor surfaces and china are not.

Touching things in the museum. The extent to which the number of photographs taken might relate to how "touchable" items were in *the museum* context seems not to be an indicator of interest (Table 1). The birds (Figure 3), the china and the diorama, cannot be touched. The birds and the diorama are situated so that most children could approach them closely, at their own level. These items possibly have an attraction in their novelty and miniature qualities.

The participating children wanted to touch things in *the museum*. There are opportunities to do this at *the museum*, although the approach of the guides varied. The opportunities to use the pump, play with toys and try costumes were all taken up by many of the children, siblings and parents. Two girls who were not offered the same opportunity both commented in their journals that they would like to touch things. Neither had visited a museum before.

Table 1: Most frequently photographed features (minimum 5 responses)

Feature	Tour feature (y/n)	Touching (y/n)	3-4 years (no. of photos)	6-7 years (no. of photos)
Decorative Features			83	82
Birds	Y	N	12	10
Floor Rugs	Y	Y	13	6
Costumes	Y	Y	14	8
Curtains	N	N	8	0
Staffordshire dogs (mantle)	Y	N	7	2
Domestic features			79	138
China	N	N	11	41
Apothecary's box	Y	N	4	8
Quills	N	N	2	7
Animal shaped doorstops	N	N	13	3
Books	Y	N	1	9
Garden tools	Y	N	6	8

Lighting	Y	N	7	13
Furnishings			81	62
Bath tubs	Y	Y	11	7
Case clock	Y	N	3	9
Four poster bed	Y	N	4	5
Commode	Y	N	5	4
Garden	N	N	93	49
Geographical context	N	N	2	14
Interpretive features			14	46
Diorama	N	N	9	14
Structural features (exterior)			79	31
Well	Y	Y	12	8
Cellar steps	N	Y	8	0
Front steps	N	Y	5	0
Structural features			54	13
(interior)	Y	Y	12	3
floorboards				
Family members	N/A	N/A	89	12

When the children's photographs were coded and paired with their interview or journal explanation, two main thematic areas arose in response to the museum features in the photographs: appreciation of the aesthetic qualities of the features and ideas that related to children's perspectives on the past (Table 2). These two thematic groups will be described in detail.

Table 2: Themes and Age Groups

Rank	6-7	3-4
1	Aesthetic appreciation (133)	Aesthetic appreciation (73)
	Colour (61)	*Colour (36)*
	Form (32)	*Pattern (15)*
	Pattern (31)	*Form (11)*
	Non-specific (14)	*Non-specific (7)*
	Smell (2)	*Tactile (6)*
2	Perspectives on the past (125)	Perspectives on the past (32)
	Comparisons to today (45)	*Comparisons to today (22)*
	Age of objects (13)	*Past people (4)*
	Past people (5)	
3	Curiosities and novelties (62)	Animals (28)
4	Animals (15)	Humour (10)
5	Function of objects (11)	Function of objects (7)
6	Humour (7)	Curiosities and novelties (6)

Aesthetic Appreciation

Children in both age groups were well able to deconstruct the appeal or interest of the museum features they photographed. A "non-specific" explanation of "It's beautiful" or "I just like it" was uncommon. Not knowing the exact way to describe their preferences was more of an issue, and children needed support. The following conversation with Carla (3 yrs 8 months) about Figure 2 is a revealing example:

Researcher:	Oh, now what were you interested in there?
Carla:	On the table
R:	On the table? What, were you interested in the plate…or were you interested in the cloth?
C:	On the ta...on the cloth and er, on the...
R:	What do you like about the cloth?
C:	Ahh…(inaudible)… some down there…
Mother:	What is it that you like about the tablecloth?
C:	Ahhh, some down there on the front (pointing along the bottom edge of the tablecloth)
R:	The lace?
C:	Yeah and some up there. (pointing along the table top edge of the image)
R:	And the embroidery?
C:	Yeah.

Figure 2: Carla's (3 years 8 months) parlour side table

Lace and embroidery. "Lace" and "embroidery" are possibly not everyday words for most nearly 4 year-olds. The same lack of vocabulary was seen in other instances as individual children tried to describe the appeal of wood grain, curved sofa arms and columns (see Figures 3, 4 , 5 and 6).

Colour, form and pattern. Colour was important but it wasn't only bright colours that were attractive (Figure 3), subtle colours were also appealing (Figure 4). The children commented on the form of many features in the museum, from furnishings and structural features to domestic objects and plants (Figures 5 and 6). Pattern was noticed in a range of contexts. Dominic, who has a significant speech delay and was determined to make himself understood, liked the bold pattern of the hall sailcloth mat, but he also liked walking on it (Figure 7).

Figure 3: Sophie (7 years 9 months) Journal entry: *I like this because it is so colourful*

Figure 4: Tanya (6 years 10 months) Document box

Tanya:	There's little bit there (pointing)... that it's coming ...becoming dark…on one side..
Researcher:	Oh I see, you're interested in the grain on the timber… the way...
Tanya:	Becoming dark and …
Researcher:	…It goes dark and light and changes colour…

Figure 5: Stefan (7 years 1 month) Sofa

Stefan:	…I liked the type of it.
Researcher:	the type of it?
Stefan:	Yes. The arms… all of it.
Researcher:	All of it? So...
Stefan:	The arms..
Researcher:	The arms? The shape of the arms?
Stefan:	Yeah.

Figure 6: Daisy (3 years 7 months) – the veranda columns

Daisy:	The house.
Researcher:	The house. What did you like about that particular shot?
Daisy:	Because it had those… (pointing)
Researcher:	Oh, you like the columns at the front of the house. Yes. What do you like about them?
Daisy:	Because they're straight.

Figure 7: Dominic (4 years 0 months) sail cloth mat

Daisy:	This one (pointing)
Researcher:	You liked the squares? The pattern?
Daisy:	Yeah
Researcher:	Yeah
Daisy:	Walking
Mother:	You liked walking on it?

Perspectives on History

Children's awareness of *the museum* representing a illustration of the past was evident in the comparisons they made between things they were seeing in *the museum* and their own experience. Parents were observed to remind children of things they had seen in the past and even songs and stories that were related to features children were seeing in *the museum.* The 6-7 years age group made more direct comparisons between the past and the present, but it was evident that the younger children noticed differences. Toileting and bathing were perhaps most commented on. Cameron (4 years 7 months) and Roly (7 years 7 months) both thought the bathtub and commode were, respectively, "funny ":

Researcher:	Oh, so it's funny because it's so different.
Cameron:	Yeah
Researcher:	Yeah...How's it different?
Cameron:	'Cause our bath is bigger.
Researcher:	Right. So you've got a much bigger bath.
Cameron:	Yeah, so then Daisy can hop in the bath.
Mother:	You wouldn't be able to have a couple of people in there would you?
Researcher:	Do you sometimes have a bath with Daisy?
Cameron:	Yeah
Researcher:	Yeah, you can fit two people in your bath.
Cameron:	But, but I have Jamie in my bath.
Researcher:	Oh, you have Jamie in your bath too?
Mother:	Three of them...Three of them.
Researcher:	(laugh)
Mother:	You wouldn't be able to fit three in, you'd squash in.
Roly:	Um, a toilet.
Researcher:	A toilet. What did you think of that?
Roly:	Um (laugh) I thought it was pretty um, funny toilet.
Researcher:	Did you? Yes....you seemed surprised to have one, a toilet in the bedroom, didn't you?
Roly:	(laugh)

The level of emotional response to these differences was marked. A humorous response, such as that recounted above, was seen in other children. It seemed to relate to children's surprise and the novelty of things they were encountering. However, some children were confronted; Barny (4 yrs 0 months), for example, by differences they could not understand or explain (Figures 8 and 9). Barny took Figure 8 outside, before commencing the museum tour. He took Figure 9 inside the house, during the tour. In his comments, his subsequent preoccupation with the bed hangings became evident as he discussed the earlier photograph.

Figure 8: Barny – (4 years 0 months) curtains in the French doors

Barny:	Yeah. I liked about the windows.
Researcher:	You like those windows did you? mmmm...what's interesting about the windows?
Barny:	Because they...because they had curtains but I don't know why the bed had a roof...

Figure 9: Barny – (4 years 0 months) four-poster bed

Barny:	Yeah, my bed's different than that bed.
Researcher:	mmmm
Barny:	My bed has curtains by the side of my bed…and behind my bed.
Researcher:	You're near the window are you?
Barny:	I do have a window. But I don't have a roof.

Then he commented:

Barny:	Oh, you shouldn't have a bath in your own room or a toilet like...

Past people. A small number of responses (9) seemed to reflect children's reaction to the tour commentary that focussed on two main figures, James Ruse and Surgeon John Harris. Harris built the house that now forms *the museum* (National Trust (NSW) 2008, 4). Some children thought the things in the house belonged to him. The children were at times bringing to bear their own, modern understandings on the past. The guide explained that Victorian gentlemen like Harris would have worn a smoking jacket and fez while smoking a pipe. Cameron (4 years 7 months) was outraged, according to his mother:

> The fact that the man was a doctor...but he smoked... that really bothered him and he didn't stop talking about it! He didn't understand why being a doctor he didn't know that smoking was bad for him. Cameron's mother (Parent Reflection)

Children's awareness of change over time. Six parents (3 for each age group) reported in the post-visit questionnaire on their children's new understandings and interest in history and ideas about change over time since visiting the museum. Responses ranged from a general awareness that things had been different in the past, to different understandings about the history of their own house and surrounding community.
Barny's father wrote:

> He talked about the rooms and that they used to grow corn. He liked the pictures at the farm too…asense of history – knowing that they used to do things there (c.g. grow corn) but didn't any more.

Thomas' (7 yrs 8 months) mother reported:

> It used to be a cattle farm where our house was built upon. We mentioned this a few times through our conversations with friends in the past. Thomas seemed to relate the idea of farming practice in an urbanised area being much more comfortable. He remarked "Where we live used to be a big farm too."

Children's Interests

The children and their families reported a wide range of interests. It would be difficult to state that there were generalised interests across the group. The most frequently reported interest was *riding bikes and scooters* (nine children). However, only Barny noticed the bicycles in the caretaker's private garden, and photographed them.

It seems that if something related to a child's particular interests or preferences was present, then the child's interest was drawn to that; children with an interest in animals or gardens in particular took many more interest-related photographs. In some cases, personal interests were applied to what children were seeing in *the museum*, if only imaginatively. Denzil (3 yrs 0 months), who wore his Superman suit to *the museum*, declared that Superman had been in the top of the Monkey-puzzle tree in the front garden as a baby. In terms of percentages of commented photos the range was 0-100%. Roxana's (7 yrs 10 months) photography was unique, in that the five photographs she took where all explained from the perspective of an individual interest. Leaving her aside, the range is from 0-31.5%, with a mean of 9.7%.

Discussion

Consistent with previous research, children were found to respond primarily on an aesthetic level to qualities they found attractive in various museum features (Danko-McGhee 2006, 228-230; Tomkins and Tunnicliffe 2007, 154). In grappling with observed differences in *the museum*, making direct comparisons between their present-day experience and the past, or recognising novelty, children in both age groups were coming to terms with this understanding (Piscitelli and Anderson 2001, 279). Partial emulation of the Kelly at al. (2007) study has provided some comparison between two different museum environments. Children's humour, imaginative response to some exhibits, the role of adults and the value for children to touch, use and see things at their own level are points of congruence between the two studies (Kelly et al. 2007, 5-8). Adults played an important role in the process of recognition and comparison. The extent to which children were given an opportunity to touch and experience things in *the museum* by guides or were reminded by parents of experiences outside *the museum* supported not only engagement but also experience on which to base thinking. Anderson et al. (2002, 229) commented that children do not necessarily make the connections between different contexts, and do need this support.

The influence of children's interests

The children's known interests are a key facet of their personal context likely to influence their prior knowledge and the attention they give to any context (Falk and Dierking 2000, 22-26; Johnson et al. 2004, 326). Many children participating in this study paid attention to museum features in some way relevant to their individual interests. The interest animals hold for young children generally, identified in other studies of young children's responses to artworks, natural history specimens and reading choices, was apparent in the photographs taken by the children in this study. (Danko-McGhee 2006, 230; Sturm 2003, 43; Tomkins and Tunnicliffe 2007). This was particularly so for those children reported to have an individual interest in animals, but also in a more general way across the group. The number of photographs most children took far outstripped the instances where individual interests could be identified as motivating the photographs. This suggests that children found much that was situationally interesting within the environment of *the museum* and the context of the tour (Krapp 2002, 388). Children were responding to *the museum* in terms of things that were familiar and known to them, and individual interests form one part of that personal context for learning and engagement.

Implications for Future Research

While this is a small study, not designed to provide generalisable results, it was evident that some children were developing new historical understandings. The National Curriculum Board (2009, 7-8) identifies museums as a key resource to support historical learning. The "payback" of a museum visit is unpredictable, but the long-term impact of museum visits and school excursions has been documented (Gross, Hayne, and Drury 2009, 966; Hudson and Fivush 1991, 356; Pace and Tesi 2004, 37-38). A longitudinal study would be valuable.

The different emotional responses of some children to comparisons was surprising in terms of their strength, and the contrast between them among participants. Although Kelly et al. (2007, 7) reported a humorous response to some exhibits in their study, affective reactions of children have not been widely researched. The affective response of children to museum visits is one standard by which teachers, for example, have been reported to judge the success of a museum visit (Anderson, Kisiel, and Storksdieck 2006, 378). How that affective response may influence learning and the long term development of attitudes is not well understood and further research would be valuable.

The importance of different facets of the museum context needs further consideration. Comparisons between young children's responses to larger, museum settings and smaller museums such as Experiment Farm Cottage needs further investigation. The influence of such variables on children as the guide commentary, sibling and peer interaction in museum environments may also be a fruitful avenue for research.

Recommendations for Practice

Museums offer a potentially rich learning environment for young children. Children in the present study learned new vocabulary and experienced a distinctive form of oral discourse in the guides' commentaries, questioning and explanation in *the museum* that will contribute positively to their language development (Sarachoa and Spodek 2007, 701-702). Educators have discussed aesthetic appreciation, based on authentic experiences, as an important co-requisite for the language development and sensory awareness that support a more formal education in aesthetics, environment and science. This also develops their sense of connection to their world and culture (Danko-McGhee 2006, 231; Eglington 2003, 35-37; Fraser and Gestwicki 2002, 102-103; MacRae 2007, 164-165; Tomkins and Tunnicliffe 2007, 154; Wooltorton 2006, 27). The experience of the museum environment with its rules and conventions introduced children to a new and different "community of practice" (Fasoli 2001, 14; MacRae 2007, 163-164). In particular, *the museum* offered children opportunities to develop historical understanding and concepts in a context related closely to their experience that made it meaningful (National Curriculum Board 2009, 6; Piscitelli and Anderson 2001, 279).

The features that children found most relevant and interesting at *the museum* seem to have been those things that had aesthetic attributes that attracted them, and for which they could make direct comparisons between their own lives and experience. Children's known personal interests were expressed in the features they chose to photograph but were not limited to those things on the whole.

Appendix 1:
Ages of children in published museum research

Unspecified	Prior to school (0-5 years)	Early Years School K-2 (5-7 years)	Primary School 3-6 (8-11yrs)	Secondary School 7-12 (12-18 yrs)**	Adults
(Hall and Bannon 2005, 2006)	(Anderson et al. 2002)* (4-7 yrs)	(Anderson et al. 2002)* 4-7 years	(Bamberger and Tal 2007) * (Yrs 4-8)	(Anderson, Lucas, and Ginns 2003) (Anderson et al. 2000) (same study)	(Cox-Petersen et al. 2003) * (Yr 2-8 & teachers)
(Hughes 2005)	(Cook and Hess 2007)	(Cox-Petersen et al. 2003) * (Yr 2-8 & teachers)	(Bowker 2002)	(Cox-Petersen et al. 2003) * (Yr 2-8 & teachers)	(Crowley et al. 2001) * (1-8 yrs & parents)
(Lucas, Macmanus, and Thomas 1986) * (one unspecified age group)	(Crowley et al. 2001) * (1-8 yrs & parents)	(Crowley et al. 2001)* (1-8 yrs & parents)	(Cox-Petersen et al. 2003) * (Yr 2-8 & teachers)	(Griffin and Symington 1997) * (Yrs 5-10)	(Kisiel 2005)
(Prosser and Eddisford 2004)	(Danko-McGhee 2006)	(Eberbach and Crowley 2005) * (mean age 7.7 yrs)	(Crowley et al. 2001) * (1-8 yrs & parents)	(Groundwater-Smith and Kelly 2003)* *(K-Yr 12)	(Melber 2007) * (4-5 yrs & mother)
(Rennie and Williams 2002)	(Eckhoff 2008) (4-5 yrs)	(Gross, Hayne, and Drury 2008)	(Eberbach and Crowley 2005) * (mean age 7.7 yrs)	(Hudson and Fivush 1991)#	(Palmquist and Crowley 2007) (parents of children aged 5-7 yrs)
	(Eberbach and Crowley 2005) *(mean age 7.7 yrs)	(Groundwater-Smith and Kelly 2003) * (K-Yr 12)	(Falk and Balling 1982)	(Kisiel 2003) *(yrs 3-11)	(Patterson 2007)* (child & parent)
	(Fasoli 2001, 2003)	(Hudson and Fivush 1991)#	(Griffin and Symington 1997)* (Yrs 5-10)	(Tunnicliffe 2000) * (4-12 yrs)	(Mulligan and Brayfield 2004)

(Kelly et al. 2007)	(Piscitelli and Anderson 2001)*(4-6 yrs)	(Groundwater-Smith and Kelly 2003) *(K-Yr 12)		(Rennie and Williams 2002)
(MacRae 2007)	(Sanford, Knutson, and Crowley 2007) * (5-12 yrs & grandparents)	(Jackson and Leahy 2005)		(Sanford, Knutson, and Crowley 2007) * (5-12 yrs & grandparents)
(Melber 2007) *(4-5 yrs & mother)	(Shine and Acosta 2000)* (4-6 yrs & parents)	(Jarvis and Pell 2005)		(Tal, Bamberger, and Morag 2005)
(Piscitelli and Anderson 2001)* (4-6 yrs)	(Speering, Rennie, and McClafferty 1997) * (3-7 yrs)	(Lucas, Macmanus, and Thomas 1986) * (8-9 yrs group)		(Tal and Steiner 2006)
(Sanford, Knutson, and Crowley 2007) *(5-12 yrs & grandparents)	(Tenenbaum and Callanan 2008)* (5-8 yrs)	(Kisiel 2003) *(Yrs 3-11)		(Valle and Callanan 2006)*(4-9 yrs & parents)
(Shine and Acosta 2000)* (4-6 yrs)	(Tunnicliffe 2000) *(4-12 yrs)	(Melber 2003)		
(Speering, Rennie, and McClafferty 1997) * (3-7 yrs)	(Tunnicliffe, Lucas, and Osborne 1997) *(5-11 yrs)	(Mortensen and Smart 2007)		
(Tunnicliffe 2000) *(4-12 yrs)	(Valle and Callanan 2006)* (4-9 yrs & parents)	(Patterson 2007)* (child & parent)		
(Valle and Callanan 2006)* (4-9 yrs & parents)	(Watson et al. 2002)* (6-8 years)	(Rapp 2005) (Special needs)		

	(Weier 2004)		(Sanford, Knutson, and Crowley 2007) *(5-12 yrs & grandparents) (Tal and Morag 2007) (Tenenbaum and Callanan 2008)* (5-8 yrs) (Tunnicliffe 1996) (Tunnicliffe 2000) * (4-12 yrs) (Tunnicliffe, Lucas, and Osborne 1997) *(5-11 yrs) (Valle and Callanan 2006)* (4-9 yrs & parents) (Watson et al. 2002)* (6-8 yrs) (Wilde and Urhahne 2008) (Xanthoudaki 1998)		
Total= 6	Total = 17	Total = 16	Total = 25	Total = 7	Total = 12

NOTE:
Study asking 12 yr-old children to reflect on a Kindergarten excursion experience
* Studies conducted with multiple/across age groups
** In the initial selection of articles there was a bias towards literature that reported research and programs involving children aged from 0-8 years, so categories relating to secondary school-aged children and adults are artificially low as a result of this selection criterion.

Appendix 2: Museum settings for research

Natural History Museums	Science museums	Art museums	History museums	Unspecified
(Anderson et al. 2002)*	(Anderson et al. 2002)*	(Anderson et al. 2002)*	(Anderson et al. 2002)*	(Shine & Acosta 2000)
(Piscitelli and Anderson 2001)*	(Piscitelli and Anderson 2001)*	(Piscitelli and Anderson 2001)*	(Piscitelli and Anderson 2001)*	
(Gross, Hayne, and Drury 2009)*	(Anderson, Lucas, and Ginns 2003; Anderson et al. 2000)	(Cook and Hess 2007)	(Gross, Hayne, and Drury 2009)*	
(Bamberger and Tal 2007)* 3 separate NH museums	(Bamberger and Tal 2007)* 1 science museum	(Danko-McGhee 2006)	(Hudson and Fivush 1991)	
(Bowker 2002)	(Crowley et al. 2001)	(Eckhoff 2008)	(Hall and Bannon 2005, 2006)	
(Cox-Petersen et al. 2003)	(Hughes 2005)	(Fasoli 2001, 2003)	(Jackson and Leahy 2005)	
(Eberbach and Crowley 2005)	(Jarvis and Pell 2005)	(MacRae 2007)	(Prosser and Eddisford 2004)	
(Falk and Balling 1982)	(Kisiel 2005)	(Mulligan and Brayfield 2004)*	(Mulligan and Brayfield 2004)*	
(Groundwater-Smith and Kelly 2003)	(Melber 2003)	(Weier 2004)		
(Griffin and Symington 1997)*	(Griffin and Symington 1997)*	(Xanthoudaki 1998)		
(Lucas, Macmanus, and Thomas 1986)*	(Lucas, Macmanus, and Thomas 1986)*			
(Kelly et al. 2007)	(Rapp 2005)			
(Kisiel 2005)	(Rennie and Williams 2002)			

(Kisiel 2003)	(Sanford, Knutson, and Crowley 2007)			
(Melber 2007)	(Speering, Rennie, and McClafferty 1997)			
(Mortensen and Smart 2007)	(Tal and Steiner 2006)			
(Palmquist and Crowley 2007)	(Tenenbaum and Callanan 2008)			
(Patterson 2007)	(Valle and Callanan 2006)			
(Tal, Bamberger, and Morag 2005; Tal and Morag 2007) 4 separate NH museums	(Watson et al. 2002)			
(Tunnicliffe, Lucas, and Osborne 1997)				
(Tunnicliffe 2000)				
(Tunnicliffe and Reiss 2000)				
(Wilde and Urhahne 2008)				
28/68 (41.2 %)	19/68 (27.9%)	12/68 (17.6%)	8/68 (11.8%)	1/68 (1.5%)

NOTE:
* Studies conducted in multiple type museum settings, each setting counted as one museum setting, thus 68 settings for 50 different studies, 54 papers: multiple dates refer to different reports about the same project.

References

Anderson, David, James Kisiel, and M. Storksdieck. 2006. "Understanding teachers' perspectives on field trips: discovering common ground." *Curator* 49 (3):365-382.

Anderson, David, K. B. Lucas, and I. S. Ginns. 2003. "Theoretical perspectives on learning in an informal setting." *Journal of research in science teaching* 40 (2):177-199. doi:10.1002/tea.10071.

Anderson, David, K. B. Lucas, I. S. Ginns, and L. D. Dierking. 2000. "Development of knowledge about electricity and magnetism during a visit to a science museum and related post-visit activities." *Science education* 84 (5):658-679.

Anderson, David, B. Piscitelli, K. Weier, M. Everett, and C. Taylor. 2002. "Children's museum experiences, identifying powerful mediators of learning." *Curator* 45 (3):213-223.

Bamberger, Yael, and Tali Tal. 2007. "Learning in a personal context: Levels of choice in a free choice learning environment in science and natural history museums." *Science Education* 91 (1):75-95. doi:10.1002/sce.20174.

Boeije, Hennie. 2002. "A purposeful approach to constant comparative method in the analysis of qualitative interviews." *Quality & quantity* 36 (4):391-409. doi:10.1023/A:1020909529486

Bowker, Rob. 2002. "Evaluating teaching and learning strategies at the Eden Project." *Evaluation & research in education* 16 (3):123-135.

Christenson, Pia, and Allison James. 2008. "Childhood diversity and commonality. Some methodological insights." In *Research with children: perspectives and practices*, edited by P. Christenson and A. James. Abingdon, Oxon: Routledge.

Cook, Tina, and Else Hess. 2007. "What the camera sees and from whose perspective: fun methodologies for engaging children in enlightening adults." *Childhood* 14 (1):29-45. doi:10.1177/0907568207068562.

Cox-Petersen, Anne M., David D. Marsh, James Kisiel, and Leah M. Melber. 2003. "Investigation of guided school tours, student learning, and science reform recommendations at a museum of natural history." *Journal of research in science teaching* 40 (2):200-218. doi:10.1002/tea.10072.

Crowley, Kevin, Maureen A. Callanan, Harriet R. Tenenbaum, and Elizabeth Allen. 2001. "Parents explain more often to boys than to girls during shared scientific thinking." *Psychological science* 12 (3):258-261.

Danko-McGhee, Katherina. 2006. "Favourite artworks chosen by young children in a museum setting." *International journal of education through art* 2 (3):223-235.

Darbyshire, Philip, Colin MacDougall, and Wendy Schiller. 2005. "Multiple methods in qualitative research with children: more insight or just more?" *Qualitative Research* 5 (4):417-436. doi:10.1177/1468794105056921.

de Gorgas, Monica Risnicoff. 2001. "Reality as illusion, the historic houses that become museums." *Museum International* 53 (2):10-15.

DeLoache, Judy S., Gabrielle Simcock, and Suzanne Macari. 2007. "Planes, Trains, Automobiles-and Tea Sets: Extremely Intense Interests in Very Young Children." *Developmental Psychology* 43 (6):1579-1586. doi:10.1037/0012-1649.43.6.1579.

Donald, Janet Gail. 1991. "The measurement of learning in the museum." *Canadian Journal of Education* 16 (3):371-382. http://www.jstor.org/stable/1494885.

Eberbach, C, and Kevin Crowley. 2005. "From living to virtual: learning from museum objects." *Curator* 29:139-154.

Eckhoff, Angela. 2008. "The Importance of art viewing experiences in early childhood visual arts: The exploration of a master art teacher's strategies for meaningful early arts experiences." *Early Childhood Education Journal* 35 (5):463-472. doi:10.1007/s10643-007-0216-1.

Eglington, Kristen Ali. 2003. *Art in the early years*. London: Routledge Falmer.

Einarsdottir, Johanna. 2005. "Playschool in pictures: children's photographs as a research method." *Early Child Development and Care* 175 (6):523 - 541: doi:10.1080/03004430500131320.

Falk, John H., and John D. Balling. 1982. "The field trip milieu: Learning and behavior as a function of contextual events." *Journal of educational research* 76 (1):21-28.

Falk, John H., and Lynn D Dierking. 2000. *Learning in museums: visitors experiences and their making of meaning.* Walnut Creek CA: Altamira Press.

Falk, John H., Carol Scott, Lynn D Dierking, L.J. Rennie, and Mika Cohen Jones. 2004. "Interactives and visitor learning." *Curator* 47 (2):171-198.

Farmery, K. 2001. "If they build it they will come." *Museums journal* (April):37-39.

Fasoli, Lyn. 2001. "Preschoolers visit the art gallery : complicating the excursions." In *Australian Curriculum Studies Association Conference*, edited by M. Brennan. ANU Canberra: Australian Curriculum Studies Association.

Fasoli, Lyn. 2003. "Reading photographs of young children: looking at practices." *Contemporary issues in early childhood* 4 (1):32-47. http://www.wwwords.co.uk.simsrad.net.ocs.mq.edu.au/pdf/validate.asp?j=ciec&vol=4&issue=1&year=2003&article=3_Fasoli_CIEC_4_1_web.

Fraser, Susan., and Carol Gestwicki. 2002. *Authentic childhood: exploring Reggio Emilia in the classroom.* Albany, NY: Delmar Thomson Learning.

Griffin, J., and D. Symington. 1997. "Moving from task-oriented to learning-oriented strategies on school excursions to museums." *Science education* 81 (6):763-779. doi:10.1002/(SICI)1098-237X(199711)81:6<763::AID-SCE11>3.0.CO;2-O.

Gross, J., H. Hayne, and T. Drury. 2008. "Drawing facilitates children's reports of factual and narrative information: implications for educational contexts." *Applied cognitive psychology (online)* Early View. Article first published online: 26 SEP 2008. doi:10.1002/acp.1518

Gross, Julien, Harlene Hayne, and Tanya Drury. 2009. "Drawing facilitates children's reports of factual and narrative information: implications for educational contexts." *Applied Cognitive Psychology* 23 (7):953-971. doi:10.1002/acp.1518.

Groundwater-Smith, S., and L. Kelly. 2003. "Seeing practice anew: improving learning at the museum." In *Australian Association for Research in Education/New Zealand Association for Research in Education Joint Conference*. Auckland: http://www.aare.edu.au/03pap/gro03195.pdf.

Hall, T, and L Bannon. 2005. "Co-operative design of children's interaction in museums: a case study in the Hunt Museum." *CoDesign* 1 (3):187-218. doi:10.1080/15710880512331392362.

Hall, T, and L Bannon. 2006. "Designing ubiquitous computing to enhance children's learning in museums." *Journal of Computer Assisted Learning* 22 (4):231-243. doi:10.1111/j.1365-2729.2006.00177.x.

Hudson, J.A., and R. Fivush. 1991. "As time goes by: sixth graders remember a Kindergarten experience." *Applied cognitive psychology* 5:347-360.

Hughes, Jill. 2005. '"Life of a Star" museum exhibit.' *TechTrends* 49 (5):61-63.

International Council of Museums (ICOM). 2008. ICOM Statutes International Council of Museums 2007 [cited 21 October 2008]. Available from http://icom.museum/statutes.html#3.

Jackson, A, and H Leahy. 2005. " 'Seeing it for real...?'—Authenticity, theatre and learning in museums." *Research in Drama Education* 10 (3):303-325. doi:10.1080/13569780500275956.

Jarvis, Tina, and Anthony Pell. 2005. "Factors influencing elementary school children's attitudes toward science before, during, and after a visit to the UK National Space Centre." *Journal of research in science teaching* 42 (1):53-83. doi:10.1002/tea.20045.

Johnson, Kathy E., Joyce M. Alexander, Steven Spencer, Mary E. Leibham, and Carin Neitzel. 2004. "Factors associated with the early emergence of intense interests within conceptual domains." *Cognitive Development* 19 (3):325-343. doi:10.1016/j.cogdev.2004.03.001.

Kawashima, Nobuko. 1999. "Knowing the public. A review of museum marketing literature and research." *Museum Management and Curatorship* 17 (1):21-39. doi:10.1016/S0260-4779(98)00030-2.

Kelly, Lynda, S. Main, S. Dockett, B. Perry, and S. Heinrich. 2007. "Listening to young children's voices in museum spaces." In *Conference of the Australian Association for Research in Education*, edited by P. L. Jeffrey. Melbourne: Australian Association for Research in Education. http://www.aare.edu.au/06pap/kel06341.pdf.

Kirchberg, Volker. 1996. "Museum visitors and non-visitors in Germany: A representative survey." *Poetics* 24 (2-4):239-258. doi:10.1016/S0304-422X(96)00007-1.

Kisiel, James. 2003. "Teachers, museums and worksheets; a closer look at a learning experience." *Journal of science teacher education* 14 (1):3-21. doi:10.1023/A:1022991222494.

Kisiel, James. 2005. "Understanding elementary teacher motivations for science fieldtrips." *Science education* 89:936- 955. doi:10.1002/sce.20085.

Krapp, Andreas. 2002. "Structural and dynamic aspects of interest development: theoretical considerations from an ontogenetic perspective." *Learning and Instruction* 12 (4):383-409. doi:10.1016/S0959-4752(01)00011-1.

Lucas, A.M., Paulette Macmanus, and Gillian Thomas. 1986. "Investigating learning from informal sources: Listening to conversations and observing play in science museums." *International journal of science education* 8 (4):341-352. doi:10.1080/0140528860080401.

MacRae, Christina. 2007. "Using sense to make sense of art: young children in art galleries. Early Years" *Journal of International Research & Development* 27 (2):159-170. doi:10.1080/09575140701425290.

Mayfield, Margie I. 2005. "Children's museums: purposes, practices and play?" *Early Child Development & Care* 175 (2):179-192. doi:10.1080/0300443042000230348.

Melber, Leah M. 2003. "Partnerships in science learning: Museum outreach and elementary gifted education." *Gifted child quarterly* 47 (4):251-258. doi:10.1177/001698620304700402.

—. 2007. "Maternal scaffolding in two museum exhibition halls." *Curator* 50 (3):341-354.

Meyer, Helen, and Steve Kroeger. 2005. "Photovoice as an Educational Action Research Tool." *Qualitative Research Journal* 5 (2):185-194. http://search.informit.com.au/documentSummary;dn=126535915027601;res=IELHSS.

Mortensen, Marianne F., and Kimberly Smart. 2007. "Free-choice worksheets increase students' exposure to curriculum during museum visits." *Journal of research in science teaching* 44 (9):1389-1414. doi:10.1002/tea.20206.

Mulligan, M. J., and A. Brayfield. 2004. "Museums and childhood: negotiating organizational lessons." *Childhood* 11 (3):275-301. doi: 10.1177/0907568204040183.

National Curriculum Board. 2009. "Shape of the Australian Curriculum: History."http://www.acara.edu.au/verve/_resources/Australian_Curriculum_-_History.pdf.

National Trust (NSW). 2008. *Experiment Farm Cottage (Draft tour script 2008)*. Unpublished document.

Pace, Stefanie, and Roger Tesi. 2004. "Adult's perception of field trips taken within Grades K-12: eight case studies in the New York metropolitan area". *Education* 125 (1):30-40.

Palmquist, Sasha, and Kevin Crowley. 2007. "From teachers to testers: How parents talk to novice and expert children in a natural history museum." *Science education* 91 (5):783-804. doi:10.1002/sce.20215.

Paris, Scott G, Kirsten M Yambor, and Becky Wai-Lang Packard. 1998. "Hands-on biology: A museum-school- university partnership for enhancing students' interest and learning in science." *The Elementary School Journal* 98 (3):267-288. http://www.jstor.org/stable/1002260.

Patterson, A. R. 2007. '"Dad, look, she's sleeping": parent-child conversations about human remains.' *Visitor studies* 10 (1):55-72.

Piscitelli, Barbara, and David Anderson. 2001. "Young children's perspectives of museum settings and experiences." *Museum Management and Curatorship 19* (3):269 - 282. doi:10.1080/09647770100401903.

Prosser, Dominic, and Susan Eddisford. 2004. "Virtual Museum Learning." *Information Technology in Childhood Education Annual* 16:281-297.

QSR International. 1999-2008. Nvivo8.

Rapp, Whitney 2005. "Inquiry-Based Environments for the Inclusion of Students With Exceptional Learning Needs." *Remedial & Special Education* 26 (5):297-310.

Rennie, L.J., and David J. Johnston. 2004. "The nature of learning and its implications for research on learning from museums." *Science education* 88 (S1):S4-S16. doi:10.1002/sce.20017.

Rennie, L.J., and Gina F. Williams. *2002.* "Science centers and scientific literacy: Promoting a relationship with science." *Science education* 86 (5):706-726. doi:10.1002/sce.10030.

Sanford, Camellia, Karen Knutson, and Kevin Crowley. 2007. '"We always spend time together on Sundays": How grandparents and their grandchildren think about and use informal learning spaces.' *Visitor Studies* 10 (2):136-151. doi:10.1080/10645570701585129.

Sarachoa, Olivia N., and Bernard Spodek. 2007. "Oracy: social facets of language learning." *Early Child Development & Care* 177 (6/7):695-705. doi:10.1080/03004430701377540.

Scaife, J. 2004. "Reliability, validity and credibility." In *Doing educational research. A guide to first time researchers*, edited by C. Opie. London: Sage.

Shine, Stephanie, and Teresa Y. Acosta. 2000. "Parent-child social play in a children's museum." *Family relations* 49 (1):45-52. http://www.jstor.org/stable/585700.

Speering, W., L. J. Rennie, and T. P. McClafferty. 1997. "Discoverland : exploring young children's interactions with science exhibits." In *Western Australian Institute for Educational Research Forum* 1997. Perth: Murdoch University. http://www.waier.org.au/forums/1997/speering.html.

Sterry, Pat, and Ela Beaumont. 2006. "Methods for studying family visitors in art museums: A cross-disciplinary review of current research." *Museum Management and Curatorship* 21 (3):222 - 239. http://www.informaworld.com/10.1080/09647770600402103.

Sturm, Brian W. 2003. "Dogs and Dinosaurs, Hobbies and Horses. Children & Libraries." *The Journal of the Association for Library Service to Children* 1 (3):39-51.

Tal, Revital, Yael Bamberger, and Orly Morag. 2005. "Guided school visits to natural history museums in Israel: Teachers' roles." *Science education* 89 (6):920-935. doi:10.1002/sce.20070.

Tal, Tali, and Orly Morag. 2007. "School visits to natural history museums: Teaching or enriching?" *Journal of Research in Science Teaching* 44 (5):747-769. doi:10.1002/tea.20184.

Tal, Tali, and Laura Steiner. 2006. "Patterns of teacher-museum staff relationships: School visits to the educational centre of a science museum." *Canadian Journal of Science, Mathematics, & Technology Education* 6 (1):25-46.

Tenenbaum, Harriet R., and Maureen A. Callanan. 2008. "Parents' science talk to their children in Mexican-descent families residing in the USA." *International Journal of Behavioral Development* 32 (1):1-12. doi:10.1177/0165025407084046.

Tomkins, Stephen, and Sue Dale Tunnicliffe. 2007. "Nature tables: stimulating children's interest in natural objects." *Journal of Biological Education* 41 (4):150-155.

Tunnicliffe, Sue D. 2000. "Conversations of family and primary school groups at robotic dinosaur exhibits in a museum: what do they talk about?" *International journal of science education* 22 (7):739- 754.

Tunnicliffe, Sue D., A.M. Lucas, and Jonathan Osborne. 1997. "School visits to zoos and museums: a missed educational opportunity?" *International Journal of Science Education* 19 (9):1039-1056. doi:10.1080/0950069970190904.

Tunnicliffe, Sue Dale. 1996. "Conversations within primary school parties visiting animal specimens in a museum and zoo." *Journal of Biological Education* 30 (2):130.

Tunnicliffe, Sue Dale, and Michael J. Reiss. 2000. 'What sense do children make of three-dimensional, life-sized "representations" of animals?' *School Science & Mathematics* 100 (3):128-138.

Valle, Araceli, and Maureen A. Callanan. 2006. "Similarity comparisons and relational analogies in parent-child conversations about science topics." *Merrill-Palmer quarterly* 52 (1):96-124.

Wang, C.C., W.K. Yi, Z.W. Toa, and K. Carovano. 1998. "Photovoice as a participatory health promotion strategy." *Health promotion international* 13 (1):75-86.

Watson, K., P. Aubusson, F. Steel, and J. Griffin. 2002. "A culture of learning in the informal museum setting?" *Australian Research in Early Childhood Education* 9 (1):125-139.

Weier, K. 2004. "Empowering young children in art museums : letting them take the lead." *Contemporary Issues in Early Childhood* 5 (1):106-116. http://www.wwwords.co.uk/pdf/freetoview.asp?j=ciec&vol=5&issue=1&year=2004&article=10_Weier_CIEC_5_1_web.

Wilde, Matthias, and Detlef Urhahne. 2008. "Museum learning: a study of motivation and learning achievement." *Journal of Biological Education* 42 (2):78-83.

Wooltorton, S. 2006. "Ecological literacy : an Australian perspective." *Social Educator* 24 (2):26-28.

Wu, Kai-Lin, Kirsten Holmes, and John Tribe. 2010. "'Where do you want to go today?' An analysis of family group decisions to visit museums." *Journal of Marketing Management* 26 (7):706 -726. doi:10.1080/02672571003780007.

Xanthoudaki, Maria. 1998. "Is it always worth the trip? The contribution of museum and gallery educational programmes to classroom art education." *Cambridge Journal of Education* 28 (2):181- 95. doi:10.1080/0305764980280204.

CHAPTER ELEVEN

WHEN A YOUNG CHILD'S INTELLECTUAL DEVELOPMENT IS ADVANCED: PROGRAM DIRECTIONS FROM THE LITERATURE AND THE FIELD

KERRY HODGE

The early childhood field in Australia has been receiving government attention and investment with the National Early Childhood Development Strategy, Investing in the Early Years initiative (Council of Australian Governments 2009). Among the initiatives is investment in practical support for early childhood services to provide a quality inclusive environment for children with the following additional needs: disability, indigenous, cultural and linguistic diversity, refugee or humanitarian interventions background.

There is another group of young Australians who have been virtually invisible in policy statements and teacher education about early childhood. They are gifted children, or more accurately potentially gifted children, since they are very young and may not yet have had the opportunity to show their capabilities (Gross 1993). They constitute between 2% and 10% of children their age, depending on the definition employed. Most Australian educational systems have adopted the developmental definition of giftedness and talent proposed by Gagné (2003). In the early childhood field, Harrison's (2003, 8) working definition is consistent with that of Gagné:

> A gifted child is one who performs or has the potential to perform at a level significantly beyond his or her age peers and whose unique abilities and characteristics require special provisions and social and emotional support from the family, community and educational context.

Early inherited potential for excellence, then, is fulfilled as later exceptional talent or achievement only if certain catalysts, including supportive teachers and parents, are present. Longitudinal research has supported this theory (Gross 2006; Freeman 2006). Therefore, it is recommended that giftedness be identified early and provision be adjusted according to evident characteristics (Koshy and Robinson 2006). Appropriate provision should be the focus, rather than labeling the child (Hertzog 2009).

Identifying Potential Giftedness

There is consensus that multiple sources of information should be used in identifying giftedness (Robinson, 2008; Robinson, Shore, and Enersen 2007). While psychometric assessment for giftedness is possible with young children, results are more reliable from the age of 6 (McCall, Appelbaum, and Hogarty 1973). This makes observation of the behavioural characteristics of giftedness, by teachers and as reported by parents, especially useful in prior-to-school settings, facilitated by a rich and "invitational" environment (Hertzog 2009; Hodge and Kemp 2002).

Research has shown that parents are generally credible identifiers of giftedness in their children (e.g. Louis and Lewis 1992; Silverman, Chitwood and Waters 1986) and has isolated a number of intellectual characteristics of giftedness that may be expressed in "positive" or "dysfunctional" ways (Porter 2005, 58). The characteristics include rapid learning; keen observation; exceptional memory; easy generalisation to other contexts; sophisticated language and reasoning; long attention span and persistence when interested; intense interests or wide interests resulting in deep or wide knowledge; early use of symbolic representation which may be evident in early interest and skill in reading, drawing, and writing; interest and skill in numbers; exceptional construction skills; questioning of authority; and early sense of social justice (Harrison 2003; Porter 2005).

Educational Provision According to the Literature

Provision for gifted children should respond to and extend the characteristics of giftedness that are evident (Maker 1986). For gifted children of school age there is an evidence base for practices such as acceleration, ability grouping and enrichment (Robinson, Shore, and Enersen 2007). There has been a very limited evidence base for an effective program for very young gifted children (Koshy and Robinson 2006).

Acceleration

Because gifted children are developmentally advanced, it can be appropriate to educate them with older children whose thinking and behaviour is similar to theirs in many ways (Robinson, Shore, and Enersen 2007). A meta-analysis by Rogers (1992) showed that early entry to school is an effective provision (effect size 0.36), provided certain guidelines are followed (Proctor, Feldhusen, and Black 1988). It is a practice that has not been readily implemented in Australia (Diezmann, Watters, and Fox 2001; Gallagher, Smith, and Merrotsy 2006).

Ability Grouping

Meta-analyses have shown ability grouping to be academically beneficial for school-aged gifted children (Kulik, 2003). Friendships may develop more easily since gifted children seek reciprocal and trusting friendships earlier than typically developing children (Gross 2002). For gifted preschoolers there is no evidence regarding ability grouping. In Australia it is rarely reported, tending to occur over a limited time (for research purposes) and in university-related settings without comparison groups (e.g. Grant 2004; Hodge and Kemp 2000, 2002).

Curriculum

Some curriculum direction has come from Australian research indicating that young gifted children seek complexity and a connection to their world (Harrison 2004) and that enrichment for all children followed by extension for self-selecting children is satisfying to children and to their parents (Grant 2004). Until there is sufficient research evidence to guide curriculum decisions in early gifted education, suggested principles and practices can be sought from the literature and from programs in the field.

There have been occasional position papers regarding the potential of "regular" early childhood curriculum approaches to meet the needs of gifted children. For example, Barbour and Shaklee (1998) and Hertzog (2001) examined the Reggio Emilia approach (Edwards, Gandini, and Forman 1993) and concluded that the following could contribute to the education of young gifted children: children's active exploration of their interests over time, expressing their thinking in varied media, and observant and intentional teachers making use of this emergent curriculum to scaffold the children's learning. The Montessori approach has been advocated for its opportunities for children to progress at their individual rates (Tittle 1984).

Direction also comes from books written to guide early childhood practitioners in identifying giftedness and providing appropriately. Publications by Harrison (2003), Hertzog (2008), Porter (2005) Sutherland (2005, 2008) and Smutny (1998) are examples. There is debate about how different adjustments to the typical early childhood curriculum need to be (Hertzog 1999, 2009; Tomlinson 1996). Maker (1986) proposed that there were many similarities between the education of young gifted children and those who are not gifted, especially when experiences allow children to participate at a variety of levels with encouragement to respond at the highest level possible. She argued that all children should be challenged to become better thinkers, which chimes with Borland's (1989) advice that provision advantageous to all children should not be reserved for gifted children. Nevertheless, Maker added that special efforts should be made when the most able are not challenged, and that these provisions can frustrate less able children.

Maker (1986) presented a framework for curriculum construction for gifted children involving the following dimensions: content (what is learned), process (the experiences that children and teachers engage in and the kinds of questions teachers ask), product (tangible or intangible outcomes of learning) and learning environment (physical and psychological). Her criteria for the development of curriculum for gifted preschoolers are listed in table 1.

Table 1: Maker's (1986) criteria for curriculum for young gifted children

Content
Abstract concepts and principles (e.g., in physical/scientific or social worlds), through concrete experiences
Complexity, integration of information from different sources or disciplines
Focus on relationships between ideas, not isolated information
Unusual content, if based on children's interests

Methods (tools, vocabulary) of experts

Skills in problem-solving, divergent thinking, prediction, evaluation

Process

Open-ended activities, questions

Discovery learning, free/guide

Freedom to choose direction and methods of inquiry

Interaction, discussion

Systematic questioning for higher order thinking

Focus on reasoning to justify/explain

Appropriate pace (fast for new learning; slower for exploration or more complex thinking)

Product

Addressing real and meaningful problems

Drawing conclusions from raw data

Presenting learning to real audience

Learning environment

Based on children's ideas and interests

Initiative and independent problem solving

Open to new ideas, people, directions, environments

Complexity of materials; challenging tasks

Mobility of children; flexible groupings

Educational Provision: Directions from the Field

Since there have been very few Australian programs to guide practice for gifted children below school age, direction was sought from overseas. In April-June 2010 the author visited a variety of separate and inclusive programs in the USA, Canada, England, and Scotland. Sites were selected on the basis of reports in the gifted or early childhood education literatures and through personal recommendations from academics or administrators involved in gifted education. Sources of information were observations of the programs, discussions with the staff, and available literature. This paper focuses on program components pertaining to intellectual development as one aspect of the Churchill Fellowship project (see Hodge 2010b).

Two settings, featured because they cater explicitly for intellectually gifted children aged 3-5 in quite different circumstances, are described and interpreted below. University Primary School (UPS) at the University of Illinois at Urbana-Champaign, Illinois in the USA offers a separate early childhood gifted program. Chelsea Open Air Nursery School and Children's Centre (COA) in London, England caters for its gifted children in a mixed-ability setting. Because of their applicability across a wide range of curriculum approaches, Maker's (1986) criteria for curriculum differentiation have been employed to interpret how UPS and COA educate young gifted children.

Separate Provision for Gifted Children: University Primary School

UPS is a program for children aged 3-7. A site to study, demonstrate and teach best practices in early childhood and gifted education, it serves families from a range of backgrounds. In the preschool classroom, 25 children attend five mornings per week with one head teacher and two paid assistants who are postgraduate students at masters or doctoral level. Program goals are to strengthen and support intellectual growth, initiate children into basic skills and challenge them to increase proficiency in academic tasks while fostering social competence.

Selection of children for the program. The school's director considers identification of giftedness to be arbitrary (Hertzog 2009). Her school's entry policy and procedures therefore focus on parents' self-selection of the program as appropriate for their child. The school's brochure lists the attributes of children likely to thrive there: a wide ranging curiosity, rapid and easy learning, problem solving ability, advanced vocabulary and sentence structure, imagination, self-reliance, and talent in one or more areas. Parents make a scheduled visit to observe the program in action and complete a questionnaire about what was observed, their own goals and their perceptions on the match between program and child. They also complete a descriptive questionnaire about the child's interests, abilities, skills and activities and supply three specified work or play samples. Balancing gender, ethnicity and age if possible, the school's placement committee meets annually to consider the applications. Children not placed can remain on a waiting list; no child is "rejected".

Curriculum. Curriculum and teaching practices are a blend of two inquiry-based approaches: the curriculum framework known as The Project Approach (Katz and Chard 2000), and Reggio Emilia (Edwards, Gandini, and Forman 1998). Assumptions underlying the UPS curriculum are that children in the early years learn best from active and interactive experiences in topics that relate to their own lives. Academic and social skills are integrated into all activities, differentiated as needed for individual children, including those who may also have a disability.

A typical 3-hour morning includes an indoor activity/project time, self-serve snack, outdoor play, small group times for the current project and for literacy ("shared reading"), and a whole group time for music/drama. The author observed a literacy group in which a Korean folktale was read. Vocabulary in both Korean and English and concepts of human behaviour were built through documented analysis of the tale's human and animal characters and its moral message.

Activity choice time is a feature that encourages even very young children to think ahead and commit to a task. As activity time ends each day the children use the choice board to make selections for the following day's activity time. Illustrated pockets display the options, which include traditional preschool child-directed experiences (e.g. puzzles), project activities (e.g. meeting with the group and its teacher to continue constructing a model) and perhaps something provided by a parent, such as an art or cooking experience. Each child has three wooden sticks coloured to indicate first, second, and third choices and with his or her photograph attached. Each child places sticks in up to three pockets; children are gently encouraged to follow through by at least trying their chosen activity if wanting to follow a spontaneous interest.

Each of the several projects per year has distinct phases. First, the teacher selects the topic of study based on the children's interests and the availability of local resources, creating a personal topic map from the teacher's own experience, knowledge and ideas. Amended throughout the project, this becomes a record of the project's progression. Phase 1 involves whole-group discussion, memory drawings and dictated stories to discover children's prior experience and knowledge about the topic. This assists the teacher to determine study groups, typically four groups with 5-6 children led by an adult. Each group decides the actual questions to which it wants to find answers.. Phase 2 is about "fieldwork", that is, making predictions, collecting data, and representing what has been learned. Each group meets daily for 15 minutes, and information sources are real objects, books, field trips and experts who visit the children. Phase 3 is called the "culminating event", in which the study groups, together, tell the story of their project to an audience (their parents). They review their learning and select the media to demonstrate this (e.g. stories, poems, murals, dances, PowerPoint® presentations).

A previously documented project, the Shoe Project carried out by 3-4 year olds, was made available by the staff involved. This project and other aspects of the UPS program evident from a three-day visit and available literature are reported in table 2 with reference to Maker's (1986) criteria. The limitations of interpretation based on a brief visit are acknowledged, although feedback on this chapter has been given by the program director.

Table 2: Comparison of UPS program with Maker's (1986) criteria for curriculum for young gifted children

Curriculum criteria	**Apparent in UPS program**
Content	
Abstract concepts and principles (e.g., in physical/scientific or social worlds), through concrete experiences	Interdependence between shoemaker/repairer and customers; human behaviour explored in Korean folk tale
Complexity, integration of information from different sources or disciplines	Complexity from study groups' separate investigations (how shoes are made, shoe repair, shoes for occupations and how shoes are bought); academic skills integrated; additional language learned

Focus on relationships between ideas, not isolated information	Concepts related in topic maps and documentation
Unusual content, if based on children's interests	Topics not prescribed by curriculum - emerge from children's interests
Methods (tools, vocabulary) of experts	Methods and terminology of shoemakers and retailers visited; research methods – ask questions, make hypotheses, collect and analyse data, share findings
Skills in problem-solving, divergent thinking, prediction, evaluation	Design and construction of shoe models; brainstorming ways shoes could be put together; predicting tools experts use; evaluating learning to share findings
Process	
Open-ended activities, questions	Activity time options open-ended; teacher questions invite diverse answers
Discovery learning, free/guided	Project learning is by discovery (for teachers also); teachers scaffold and facilitate skill development as needed
Freedom to choose direction and methods of inquiry	Study groups choose questions to investigate
Interaction, discussion	Throughout program.
Systematic questioning for higher order thinking	Questioning encourages analysis (e.g., difference between predicted and actual tools for shoemaking), evaluation, creative thinking
Focus on reasoning to justify/explain	Interpretation of graph of friends' thoughts on how shoes are put together (e.g., "Five thought sewing, only 2 thought glue. They thought glue would be too messy.")
Appropriate pace (fast for new learning; slower for exploration or more complex thinking)	New Korean vocabulary frequently; project lasts several months for deep thinking and problem solving
Product	
Addressing real and meaningful problems	Projects arise from children's interests and questions
Drawing conclusions from raw data	Interpretation of graph from survey; direct observation of experts' tools and practices

Presenting learning to real audience	Culminating event - display of real tools and children's representations, measuring parents' shoe sizes, demonstration of water-proofing experiment, shoe care station, own shoe store to 'sell' shoes to parents
Learning environment	
Based on children's ideas and interests	Through project phases and activity time options
Open to new ideas, people, directions, environments	Projects and study group questions are fresh (not repeated annually); experts met in new environments and own setting
Complexity of materials; challenging tasks	Wide range of book genres; rich art and construction materials; project tasks appear challenging for 3-4 year olds
Mobility of children; flexible groupings	Free movement in activity time and outdoor play; new groupings for each project then stable throughout project

Inclusive Provision: Chelsea Open Air Nursery School and Children's Centre

As in Australia, gifted children below school age in the UK are educated in inclusive programs. Enrolling children across a wide range of abilities and disabilities, COA is a state-funded nursery school with families from a very wide range of cultural and socio-economic backgrounds. It caters for 60 children aged 3-5 across the week, with the younger children attending half-days and the older ones for a full day. Four "keyworkers" (two university-qualified teachers and two nursery officers with up to 2 years diploma training) each monitor a mixed-ability group of children.

COA openly acknowledges giftedness as one of a range of additional needs that require some adjustments to be made. This is explicit in the parent handbook and in an optional parent meeting on the topic. A written policy on giftedness (since 2002) specifies procedures and staff responsibilities, as well as the role of the nursery's governing body in supporting these children, such as enabling relevant staff training and a resource budget.

Identification of children for curriculum differentiation. Identification comes from teachers' observations of children responding to the curriculum and from parent information invited during enrolment. Teachers keep detailed records of all children's progress, called learning journeys, and note rapid learning, deep interests, consistent persistence and reflection, as well as an awareness of self and others. These are discussed during a regular segment of staff meetings. An observational protocol of gifted characteristics, Nebraska Starry Night Protocol (Griffin and McKenzie 1993), is used to document the development of these children and to plan suitable objectives and extension. There is awareness that a child who has other additional needs may also be gifted.

Curriculum. COA follows England's statutory Early Years Foundation Stage (EYFS, Department for Educational Studies 2007) curriculum for children from birth to 5 years. Its framework is developmental, providing a continuum of stages in which there are milestones reflecting average expectations for particular age ranges, with recognition that the nature and rate of individual children's progress varies. There are "early learning goals" specified in each of six areas of learning and development: personal, social and emotional development; problem solving, reasoning and numeracy; communication, language and literacy; knowledge and understanding of the world; physical development; creative development. Play and exploration are the main processes by which children progress towards these goals. As a result of the Effective Provision of Pre-School Education (EPPE) study (Siraj-Blatchford et al. 2003), teachers in England and elsewhere are being encouraged to supplement child-initiated activities with more teacher-led activities and to intervene more in child-initiated activities to extend children's thinking. Siraj-Blatchford et al. (2003, no pagination) referred to this as "sustained shared thinking", in which "two or more individuals work (often playfully) together in an intellectual way to solve a problem clarify a concept, evaluate activities, or extend a narrative".

The COA curriculum has preceded but appears to be consistent with England's "guidance" for early gifted education (Department for Children, Schools and Families, 2010). This document promotes the provision of a rich and challenging environment for all children in any community, followed by extension for children identified as needing it. The COA environment is indeed rich and varied. The garden is a major focus regardless of the weather, with long periods daily of simultaneous indoor and outdoor play. Mature deciduous trees, a pond and gardens for flowers, herbs and vegetables enable a connection to the natural world in an urban environment. Visiting artists and professionals are engaged to work with the children, although the interactive process of planning and executing the in-depth projects is considered more important than the products. To date, a poet, sculptor, gardener, photographer, composer and chef have been involved.

Extension occurs in several ways for individual children or in small groups. This can occur daily during play or in the ability-grouped language/story experiences, and once or twice a week teachers provide an extension group for a small number of children of any age. In the second half of the year a weekly philosophy group is introduced. The teacher uses a toy, Philosophy Bear, to help a small group of children to think abstractly, to frame and answer questions precisely and to develop an argument. From time to time an "expedition" into the local or wider community is planned for a small group with a teacher and parent in order to extend an interest. Younger more able children are allowed to join older children when staffing permits, following staff discussion and consultation with parents.

Presented in table 3 is the author's interpretation of the COA program with reference to Maker's (1986) criteria. Interpretation is based on a one-day visit and available literature, the limitations of which are acknowledged, although an earlier draft of this section has been revised in response to feedback from the COA Head teacher.

Table 3: Comparison of COA program with Maker's (1986) criteria for curriculum for young gifted children

Curriculum criteria	Apparent in COA program
Content	
Abstract concepts and principles through concrete experiences	Philosophical exploration of abstract concepts through objects and pictures; expeditions (e.g., palace with clothes decorated with symbols of strength and power)
Complexity, integration of information from different sources or disciplines	Activities on-site and on expeditions cross-curricular where possible
Focus on relationships between ideas, not isolated information	Involvement in planning, implementation and documentation of projects with visiting professionals

Unusual content, if based on children's interests	Unusual interests respected and nurtured (e.g., pond creatures, bridges, church architecture)
Methods (tools, vocabulary) of experts	Participation in projects of visiting professionals; during expeditions
Skills in problem-solving, divergent thinking, prediction, evaluation	Embedded in adult-child interactions in play and group activities; weekly voting for proposed activity for following week; comparing pre-expedition drawings with on-site sketches; pictorial self assessment before school transition
Process	
Open-ended activities, questions	During play and group times; a feature of sustained shared thinking
Discovery learning, free/guided	Exploration and testing theories in play and expeditions; teachers' observation and playful participation; mistakes are learning opportunities
Freedom to choose direction and methods of inquiry	Long periods daily of play and exploration
Interaction, discussion	Throughout program; structured in philosophy group to allow turns to speak and listen
Systematic questioning for higher order thinking	In sustained shared thinking and extension group
Focus on reasoning to justify/explain	Staff guide children in thinking about thinking; learning to ask and answer 'how' and 'why' questions
Appropriate pace (fast for new learning; slower for exploration or more complex thinking)	New learning not observed; unhurried pace in exploration of interests and philosophy group
Product	
Addressing real and meaningful problems	Expeditions arise from children's interests, questions
Drawing conclusions from raw data	Sketches made during expeditions
Presenting learning to real audience	Books made from photographs and drawings from expeditions and shared with families and children

Learning environment	
Based on children's ideas and interests	Basis for enrichment and extension
Initiative and independent problem solving	Rich and changing environment encourages initiative; teachers scaffold towards independence
Open to new ideas, people, directions, environments	Meeting visiting artists, professionals onsite and in community; participation in community-based projects
Complexity of materials; challenging tasks	Create own challenges from wide range of materials (e.g., bicycle to disassemble); extension group tasks (e.g., on computer); expedition as a serious intellectual, physical, social and emotional challenge
Mobility of children; flexible groupings	Free play indoors and out for extensive periods with companions of their choice; membership of philosophy and extension groups changes according to observed responses.

Discussion

It appears from this interpretation of just two programs from the field that different approaches to the education of gifted preschoolers can "work", although research is needed to determine outcomes and contributing components. Aspects of the observed programs are discussed below with reference to the Australian early childhood context and, in particular, the new national Early Years Learning Framework (EYLF) (Department of Education, Employment and Workplace Relations, DEEWR 2009), entitled Belonging, Being and Becoming. As Australian teachers examine this new framework and its implications for their settings, it is pertinent to consider how, among all children, those with advanced development can belong, be, and become.

Direction from Observed Programs: Shared Aspects

Both UPS and COA programs are intentional and explicit in catering for children with advanced intellectual development and treat them, and their parents, seriously. The extent to which Australian preschool and childcare settings do this is unknown, but in a recent study in New South Wales only 42% of 73 surveyed teachers worked in a setting where there was a policy for gifted children, either stand-alone or embedded in an additional needs policy (Hodge 2010a).

Both programs use processes consistent with recommended practice in gifted education as outlined by Robinson (2008). They make use of known characteristics of giftedness in order to identify children who are in need of intellectual challenge and complexity; both acknowledge that giftedness and other additional needs can co-exist. Parents' perceptions are valued, and teachers' observations are the basis for determining the type and degree of differentiation for individual children. In Australian early childhood settings, observation of children has long been a skill of teachers and is increasingly focused on children's strengths (Arthur et al. 2008). Nevertheless, teachers may not be familiar with characteristics of giftedness. Fewer than half of the teachers in Hodge's (2010a) study had had pre-service input or professional development in gifted education, and more than half did not feel confident in identifying giftedness in a young child.

In many ways both programs are high quality, child-centred programs in which any child might thrive. UPS and COA allow participation at a variety of levels with, as suggested by Maker (1986), encouragement to respond at the highest level possible. A combination of teacher-initiated group work and children's free play, as well as teachers' scaffolding of children's thinking during interactions, indicates effectiveness according to Siraj-Blatchford et al. (2003). Children's interests are respected, and children are supported to actively seek answers to the questions they are curious about. These practices are consistent with the principles of the EYLF regarding the development of dispositions that build confident and involved learners (DEEWR 2009, 33-34). Children's documentation of their learning is strong in UPS projects and COA children's learning journeys. This, too, is encouraged in Australian settings (Arthur et al. 2008) and in the EYLF learning outcome "Children express ideas and make meaning using a range of media" (DEEWR 2009, 42).

However, the UPS and COA programs reach beyond the enrichment that benefits all; they provide challenge and complexity in ways that, as Maker (1986) advised, could frustrate preschoolers whose development is more typical. For example, all UPS children pursue investigations daily over months; COA introduces philosophical thinking with which typically developing children of the same age would struggle. Teachers are aiming high for these children in response to observations of what they are able to do, and with attention to individual differences. High expectations are a feature of the EYLF (DEEWR 2009, 13), and teachers are encouraged to reflect on whether there is sufficient challenge for all children (DEEWR 2009, 18). Teachers could gain direction from the UPS and COA programs to provide challenge for children whose development is so advanced that they already have achieved to a high degree the learning outcomes specified in the EYLF, that is, provide challenge for highly curious, persistent, creative children who can spontaneously transfer what they have learned to a new situation, take responsibility for their learning (DEEWR 2009, 33-37) and are already sophisticated in their communication through a variety of media and symbol systems (DEEWR 2009, 38-44).

The gifted child's desire for connection to the physical and social aspects of the world, as noted by Harrison (2004), is recognised and nurtured in both programs. Children venture beyond the settings in small groups, and interesting people visit and connect with them. They can pursue questions that matter to them, collect data about the world and interpret it. Both programs are situated in communities with ample possibilities for community connections; teachers in settings not so well situated would need to be resourceful and creative with what is available to them. Generous staff-to-child ratios, easy access to information technology and parents happy to volunteer their time all facilitate connections.

Inclusive or separate provision

Education in inclusive settings or systems where all children have access to an enriching environment does not require prior identification of who will benefit, and reduces potential jibes of provision for gifted children as elitist. Extension that occurs for particular children, perhaps in groups, can be justified in terms of the children's response to enrichment, especially if the setting is transparent about its policies and practices in catering for giftedness as an additional need. Potentially, provision in inclusive settings reaches a greater number of gifted children without the need for families to invest time and financial resources in travel to a "gifted program", if one is available. This is especially important in economically-disadvantaged communities where there may be fewer sources of recreational enrichment and limited family resources to afford them, which is the case for many COA children. However, inclusive provision also requires that many, if not all, teachers are knowledgeable about recognising and nurturing giftedness.

When provision is separate there is an opportunity to tailor the curriculum content and processes to a relatively homogeneous group of children who can concentrate on complex, challenging concepts or tasks and sustain focus over months, although the children's differing temperaments, strengths and interests will require varying strategies and responses from teachers. Separate provision increases the likelihood that gifted children can find satisfying friendships. While separate provision requires some screening to determine who will benefit from the program, the UPS process indicates that this can be done in a sensitive, family-friendly and developmentally appropriate manner, tapping into the observations of parents who know their child best. Again, teachers need to be knowledgeable about gifted education.

Inclusive provision is almost universal in Australia. However, separate provision could occur, perhaps on a part-time basis or within an inclusive program, if a cluster of gifted children was enrolled. The latter may be more socially acceptable in our egalitarian society in which debate continues about "selective" education for gifted children (e.g. Tovey 2008).

Regardless of provision style, it appears that the quality of the program and its differentiation for individual children with advanced development are important. Conceptually, the kind of provision that occurs in UPS and COA appears to sit comfortably with the EYLF. However, a policy that is explicit about giftedness as an additional need is required in Australia so that gifted children will not be invisible and forgotten. In addition, teachers need opportunities, pre-service and during their careers, to develop knowledge, skills (and attitudes) that will assist them to recognise and provide for gifted children.

Conclusion

Although gifted children are enrolled in Australian preschools and childcare centres, they have been barely visible in policy and in teacher education. While early gifted education has much in common with high quality education for all children, it goes beyond to ensure the complexity, challenge and connection on which intellectually gifted children appear to thrive. The overseas UPS and COA programs show how curriculum differentiation for gifted preschoolers can take different paths. As much needed research is conducted, clearer directions will emerge. In the meantime, there are indications from the literature, such as Maker's (1986) criteria, and from the field to guide teachers' endeavours. The principles and practices of the new EYLF appear compatible with early gifted education and present an opportunity to consider appropriate differentiation for children whose development is advanced.

Acknowledgement

This chapter is based on information gathered during the author's traveling fellowship to the USA, Canada, and the United Kingdom in April-June 2010. The 2009 Nancy Fairfax Churchill Fellowship was awarded to investigate innovative programs for intellectually gifted preschoolers and teacher training in early gifted education. The author gratefully acknowledges the generosity of the Vincent Fairfax Family Foundation as sponsor of this fellowship and the willingness of personnel from the visited sites to share their knowledge and expertise.

References

Arthur, Leonie, Bronwyn Beecher, Elizabeth Death, Sue Dockett, and Sue Farmer. 2008. *Programming and Planning in Early Childhood Settings.* 4th ed. South Melbourne: Thomson.

Barbour, Nancy, and Beverly Shaklee. 1998. "Gifted Education Meets Reggio Emilia: Visions for Curriculum in Gifted Education for Young Children". *Gifted Child Quarterly* 42 (4): 228-237. doi: 10.1177/001698629804200406

Borland, James. 1989. *Planning and Implementing Programs For the Gifted.* New York: Teachers College, Columbia University.

Council of Australian Governments (2009). *National Early Childhood Development Strategy, Investing in the Early Years.* Retrieved from http://www.deewr.gov.au/Earlychildhood/Policy_Agenda/Pages/EarlyChildhoodDevelopmentStrategy.aspx

Department for Children, Schools and Families 2010. *Finding and Exploring Young Children's Fascinations: Strengthening the Quality of Gifted and Talented Provision in the Early Years.* Retrieved from http://teachfind.com/search/apachesolr_search/finding%20and%20exploring

Department for Educational Studies. 2007. *Early Years Foundational Stage Curriculum.* Retrieved from http://nationalstrategies.standards.dcsf.gov.uk/earlyyears

Department of Education, Employment and Workplace Relations (DEEWR) (2009). *Belonging, Being and Becoming: The Early Years*

Learning Framework for Australia. Canberra, ACT: Commonwealth of Australia. Retrieved from http://www.deewr.gov.au/EarlyChildhood/Policy_Agenda/Quality/Pages/EarlyYearsLearningFramework.aspx

Diezmann, Carmel, James Watters, and Kathryn Fox. 2001. "Early Entry to School in Australia: Rhetoric, Research and Reality". *Australasian Journal of Gifted Education* 12 (2): 5-18.

Edwards, Carolyn, Lella Gandini, and George Forman. eds. 1998. *The Hundred Languages of Children: Advanced Reflections.* 2nd ed. Greenwich, Conn: Ablex.

Freeman, Joan. 2006. "Giftedness in the Long Term." *Journal for the Education of the Gifted* 29: 384-403. Retrieved from http://journals.prufrock.com/IJP/b/journal-for-the-education-of-the-gifted

Gagné, Françoys. 2003. "Transforming Gifts into Talents: The DMGT as a Developmental Theory." In *Handbook of Gifted Education.* 3rd ed., edited by Nicholas Colangelo, and Gary A. Davis, 60-74. Boston: Allyn and Bacon.

Gallagher, Selena, Susen Smith, and Peter Merrotsy. 2006. "Early Entry: When Should a Gifted Child Start School?" *Australasian Journal of Gifted Education* 19 (1): 16-23.

Grant, Anne. 2004. "Picasso, Physics and Coping with Perfectionism: Aspects of an Early Childhood Curriculum for Gifted Preschoolers." *Journal for Australian Research in Early Childhood* 11 (2): 61-19. Retrieved from http://search.informit.com.au/fullText;dn=133831;res=AEIPT

Griffin, Norma. S., and J. McKenzie. 1993. *Nebraska Starry Night: A Behavior-based Observation Protocol, Version 8.893.* Lincoln: University of Nebraska-Lincoln.

Gross, Mirica. 1993. *Exceptionally Gifted Children.* London: Routledge

—. 1999. "Small Poppies: Highly Gifted Children in the Early Years." Roeper Review 21(3): 207-. Retrieved from http://web.ebscohost.com/ehost/detail?hid=18&sid=191d00c6-9d14-486e-a20f-46def1da4a4a%40sessionmgr14&vid=1&bdata=JnNpdGU9ZWhvc3QtbGl2ZQ%3d%3d#db=f5h&jid=ROE#db=f5h&jid=ROE

—. 2002. "Play Partner or Sure Shelter? What Gifted Children Look for in Friendship." *Gifted* 124: 1, 11. Retrieved from http://search.informit.com.au/documentSummary;dn=122157;res=AEIPT

—. 2006. "Exceptionally Gifted Children: Long-term Outcomes of Acceleration and Non-acceleration." *Journal for the Education of the Gifted* 29: 404-429. Retrieved from http://journals.prufrock.com/IJP/b/journal-for-the-education-of-the-gifted

Harrison, Cathie. 2003. *Giftedness in Early Childhood.* 3rd ed. Sydney: Gifted Education Research, Resource and Information Centre, University of New South Wales.

—. 2004. "Giftedness in Early Childhood: The Search for Complexity and Connection." *Roeper Review* 26 (2): 78-84. Retrieved from http://web.ebscohost.com/ehost/detail?hid=18&sid=191d00c6-9d14-486e-a20f-46def1da4a4a%40sessionmgr14&vid=1&bdata=JnNpdGU9ZWhvc3QtbGl2ZQ%3d%3d#db=f5h&jid=ROE#db=f5h&jid=ROE

Hertzog, Nancy. 1999. "Gifted Education in an Early Childhood Context: A Secret We Should Share." In *Perspectives in Gifted Education: Young Gifted Children,* edited by Norma Lu Hafenstein and Brooke Walker, 36-49. Denver, CO: Institute for the Development of Gifted Education.

—. 2001. "Reflections and impressions from Reggio: "It's not about art!"." *Early Childhood Research and Practice* 3 (1). Retrieved from http://ecrp.uiuc.edu/v3n1/hertzog.html

—. 2008. *Early Childhood Gifted Education.* Waco:TX: Prufrock Press.

—. 2009. "The Arbitrary Nature of Giftedness". In *International Handbook on Giftedness,* edited by Larissa V. Shavinina, 205-214. Baltimore, MD: Johns Hopkins University.

Hodge, Kerry. 2010a. "Goodwill or Irritation? The Beliefs and Experiences of Preschool and Childcare Teachers in NSW Regarding Parents Who View their Child as Gifted." Paper presented at the 11th Asia-Pacific Conference on Giftedness, Sydney, Australia, July 29 – August 1.

—. 2010b. *The Winston Churchill Memorial Trust of Australia Report by Kerry Hodge – 2009 Churchill Fellow.* Retrieved from http://www.churchilltrust.com.au/fellows/reports/education/early-childhood/

Hodge, Kerry, and Coral Kemp. 2000. "Exploring the Nature of Giftedness in Preschool Children." *Journal for the Education of the Gifted* 24: 46-73. Retrieved from http://journals.prufrock.com/IJP/b/journal-for-the-education-of-the-gifted

—. 2002. "The Role of an Invitational Curriculum in the Identification of Giftedness in Young Children. *Australian Journal of Early Childhood* 27 (1): 33-38. Retrieved from http://search.informit.com.au/browseJournalTitle;res=AEIPT;issn=0312-5033

Katz, Lilian, and Sylvia Chard. 2000. *Engaging Children's Minds: The Project Approach.* Stamford, CT: Ablex.

Koshy, Valsa, and Nancy M. Robinson. 2006. "Too Long Neglected: Gifted Young Children." *European Early Childhood Education Research Journal* 14 (2): 113-126. doi: 10.1080/13502930285209951

Kulik, James A. 2003. "Grouping and Tracking. In *Handbook of Gifted Education.* 3rd ed., edited by Nicholas Colangelo and Gary A. Davis, 268-281. Boston: Allyn and Bacon.

Louis, Barbara, and Michael Lewis. 1992. "Parental Beliefs About Giftedness in Young Children and their Relation to Actual Ability Level." *Gifted Child Quarterly* 36: 27-31. doi:10.1177/001698629203600107

Maker, C. June. 1986. "Suggested Principles of Gifted Preschool Curricula." *Topics in Early Childhood Special Education* 6 (1): 62-73. doi:10.1177/027112148600600109

McCall, Robert. B., Mark I. Appelbaum, and Pamela S. Hogarty. 1973. "Developmental Changes in Mental Performance." *Monographs of the Society for Research in Child Development* 38 (3), Serial No. 150.

Porter, Louise. 2005. *Gifted Young Children: A Guide for Teachers and Parents.* 2nd ed. Sydney: Allen and Unwin.

Proctor, Theron B., John F. Feldhusen, and Kathryn N. Black. 1988. "Guidelines for Early Admission to Elementary School." *Psychology in the Schools* 25: 41-43. DOI: 10.1002/1520-6807(198801) 25:1<41::AID-PITS2310250107>3.0.CO;2-J

Robinson, Nancy. M. 2008. "Early Childhood." In *Critical Issues And Practices In Gifted Education: What The Research Says*, edited by Jonathan A. Plucker and Caroline M. Callahan, 179-194. Waco, TX: Prufrock Press.

Robinson, Ann, Bruce M. Shore, and Donna L. Enersen. 2007. *Best Practices in Gifted Education: An Evidence-based Guide.* Waco, TX: Prufrock Press.

Rogers, Karen. 1992. "A Best-evidence Synthesis of the Research on Acceleration Options for Gifted Learners." In *Talent Development: Proceedings from the 1991 Henry B. Wallace and Jocelyn Wallace National Research Symposium on Talent Development*, edited by Nicholas Colangelo, Susan G. Assouline, and DeAnn. L. Ambroson, 406-409. Unionville, NY: Trillium Press.

Silverman, Linda. K., Donna G. Chitwood, and Jana Leigh Waters. 1986. "Young Gifted Children: Can Parents Identify Giftedness?" *Topics in Early Childhood Special Education* 6: 23-38. doi:10.1177/027112148600600106

Siraj-Blatchford, Iram, Kathy Sylva, Brenda Taggart, Edward Melhuish, Pam Sammons, and Karen Elliot. 2003. "The Effective Provision of Pre-school Education (EPPE) Project (1997-2003)" Technical Paper 10 'Intensive case studies of practice across the foundation stage'. Brief No. RBX16-0 Retrieved from http://www.dfes.gov.uk/research/

Smutny, Joan. F. ed. 1998. *The Young Gifted Child: Potential and Promise, an Anthology*. Cresskill, NJ: Hampton Press.

Sutherland, Margaret. 2005. *Gifted and Talented in the Early Years: Practical Activities for Children Aged 3 to 5*. London: Paul Chapman.

—. 2008. *Developing the Gifted and Talented Young Learner*. London: Sage.

Tittle, Bess. 1984. Why Montessori for the Gifted? *G/C/T* 33: 3-7.

Tomlinson, Carol Ann. A. 1996. "Good Teaching for One and All: Does Gifted Education Have an Instructional Identity?" *Journal for the Education of the Gifted* 20 (2): 155-174.

Tovey, Josephine. 2008. "Selective Schools: Gifted Kid's Choice". *Sydney Morning Herald*, 10 April. http://www.smh.com.au/lifestyle/lifcmatters/selective-schools-gifted-kids-choice-20090407-9ypo.html,

CHAPTER TWELVE

USING PICTURE BOOKS TO INTEGRATE MATHEMATICS IN EARLY LEARNING

JENNIE MARSTON AND JOANNE MULLIGAN

Introduction

Young children's experiences with picture books play an important role in developing literacy skills. Picture books often include mathematical ideas, images, linguistic terms and symbols, either intentionally or unintentionally, that may offer opportunities for mathematical learning. In the early years (both prior-to-school and formal school), picture books have always been widely used. However, since the importance of picture books in literacy and numeracy development has been documented (Anderson, Anderson, and Shapiro 2005; Giorgis and Glazer 2009; van den Heuvel-Panhuizen and van den Boogaard 2008), the purposeful inclusion of picture books in the curriculum is more actively encouraged. The Early Years Learning Framework (Australian Government, Department of Education, Employment and Workplace Relations, DEEWR, 2009) advocates the use of picture books to promote an integrated approach to literacy and numeracy across the curriculum.

The Early Years Learning Framework (DEEWR 2009) has been developed by the Council of Australian Governments "to assist educators to provide young children with opportunities to maximise their potential and develop a foundation for future success in learning" (DEEWR 2009, 5). "It has a specific emphasis on play-based learning and recognises the importance of communication and language (including early literacy and numeracy)" (DEEWR 2009, 5). While the five learning outcomes are "broad and observable" (p.19) two key learning outcomes encourage the development of children as "confident and involved learners" and children as "effective communicators" (DEEWR 2009, 19). The use of picture books to promote enquiry and play-based approaches to learning aligns with these outcomes. Picture books can encourage students to "make predictions and generalisations" and use "mathematical language and symbols" (DEEWR 2009, 35), as demonstrated later in this chapter.

This chapter first defines "mathematical" picture books, and describes three different types: perceived, explicit and embedded. Examples of each type typically used to engage young children are provided. Next, a rationale is provided to guide professionals in selecting and using picture books to develop children's understanding of mathematical concepts. The important role of the visual images in picture books is also highlighted. A framework, that identifies seven categories encompassing curriculum, pedagogy and implementation for mathematics learning, is then described. The framework was developed as the initial phase of a broader research project on the role of different types of mathematical picture books in young children's mathematical development (Marston 2010). Examples of how three different types of "mathematical" picture books are classified using three key framework categories are then included.

Classifying "Mathematical" Picture Books

A picture book is defined as a book suitable for very young children, containing multiple visual images. It usually includes a simple narrative or descriptive text, which is intended to be read aloud and shared between an adult and child, or group of children (Muir 1982; Reeder 1997).

Theissen and Matthias (1992) compiled a list of books containing mathematical concepts and divided them into two groups. The first group consisted of those that included mathematics as their emphasis, such as concept books, and the second where the mathematics was incidental. However, they found that the division was unclear (Theissen and Matthias 1992). Gailey (1993) described four types of mathematical picture books: counting books, number books, miscellaneous story books (where the author touches on a mathematics concept), and concept or information books. Schiro (1997) recognised two groups of mathematical picture books: "trade" books, that is "any book that has a plot built around a mathematical concept or that directly poses a mathematical problem to its characters or the reader" and "those that a mathematically inclined person could build a mathematics problem around even though no mathematics is contained in the book" (Schiro 1997, viii).

Following a review of 138 contemporary picture books, Marston (2010) defined "mathematical" picture books as those with mathematical content and language present in both the text and images. The text may be either descriptive or narrative, with the mathematical content *perceived, explicitly referenced* or *embedded.* Picture books with perceived mathematical content are books written principally to entertain; the mathematical concepts are unintentional and incidental, for example, *Grandpa and Thomas* (Allen 2003). Picture books with explicit mathematical content are books written in picture book format to specifically teach or develop one or more mathematical concepts. These include counting books and "trade" books, for example, *One Hundred Hungry Ants* (Pinczes 1993), or in series such as *Sir Cumference* (Neuschwander 1997). Picture books with embedded mathematical content are quality picture books principally written to entertain but include purposefully-embedded mathematical ideas, for example, *The Waterhole* (Base 2003). Like Theissen and Matthias (1992) Marston has also found that. on occasion, the distinction between embedded and explicit books and between embedded and perceived books can be blurred. Moreover, without knowing the author's explicit intention it may not be possible to accurately assign a precise class.

Rationale: Selecting and Using Picture Books to Develop Mathematical Concepts

Whitin (1992) claims that children's literature is fundamental to mathematical learning; it helps children "better understand mathematical ideas and their application to real-world situations" (Whitin 1992, 28). If children find the context of their mathematics learning meaningful and part of their everyday lives they will be motivated, more mathematically confident, and encouraged to value mathematics more than they would otherwise (Hong 1996; Whitin and Gary 1994). For example, Amy and Louis (Gleeson 2006) depicts two young children engaged in real-world activities with three-dimensional objects and in discussion with parents about time differences across the world. Meaningful contexts provided by picture books also afford opportunities for problem-solving and mathematical reasoning (Schiro 1997; Welchman-Tischler 1992) as well as the development of play and structured-play activities (Hong 1999; DEEWR 2009).

An integrated approach to early childhood curriculum and programming is considered appropriate because young children do not see their world divided into separate "cubbyholes" or subject areas (National Association for the Education of Young Children (NAEYC), 7; DEEWR 2009). The NAEYC (2010) recognises the importance of weaving mathematics into children's experiences with literature and other curriculum areas. The EYLF (DEEWR 2009) and the Australian National Curriculum (Australian Curriculum Assessment and Reporting Authority (ACARA) 2010) encourage the integration of literacy and numeracy through children's literature.

The Role of Visual Images in "Mathematical" Picture Books

Visual images are neither an adjunct nor an aid to comprehension of the written text, but rather the visual images and written text together construct the meanings in the picture book (Kress and van Leeuwin 1996; Lewis 2001). Combining visual images and narrative to promote mathematics affords rich learning opportunities where children can see mathematical concepts represented graphically (Steinberger, 1998) and form representations of mathematical ideas.

Recent research has shown the important role of visual images and representations in picture books that are thought to impact on young children's mathematical concept development. Some key studies have found that most of the responses by young children interacting with picture books related to the illustrations rather than the written narrative (Anderson, Anderson, and Shapiro 2005; Moschovaki and Meadows 2005a, 2005b; Van den Heuvel-Panhuizen and Van den Boogaard 2008). Therefore, when purposefully selecting picture books to develop mathematical concepts it is not only important to consider the mathematical content and the text, but also the role and purpose of the visual images. The framework described in this chapter reflects this relationship between text and visual images. For example, in the category of Mathematical Content, (Table 1, following) the framework considers both the mathematical accuracy of the text, the accuracy of the visual images, and whether they relate to each other.

How then do teachers of young children select books to facilitate mathematical learning experiences? Sometimes the title of a picture book indicates the mathematical content of the book, e.g. Patterns in Peru (Neuschwander 2007). However, this does not necessarily guarantee sufficient quality content for effective use. Other times, opportunities for mathematical learning experiences are not clearly evident in the title, such as with Grandpa and Thomas (Allen 2003). This book is rich in opportunities to engage children both in an interesting story and mathematical language and ideas. Therefore, the development of an informative framework that evaluates picture books will support professionals to promote early mathematics learning through picture books in both prior-to-school and school settings.

Frameworks have previously been designed to assist teachers in their selection and evaluation of mathematical "trade" picture books (Schiro 1997; Halsey 2005; Whitin and Whitin 2001; 2004). These have included relevance of the mathematics concepts, age appropriateness, suitability for integration, accessibility of resources, and literacy quality (Donoghue 1996). Teacher resources have also been developed and widely used in Australia and internationally (Griffiths and Clyne 1988; Theissen and Matthias 1992). However, there has not been an evaluative framework developed that incorporates the three different types of mathematical picture books described earlier in this chapter.

The Framework

Development of the Framework

Marston (2010) sourced 138 books including 114 picture books and 10 mathematical "trade" books. To ensure currency and quality, a list of 240 books that had won Australian or international awards in the past ten years was compiled. Two recent books by award-winning authors with researcher-identified "embedded" mathematics, and 12 books widely used by teachers for mathematics learning (e.g. Alexander's Outing, Allen, 1993) were added to the collection.

The books were then read, classified and analysed for features previously illustrated in the literature. The procedure involved labelling visible mathematical concepts in the text and visual images, identifying the interaction between text and visual images, recording mathematical inaccuracies, and noting opportunities for learning experiences.

The framework, containing seven categories, is presented in Table 1 (Marston 2010). The elaboration of the framework also provides examples drawn from picture books displaying a particular element of these categories.

Table 1: Framework Classification Scheme

Code	Categories	Definition
MC	Mathematical Content	The content is visible, displayed with accuracy and authenticity in mathematical contexts, and provides opportunities for developing mathematical language.
CPP	Curriculum Content, Policies, and Principles	Mathematical content is consistent with relevant curricula and reflects policies of gender equity, cultural and socioeconomic diversity, inclusiveness, and environmental awareness.
IMC	Integration of Mathematics Content	Mathematical content is linked within and across mathematical strands, across other disciplines, and with Information and Communication Technology.
MM	Mathematical Meaning	The text and visual images are presented in authentic contexts; concepts are developed in an effective, sequential, and interrelated way.
MPS	Mathematical Problem Solving and Reasoning	The text and images afford opportunities for problem solving, problem posing, co-operative strategies, and creative multiple solution paths.
AML	Affordance for Mathematics Learning	The learning experience is motivating, engaging, and enjoyable, and promotes positive values and attitudes towards mathematics and creative intellectual endeavour.
PI	Pedagogical Implementation	The mathematical content in quality picture books is applicable to a variety of learning situations.

During this process it became clear that the three types of mathematical picture books previously defined were evident. To test Marston's initial classification, a total of 50 books from the original collection were randomly chosen (34 with perceived mathematics, eight with explicit mathematics and eight with embedded mathematics) and classified by an independent coder. An intercoder reliability of 0.92 was achieved.

Like Schiro (1997) every book that was categorised was found to have some degree of mathematical content. For example, simple counting of objects or comparison of sizes of objects was possible with all books, but others contained potential for rich mathematical explorations. However, the quantity, quality, and potential use of each book for mathematical learning needed to be evaluated using the framework.

Using the Framework to Select and Evaluate Picture Books

Several picture books have been selected to exemplify how the framework can be used to articulate particular categories and their elements. Three of the seven categories are selected for illustration here: Mathematical Content; Curriculum Content, Policies, and Principles; and Integration of Mathematics Content.

Example 1: Mathematical Content

The category of Mathematical Content (Table 2) and its four elements describes the mathematical content (perceived, explicit or embedded) presented within the text and visual images.

Table 2: Mathematical Content

Code	Element	Definition
AMC1	Mathematical representation: visibility	Mathematics is easily seen/ recognised by the reader in the title, text or representations (symbols, diagrams, pictures, actions).
AMC2	Mathematical content: accuracy	Mathematical content, linguistic terms, concepts, calculations and representations are accurate and consistent with school mathematics curricula.
AMC3	Mathematical contexts: authenticity	The mathematical content (text and/or visual images) is presented in authentic everyday contexts.
AMC4	Mathematical language	The text and visual images provides opportunities for the child to verbalise mathematics ideas using mathematical language.

One Hundred Hungry Ants (Pinczes 1993) is a "trade" book purposefully written to include mathematical concepts. Here, 100 ants set off to a picnic in single file but discover different formations may get them to their destination more quickly i.e. 2 rows of 50, 4 rows of 25, 5 rows of 20 and finally 10 rows of 10.

> "Stop!" yelled the littlest ant.
> "we're moving way too slow!
> More of the food will be gone
> unless we hurry up. So…
> with 4 lines of 25
> we'd get there soon, I know." (Pinczes 1993, unpaged)

The mathematical intent is clear from the title and in the ensuing pages (MC: Visibility). Opportunities are provided in both the text and visual images for students to use mathematical language (MC5/6: Language), for example, "arrays". Although the mathematical calculations are correct within the text, the terms "line" and "row" are interchanged throughout the book, which could lead to some confusion in conceptual understanding (MC: Accuracy). It could also be questioned whether all possible combinations of 100 are discussed or displayed in the book; the commutative properties of each given formation are also possible, for example 4 rows of 25 are shown, but 25 rows of 4 are also possible. This, however, could be viewed as a positive feature of the book, as it provides opportunities for mathematical problem-solving (MPS: Problem solving opportunities) and development of multiplication and division concepts.

In most instances the actual number of ants presented on the page is correct, and the visual images reflect the text on the pages (e.g. Figure 1).

However, there are several instances of inconsistency between text and visual images; first, when 100 ants set off to the picnic, there are only 20 depicted, then in the final page when it states "Ninety-nine ants are swarming from each and every row", there are only 26 ants shown. The back cover also shows many more than 100 ants (MC: Accuracy).

It is unclear from reading the book whether the author's intent is to also teach about arrays or only the combinations of 100. Most of the depictions (e.g. 5 lines of 20 ants) are portrayed correctly, but most of the formations (rows and columns) are not always clearly displayed as used in an array. Young children (aged five to eight years) would find it difficult to visually align the ants for quick calculation as used in an array. Again, these misrepresentations are not necessarily a disadvantage as they offer opportunities for mathematical discussion between teacher/reader and child, for example do the rows and columns in an array need to be straight, and perpendicular to each other?

Figure 1: From *One Hundred Hungry Ants* by Elinor J. Pinczes, illustrated by Bonnie MacKain. Text copyright (c) 1993 by Elinor J. Pinczes. Illustrations copyright (c) 1993 by Bonnie MacKain. Reprinted with permission of Houghton Mifflin Harcourt Publishing Company. All rights reserved.

The title and general reading of *One Hundred Hungry Ants* (Pinczes 1993) may suggest its suitability for mathematical concept development. The use of the framework category, Mathematical Content, has identified both opportunities and mathematical inconsistencies. However, use of the framework to evaluate the book has also highlighted further possibilities, particularly with problem-solving activities.

Example 2: Curriculum Content, Policies, and Principles

Using the category of *Curriculum Content, Policies, and Principles* (Table 3), the reader can consider how well the content, text and visual images are aligned with relevant state or national curriculum documents (e.g. EYLF, ACARA). Issues regarding gender equity, cultural and socioeconomic equity, inclusiveness, and environmental awareness and sustainability are also important components of contemporary curriculum documents, and therefore impact on the goals of bodies such as the EYLF and Australian National Curriculum. For example, Outcome 1 of the EYLF (DEEWR 2009, 24): *Children have a strong sense of identity* refers to the importance of inclusion. Therefore, consideration of issues such as inclusiveness should be made when evaluating picture books with the framework.

Table 3: Curriculum Content, Policies and Principles

Code	Element	Definition
ACPP1	School and Early Years Mathematics	Content described in mathematics curricula and Early Years Frameworks such as number, algebra, measurement, geometry, statistics and probability and process/ problem solving is included.
ACPP2	Developmental appropriateness	Mathematical content and processes are developmentally appropriate to a particular age level and consistent with the relevant mathematics curriculum.
ACPP3	Equity and Inclusiveness	The text, visual images and the mathematical concepts are not exclusive to any gender, cultural, disability or socioeconomic group and include appropriate representations of these.
ACPP4	Environmental Awareness	The text, visual images and the mathematical concepts provide opportunities or contexts for developing environmentally sustainable principles.

Grandpa and Thomas (Allen 2003) is a story about a day at the beach for Thomas and his grandfather. Although a book that contains perceived mathematical content, it offers many opportunities for teachers to explore several mathematical concepts in a story that is an authentic everyday experience (MC: Authenticity). There is only one instance when mathematics (the concept of addition) is clearly evident in the text, (Figure 2) and this number story could be used as a base for other addition activities. However, there are many other opportunities for mathematical investigations (e.g. patterning), that are developmentally appropriate (CCP: Developmental appropriateness). The use of the repeated words, “swish, swash, swoosh, sings the sea”, throughout the book is an example of simple repetition (patterning). Other text and visual images suggest mathematical activities involving the concept of volume, such as when Grandpa and Thomas eat their sandwiches from their lunch box (What else would fit in Thomas'/your lunch box?). The concept of capacity could be explored using the page where Thomas fills his bucket with water and Grandpa digs a hole (How many buckets of water does Thomas need to fill Grandpa's hole?). Other examples would include length (How high is the sandcastle in Figure 2) and area (How big is their picnic rug?) (CCP: School and Early Years Mathematics).

Figure 2: From: Allen, Pamela. 2005. *Grandpa and Thomas* by Pamela Allen, 2005. Reproduced with permission of Penguin Group (Australia).

The Early Years Learning Framework (DEEWR 2009) emphasises a sense of belonging and learning through play. The ability to explore, discover and challenge children's thinking can promote positive dispositions towards mathematical learning (DEEWR 2009) (Affordances for Mathematical Learning: AML, Table 1). Grandpa and Thomas (Allen 2003) illustrates the grandfather/grandchild relationship and encourages further explorations through play (CCP3: Developmental appropriateness).

Although the simple depictions of the main characters are males of a particular cultural group, the story and the relationship between Thomas and his grandfather are not gender specific (CCP: Equity and Inclusiveness). This situation may not be common to all cultural and socioeconomic groups or those with a disability (CCP), but may provide a springboard for students and teachers to incorporate similar mathematical activities appropriate to authentic contexts. Although there are opportunities for integration with other learning areas (IMC: Integration across other disciplines and with ICT) e.g. the care of the marine environment and sun and beach safety, there are scant opportunities for raising environmental awareness issues related to the actual mathematics of the text and visual images (CPP: Environmental awareness). An example, however, is when Grandpa and Thomas use the shells to count and decorate their sandcastle, as shown in Figure 2. This could link to discussion of whether shells should be removed from their natural environment.

Grandpa and Thomas (Allen 2003) meets the criteria of the first two elements of the category and several other categories, including the *Integration of Mathematical Content* and *Affordances for Mathematical Learning* (Table 1)

Example 3: Integration of Mathematics Content

The category of *Integration of Mathematics Content*, (Table 4) focuses on how the picture book integrates several mathematical concepts within the story. Typically, this might include examples where counting and measurement ideas are interrelated in a situation (IMC: Integration within and across the mathematics curriculum). It also relates particularly to how the mathematics (explicit, perceived or embedded) in the book can be integrated into cross-curricula explorations, and more broadly how situations and ideas evidenced in the story embed concepts that are cross-curricula.

The Waterhole (Base 2001) is principally designed to entertain readers and was originally intended as a "simple story about the cycle of seasons" (Base 2001, inside front cover). However, it evolved into a "fusion of counting book, puzzle book, storybook and art book" (Base 2001, back cover). It can be inferred that the main purpose here is not to teach mathematical concepts but to use the book as a vehicle for a story and environmental message. Therefore, the mathematics could be said to be *embedded*. Each double-page spread forms the storyline as an ever-increasing number of animals come to drink from a waterhole. The waterhole gets smaller and smaller until it disappears before being finally replenished by rain. The text on each double spread contains a large number symbol, and the number word, while the visual image reflects the number of animals in the text (see Figure 3). Many more animals are hidden in the artwork, consistent with Base's usual style. The visual images offer the possibility for return visits from the reader, although not necessarily for the mathematical content (*Affordances for Mathematical Learning*).

Table 4: Integration of Mathematics Content

Code	Element	Definition
AIMC1	Integration **within and across** the mathematics curriculum	Evidence of connected concepts **within** the same content or process strand e.g., area and length within measurement or **across** content and/or process strands e.g., number and measurement.
AIMC2	Integration **across other disciplines and with ICT**	Evidence of integration links **across disciplines** e.g., Mathematics and Science and incorporation of Information and Communication Technology (ICT) into mathematical contexts.

Figure 3: From Base, Graeme. 2003. *The Waterhole* by Graeme Base, 2003. Reproduced with permission of Penguin Group (Australia).

The complexities of both the visual images and mathematical concepts allow for the book to be used at a variety of levels, dependent on the intended age group. There are obvious opportunities to use *The Waterhole* as a counting experience, but there are additional opportunities to explore volume, capacity and proportion through learning engagements based on the children's interests (see, for example, Figure 3) (IMC: Integration within and across the mathematics curriculum).

The Waterhole offers opportunities for a range of learning engagements from across the mathematics curriculum and beyond. However, other benefits of this book are the integration it affords with an environmental theme, a study of the different continents of the world, different animals and their habitats, or a visual arts study, none of which are necessarily mathematics-based. Using the framework in this case has aided identification of the book's potential beyond the counting and environmental themes suggested by initial reading.

Implications of the Framework for Mathematical Concept Development

Using the framework to evaluate picture books may facilitate a deeper understanding of the range and quality of possible opportunities for learning. In this chapter, the process of evaluating books using the categories of *Mathematical Content, Curriculum Content, Policies and Principles* and *Integration of Mathematics Content* has been explored. Using picture books in an integrated curriculum is warranted, but the place of mathematics can be made more explicit. This framework has the potential to assist teachers in identifying affordances for concept development that may not yet have been realised.

The framework is designed to facilitate appropriate book selection for developing mathematical concepts. This may be a book that the teacher is already using to develop literacy skills or other curriculum content. The framework draws attention to the accuracy of mathematical content, relevance of curriculum policies and principles, integration of content, mathematical meaning, problem-solving opportunities, affordances for mathematics learning and implementation of pedagogy reflected by the use of the particular book. The efficacy of the framework depends also on the perception that the teacher has about mathematics learning. If this view is limited to counting and number concepts, the usefulness of the framework too, may be limited.

Acknowledgement

The authors wish to acknowledge the expert advice of Associate Professor Jane Torr of the Institute of Early Childhood, Macquarie University, on the subject of visual literacy in the early stages of the research project.

References

Allen, Pamela. 1993. *Alexander's Outing*. Ringwood, Victoria: Viking.

—. 2005. *Grandpa and Thomas.* Camberwell, Victoria: Puffin.

Anderson, Ann, Jim Anderson, and Jon Shapiro. 2005. "Supporting Multiple Literacies: Parents' and Children's Mathematical Talk within Storybook Reading." *Mathematics Education Research Journal* 16(3):5-26.

Australian Curriculum Assessment and Reporting Authority [ACARA]. (2010). Australian Curriculum: Mathematics. Retrieved January 11, 2011, from www.australiancurriculum.edu.au/Mathematics/Curriculum/F-1

Australian Government, Department of Education, Employment and Workplace Relations. (2009). *Belonging, Being and Becoming: The Early Years Learning Framework for Australia.* Retrieved from http://www.deewr.gov.au/Earlychildhood/Policy_Agenda/Quality/Documents/Final%20EYLF%20Framework%20Report%20-%20WEB.pdfBase, Graeme. 2003. *The Waterhole.* Melbourne: Penguin Group.

Donoghue, Mildred R. 1996. "Literature Connections in Six Current Math Series for Grades K – 2". Paper presented at the Annual Literacy Conference, Anaheim, CA. Accessed April 10, 2010. http://www.eric.ed.gov/PDFS/ED396286.pdf

Gailey, Stavroula K. 1993. "The Mathematics-Children's Literature Connection." *Arithmetic Teacher* 40:258-61.

Giorgis, Cyndi, and Joan I. Glazer. 2009. *Literature for Young Children: Supporting Emergent Literacy, Ages 0-8.* 6th Edition. Upper Saddle River, N.J.: Pearson/Prentice Hall.

Gleeson, Libby. 2006. *Amy and Louis.* Lindfield, N.S.W.: Scholastic Press.

Griffiths, Rachel, and Margaret Clyne. 1988. *Books You Can Count On: Linking Mathematics and Literature.* Melbourne: Nelson.

Halsey, Pamela. 2005. "Assessing Mathematics Trade Books: Do They Measure Up?" *Reading Improvement* 42(3):158-163.

Hong, Haekyung. 1996. "Effects of Mathematics Learning through Children's Literature on Math Achievement and Dispositional Outcomes." *Early Childhood Research Quarterly* 11:477-94.

—. 1999. "Using Storybooks to Help Young Children Make Sense of Mathematics." Chapter 18 in *Mathematics in the Early Years*, edited by Juanita V. Copley, Reston, VA: National Council of Teachers of Mathematics.

Kress, Gunther, and Theo van Leeuwen. 1996. *Reading images: The grammar of visual design.* London: Routledge.

Lewis, David. 2001. *Reading Contemporary Picture Books: Picturing text.* London: Routledge Falmer.

Marston, Jennifer. 2010. "Developing a Framework for the Selection of Picture Books to Promote Early Mathematical Development." pp.383-90 in *Shaping the Future of Mathematics Education: Proceedings of the 33rd Annual Conference of the Mathematics Education Research Group of Australasia Incorporated,* vol. 2 edited by Len Sparrow, Barry Kissane and Chris Hurst. Fremantle, WA: MERGA.

Moschovaki, Eleni, and Sara Meadows. 2005a. "Young Children's Spontaneous Participation during Classroom Book Reading: Differences According to Various Types of Books." *Early Childhood Research and Practice* 7(1). Accessed July 4, 2008. http://ecrp.uiuc.edu/v7n1/moschovaki.html

Moschovaki, Eleni, and Sara Meadows. 2005b. "Young Children's Cognitive Engagement during Classroom Book Reading: Differences According to Book, Text Genre, and Story Format." *Early Childhood Research and Practice* 7(2). Accessed July 4, 2008. http://ecrp.uiuc.edu/v7n2/moschovaki.html

Muir, Marcie. 1982. *A history of Australian Children's Book Illustration.* Melbourne: Oxford University Press.

National Association for the Education of Young Children (NAEYC). 2010. "Early Childhood Mathematics: Promoting Good Beginnings." Accessed August 25, 2010. http://www.naeyc.org/files/naeyc/file/positions/psmath.pdf

Neuschwander, Cindy. 1997. *Sir Cumference and the First Round Table.* Watertown MA.: Charlesbridge.

—. 2007. *Patterns in Peru.* New York: Henry Holt and Company.

Pinczes, Elinor J. 1993. *One Hundred Hungry Ants.* New York: Houghton Mifflin Company.

Reeder, Stephanie O. 1997. "Drawing the Line: Defining Children's Picture Books." *Orana. Journal of School and Children's Librarianship* 33(2): 91-98.

Schiro, Michael. S. 1997. *Integrating Children's Literature and Mathematics in the Classroom: Children as Meaning Makers, Problem Solvers, and Literary Critics.* New York: Teachers College Press.

Steinberger, K. 1998. "Picture Book Maths." *Literature Base*, *9*:4.

Thiessen, Diane, and Margaret Matthias. 1992. *The Wonderful World of Mathematics.* Reston, VA: National Council of Teachers of Mathematics.

Van den Heuvel-Panhuizen, Marja, and Sylvia van den Boogaard. 2008. "Picture Books as an Impetus for Kindergarteners' Mathematical Thinking." *Mathematical Thinking and Learning* 10:341-73.

Welchman-Tischler, Rosamond. 1992. *How to Use Children's Literature to Teach Maths.* Reston, VA: National Council of Teachers of Mathematics Inc.

Whitin, David. J. 1992. "Explore Mathematics Through Children's Literature." *School Library Journal,* 38(8): 24-28.

Whitin, David, J., and Cassandra C. Gary. 1994. "Promoting Mathematical Explorations through Children's Literature." *Arithmetic Teacher* 41:394-99.

Whitin, David J., and Phyllis Whitin. 2001. "What Counts in Math-Related Books for Children." *Journal of Children's Literature* 27(1): 49-55.

CONTRIBUTORS

Anita Bundy is a Professor of Occupational Therapy at the University of Sydney, Australia. She is known internationally for her work in occupational therapy assessment and intervention. She has published widely in these areas and given invited lectures and courses on five continents. She is best known for developing theory and research in play with children who have disabilities and in sensory integration. She has a strong interest in the everyday lives of children with disabilities.
Email anita.bundy@sydney.edu.au

Sheila Degotardi is a Senior Lecturer at the Institute of Early Childhood, Macquarie University, Australia. She has a research interest in the qualities of children's relationships and inter-personal relatedness and specialises in infant-toddler pedagogy, curriculum and learning. As well as supervising research students, she teaches about children's play, inquiry and early childhood pedagogy in undergraduate and post-graduate early childhood programs.
Email: sheila.degotardi@mq.edu.au

Katey De Gioia lectures in professional experience at the Institute of Early Childhood, Macquarie University, Australia. Her research interests include addressing transition to school and into school for migrants and refugee children and families from a community perspective. She also advocates for the importance of family- teacher relationships to ensure cultural practices are respected in the early years. More recently Katey has been engaging in practitioner enquiry research, shifting the focus to teachers' practices as key in outcomes for children and families within local communities.
Email: katey.degioia@mq.edu.au

Rosemary Dunn is a PhD candidate in the Department of Education at Macquarie University, Australia, She worked as an English and History teacher in NSW high school settings before retraining as an Early Childhood teacher at the Institute of Early Childhood. Rosemary's research encompasses young children's perspectives on and experiences of

museums and their understandings of history and issues around the inclusion of children with a disability and/or challenging behaviours.
Email: rosemary.dunn@mq.edu.au

Lina Engelen is a Research Fellow in the Faculty of Health Sciences, University of Sydney, Australia. She manages the Sydney Playground research project, aimed at increasing physical activity and social skills in primary school children by means of a school playground intervention. Lina's research interests span children's health, physical activity, oral physiology, the interaction and perception of food, and nutrition. She is the author of journal articles and book chapters and her research has been presented at international conferences.
Email: lina.engelen@sydney.edu.au

Frances Gibson is a Lecturer in child development at the Institute of Early Childhood, Macquarie University, Australia. With a professional background in psychology, she has worked as a clinical and research psychologist in the health sector involved in the long-term developmental follow-up of babies born at high risk (extremely premature) and in disability. Frances has particular interest in social emotional development, parent-child relationships and children's learning and adjustment at school.
Email: frances.gibson@mq.edu.au

Fay Hadley is a Lecturer at the Institute of Early Childhood, Macquarie University, Australia where she supervises research students and teaches in the undergraduate early childhood program. Fay's research interests include partnerships with families in early childhood settings, supporting needs of CALD families, supporting the professional learning of early childhood teachers, analysing the support that pre-service students require (including international students and students who enter university through different pathways). Recently she has been supporting early childhood teachers from several early childhood organisations in practitioner inquiry action research projects.
Email: fay.hadley@mq.edu.au

Kerry Hodge is an Honorary Associate of the Institute of Early Childhood at Macquarie University, Australia where she is also a member of the Children and Families Research Centre. Kerry's research interests include the identification of giftedness in young children and early gifted education from the perspectives of educators, parents and the children themselves. Her work has been published in journal articles and book

chapters. Kerry has taught in undergraduate and postgraduate teacher education programs in early childhood and special education.
Email: kerry.hodge@mq.edu.au

Rozanna Lilley is a social anthropologist currently researching maternal perspectives on autism diagnosis, early intervention and schooling. Graduating from the University of Sydney in 1988 with a BA(Honours) degree and a University Medal, Rozanna was awarded a PhD (Anthropology) from the Australian National University in 1994. In 2009 she embarked on a second PhD (in Early Childhood) at the Children and Families Research Centre, Macquarie University, Australia, on the experiences of mothers whose children with autism are transitioning to primary school in New South Wales. She has published widely in scholarly journals, books and popular parenting magazines.
Email: roselilley@fastmail.fm

Helen Little is a Lecturer at the Institute of Early Childhood, Macquarie University, Australia where she teaches on undergraduate and postgraduate units in child development. She is a trained early childhood teacher and previously taught in preschools and primary schools in Sydney. She has been investigating children's risk-taking over the past six years and her doctoral thesis examined the influence of individual, social and environmental factors on children's engagement in risk-taking behaviour in outdoor play. Current focus relates to how the space and physical features available in the outdoor environment impact on children's experiences of risk taking in play.
Email: helen.little@mq.edu.au

Jennie Marston is a Lecturer at Macquarie University, Australia. Her teaching includes undergraduate programs in teacher education, with a particular emphasis on mathematics education, and teaching the gifted and talented student. Jennie is currently completing her PhD in Education titled, *The role of picture books in young children's development of mathematical concepts*, under the supervision of A/Prof. Joanne Mulligan. She is the author of articles on the integration of numeracy and literacy and is often asked to speak on this topic and to assist in the establishment of gifted and talented programs.
Email: jennie.marston@mq.edu.au

Zinnia Mevawalla is a doctoral candidate at the Institute of Early Childhood, Macquarie University, Australia. Her doctoral research is focused on early childhood community development and the accountability of aid in low- and middle-income contexts. Zinnia's other research interests include early childhood advocacy, complexity theory and early childhood social networks.
Email: zinnia.mevawalla@mq.edu.au

Joanne Mulligan is Associate Professor of Education in the Department of Education, Macquarie University, Australia. She leads research projects and professional development initiatives specialising in early mathematics learning. Her teaching involves supervision of research students and undergraduate and postgraduate programs in mathematics education and teacher education. She is internationally renowned for her research on early mathematical development and is an established author and invited speaker to international meetings. She currently leads the Reconceptualising Early Mathematics Learning project funded by the Australian Research Council.
Email: joanne.mulligan@mq.edu.au

Geraldine Naughton is Director of the Centre of Physical Activity Across the Lifespan at Australian Catholic University. She is a paediatric exercise scientist with a background of projects aiming at improvements in physical activity pathways for a range of young populations from overweight and obese children to intensively training adolescents.
Email: geraldine.naughton@acu.edu.au

Jo Ragen is a Senior Research Associate in the Faculty of Health Sciences, University of Sydney, Australia. Current project interests include children and play; parent and teacher perceptions of risk for children, developing risk attitudes and their effect on practice; perceptions of everyday risk for children and young adults with disability.
Email: jo.ragen@sydney.edu.au

Ellen Beate Hansen Sandseter is an Associate Professor in the Department of Physical Education at Queen Maud University College of Early Childhood Education in Trondheim, Norway. Her primary research focus is on risky play among children in early years settings, exploring what risky play is, why children engage in this kind of play and how preschool constitute an arena for risky play. She has cooperated with early childhood

researchers from both England and Australia to study cultural differences in provision of risky play in early years settings.
Email: ebs@dmmh.no

Anthony Semann is Director of Semann & Slattery, a consulting, research and professional development firm focused on transforming individuals and organisations. Working across both government and non-government organisations Anthony's research interesting include critical approaches to leadership, organisational change, pedagogy and leader identity. Anthony is currently completing a PhD at Macquarie University, Australia titled 'of courage: a critical and post-structural analysis of courage and leadership'.
Email: anthony@semannslattery.com

Wendy Shepherd is a graduate of the Institute of Early Childhood, Macquarie University and the University of Sydney. A member of the Social Justice in Early Childhood advocacy group, she has taught Kindergarten, Year One and Year Two children, was the Director of a preschool and then an advisor for preschool, long day care and out of school hours programs. Wendy is the Director of Mia Mia Child and Family Studies Centre at the Institute of Early Childhood, Macquarie University, Australia where she is also a Lecturer.
Email: wendy.shepherd@mq.edu.au

Elspeth Stephenson is a Lecturer in Professional Studies at the School of Education, University of Tasmania. She has more than 20 years experience in the field of education, working with children aged from 6 weeks to 16 years and is now working in the area of pre-service teacher education. Her passion lies with the early years, particularly in the areas of children's rights, and children's voice. Elspeth is currently undertaking her PhD in Early Childhood; her research focus is the voice of the young child in educational research, particularly in the area of wellbeing during transition.
Email: elspeth.stephenson@utas.edu.au

Paul Tranter is Associate Professor in Geography at UNSW@ADFA (the Australian Defence Force Academy), Australia, where his research and teaching interests are in social and transport geography, and global change. His research has made a pioneering contribution to the literature in areas of child-friendly environments, active transport, and healthy and sustainable cities. These themes are brought together in a recent book – *Children and*

Their Urban Environment: Changing Worlds, which Paul has co-authored with Claire Freeman.
Email: paul.tranter@adfa.edu.au

Peter Whiteman is Associate Director of The Children and Families Research Centre at the Institute of Early Childhood, Macquarie University, Australia. He supervises research students and teaches in undergraduate and postgraduate early childhood programs. Peter's research interests span early childhood music education and musical development, musical cultures, emergent symbol systems and reconstructed childhoods. He is the author of journal articles and book chapters and his research has been presented in a range of international settings.
Email: peter.whiteman@mq.edu.au

Shirley Wyver is a Senior Lecturer in child development at the Institute of Early Childhood, Macquarie University, Australia. Her research interests are in early play and cognitive/social development. She also conducts research in the area of blindness/low vision and development.
Email: shirley.wyver@mq.edu.au

Christine Zuvela graduated from Macquarie University, Australia in 2009 with the degree of Bachelor of Education (Early Childhood Education) (Honours). Currently, she is working as an Early Childhood Teacher at SDN Beranga which is a demonstration Early Childhood Education and Care service for children with an Autism Spectrum Disorder. Christine's interests include play therapy, early intervention, inclusion, autism spectrum disorders and working within a multi-disciplinary team.
Email: c.zuvela@sdn.org.au